STARING

AT

SOUND

ALSO BY

JIM DeROGATIS

LET IT BLURT:
THE LIFE AND TIMES OF LESTER BANGS,
AMERICA'S GREATEST ROCK CRITIC

MILK IT!
COLLECTED MUSINGS ON THE
ALTERNATIVE MUSIC EXPLOSION OF THE '90S

TURN ON YOUR MIND:
FOUR DECADES OF GREAT PSYCHEDELIC ROCK

KILL YOUR IDOLS:
A NEW GENERATION OF ROCK WRITERS
RECONSIDERS THE CLASSICS (EDITOR, WITH CARMÉL CARRILLO)

STARING

JIM DeROGATIS

BROADWAY BOOKS

NEW YORK

AT SOUND

THE TRUE STORY OF OKLAHOMA'S FABULOUS

flaming Lips

B
BROADWAY

BROADWAY BOOKS and its logo, a letter B bisected on
the diagonal, are trademarks of Random House, Inc.

Visit our Web site at www.broadwaybooks.com

Excerpts from Wayne Coyne's "Jesus Freak" poem
and Boom Box Experiment program notes used by
permission of Wayne Coyne.

Book design by Terry Karydes

Library of Congress Cataloging-in-Publication Data

DeRogatis, Jim.
Staring at sound : the true story of Oklahoma's fabulous
Flaming Lips / by Jim DeRogatis.
    p.   cm.
1. Flaming Lips (Musical group) 2. Rock musicians—
Oklahoma—Biography. I. Title.

ML421.F557D47 006
782.42166092'2—dc22
[B] 2005045691

ISBN-13: 978-0-7679-2140-4
ISBN-10: 0-7679-2140-2

PRINTED IN THE UNITED STATES OF AMERICA

10 9 8 7 6 5 4 3 2 1

First Edition

For Carmél:

Usted es mi verdadera amor.

THE UNITED STATES HAS A HABIT OF MAKING HEROES OUT OF ANYTHING AND

ANYBODY. YOU COULD DO ANYTHING HERE. OR DO NOTHING. BUT I ALWAYS

THINK YOU SHOULD DO SOMETHING. FIGHT FOR IT, FIGHT, FIGHT.

— ANDY WARHOL

IF YOU WANT TO BE SUCCESSFUL, KNOW WHAT YOU ARE DOING,

LOVE WHAT YOU ARE DOING, AND BELIEVE IN WHAT YOU ARE DOING.

— WILL ROGERS

(OKLAHOMA PHILOSOPHER)

CONTENTS

"TIME BEGINS AGAIN."
THE FLAMING LIPS AT
MADISON SQUARE GARDEN,
NEW YEAR'S EVE, 2004–2005.
CLOCKWISE FROM TOP LEFT:
MICHAEL IVINS, WAYNE
COYNE, AND STEVEN DROZD.

WHEN Led Zeppelin performed at New York City's legendary Madison Square Garden in July 1973, the band members arrived in stretch limos moments before walking onstage as conquering heroes and self-proclaimed golden gods, as seen in their famous concert film *The Song Remains the Same*. More than thirty years later, as the Flaming Lips prepared to play the same venue on the last day of 2004, they arrived seven hours before showtime, helping to haul their own gear, carrying boxes full of balloons, confetti, and furry animal costumes, and armed with rolls of duct tape.

Wayne Coyne and Michael Ivins had logged hundreds of thousands of miles performing around the world since the Flaming Lips first played in public at a black cowboy bar in their hometown of Oklahoma City two decades earlier. For the last twelve years of that long, strange trip, Steven Drozd had been at their side, and together they were about to cap the most successful period of their career to date, which started in July 2002 with the release of *Yoshimi Battles the Pink Robots* and ended here on the stage where so many of their heroes had made history.

Along the way, if the Flaming Lips hadn't quite reached the level of fame and fortune achieved by Led Zeppelin, Pink Floyd, or the Who, they had at least secured their position as one of the best-selling bands in the rock underground, and as one of the most imaginative, groundbreaking, and wonderfully weird groups in the pop mainstream. They hardly took this for granted, though. Backstage in their dressing room before the show, someone had scrawled the evening's agenda on a dry-erase bulletin board.

> Rule #1: Try not to suck.
> Rule #2: I told you not to suck, assface!
> Rule #3: Fuck you.

An hour and a half before midnight, after an opening set by Sleater-Kinney, the indie-rock darlings who had just recorded with the Flaming Lips' longtime producer, Dave Fridmann, the Lips took the stage to the taped strains of a lush orchestral fanfare—Wayne in a three-piece gray pinstriped Dolce & Gabbana suit, Steven in a pink elephant costume, and Michael in a black-and-white zebra outfit—accompanied by three dozen fans dressed as plushy pandas, baboons, lions, tigers, and bears waving powerful handheld spotlights; six gyrating strippers in pasties and G-strings; a giant inflatable sun; clouds of smoke; a barrage of lights and video; and a nonstop rain of confetti.

Standing backstage as the group's roadies bounced dozens of colorful, oversized balloons from a holding bin out into the crowd, one of the Garden's veteran stagehands shook his head in amazement. "I ain't seen nothin' like this," he said—impressive testimony from a Teamster who'd worked countless concerts and pro sporting events, the Westminster Kennel Club's 128th Annual Dog Show, the 2004 Republican National Convention, and the yearly visit from the Ringling Bros. and Barnum & Bailey Circus.

"Hello, everybody! It is truly an honor to be here with you guys tonight welcoming in 2005 at Madison Square Garden," Wayne announced as the introductory music, an instrumental that Steven called "Plinkee," ended. The band's leader took his place behind the vocal mike at center stage, flanked by Steven on keyboards and guitar at his right, Michael on bass and keyboards seated at his left, and touring drummer Kliph Scurlock at the rear behind a transparent pink plastic drum set. "We're gonna make this the best fuckin' show you could have ever gone to," Wayne promised.

With that, the group launched into a triumphant version of "Race for the Prize," a song that Wayne describes as his ideal combination of Frank Sinatra and Led Zeppelin, and which neatly encompasses several of his recurring themes: Seize the moment; dare to live life to the fullest; believe in yourself, work hard, and you can accomplish anything. These maxims sound less like Dale Carnegie aphorisms and more profound in his fanciful lyrics about two scientists trying to save the world. During the bridge, many in the audience of eleven thousand augmented his hoarse, off-key, but endearing voice by adding their own: "Theirs is to win, if it kills them/They're just humans with wives and children."

"That's the way a fuckin' rock show should begin, huh?" Wayne asked after the song had thundered to a close, and the crowd roared its approval.

Wayne is the first to admit that he isn't much of a singer, and that he relies on his charisma to carry the show. During the years the group has spent developing the uplifting multimedia circus of its current concerts, he has honed the philosophical edge of his lyrics, and he has acquired along the way a near-messianic appeal, with fans cheering every time he raises his arms on-stage, or even when he strolls out before the performance to duct-tape the guitar cords to the floor. A dedicated fan of what he calls "the weird religiosity" of the Who, he's aware of the downside of gurudom, as described in Pete Townshend's epic rock opera *Tommy,* and Wayne will brook no mythologizing of his role as the group's leader. He insists that people just want to come together to celebrate, and he is simply their designated cheerleader, employing an analogy that's more convincing when you know he spent eleven years as a fry cook at a fast-food restaurant before becoming his own thrift-store, do-it-yourself golden god.

"Anybody with as much luck and determination as me could do this," Wayne maintains. "I'm making chicken, and you like chicken. You think I'm making chicken because you like it, Jim, but I'm just making chicken because I like to make chicken."

Even if you dislike the Flaming Lips' particular brand of poultry, it's hard to deny that they are the ideal band to lead a round of "Auld Lang Syne." The group thought it had ended the touring cycle supporting *Yoshimi Battles the Pink Robots* with a show opening for their admirers the White Stripes at Chicago's Aragon Ballroom on New Year's Eve, 2003–2004, but the album continued to grow in popularity, and the band had spent another year on the road. Now it was ushering in 2005—or, as Wayne noted on the poster he designed for the show (he's always done almost all of the band's artwork), celebrating the night when "Time Begins Again"—as co-headliners with Wilco. Like many acts that have shared a stage with the Flaming Lips, the Chicago-based alternative country/art-rock group felt a twinge of regret in deciding to follow the Oklahoma band. "I don't know how *anyone* can follow that," Wilco bassist John Stirratt sighed as he watched the Flaming Lips' bacchanal from the side of the stage, though once the Teamsters had swept up the confetti, Wilco did just fine.

As influential critical and cult favorites on the brink of full-fledged mainstream success, Wilco and the Flaming Lips have few peers on the current music scene, and the bands had once been label mates, though technically Wilco recorded for Reprise Records, while the Flaming Lips record for Warner Bros. proper. Wilco famously split with its label's corporate parent company in an acrimonious dispute over the commercial potential of its 2002 album, *Yankee Hotel Foxtrot.* In an era of shrinking artistic experimentation and growing number-crunching, some of the company's executives had decided it was no longer enough for a well-respected band to sell merely a few hundred thousand albums. "I can't believe I'm going to say this to you and you're going to write this in a book, but I'll say it anyway: I think it could have happened to the Lips, too," said Deb Bernardini, Wilco's publicist, who had spent several years working in the same role for the Flaming Lips before leaving Warner Bros.

In fact, Warner Bros. nearly dropped the Flaming Lips several times over the last decade and a half, but by keeping their heads low, their expectations realistic, and their relations cordial, and relying on the charm and cunning of their manager, Scott Booker, the musicians persevered to the point where their attorney, Bill Berrol, said they will be the only band he has represented during thirty years in the music business to fulfill the terms of their contract, delivering all seven of the albums the label optioned when they signed in 1990. By all rights, the group should have broken up at any of a half-dozen critical junctures, but the band members say they forged ahead because they simply had no other choices. Nonsense. The truth is that they always believed in themselves, their music, and Wayne's vision, and this faith finally paid off when *Yoshimi Battles the Pink Robots* sold almost a million copies worldwide.

A band that produces an artistic triumph as well as its most commercially successful effort on its tenth album is nearly unprecedented in rock 'n' roll, an art form where most acts have a shelf life of Andy Warhol's proverbial fifteen minutes. But then the Flaming Lips' unlikely career resembles few others, with the possible exception of Pink Floyd's, which evolved from the Syd Barrett–driven psychedelic pop of the mid-sixties to the trippy art rock of the early seventies to the platinum success that followed *The Dark Side of the Moon*. Like their heroes Pink Floyd, the Flaming Lips always have used the recording studio as a tool to create beautiful sounds far beyond their own technical abilities, and they have been several distinctly different bands in the process: the noisy indie-rock group of the mid-eighties, the expansive psychedelic combo of the early alternative era, and the strange orchestral pop band of recent years.

Just as a wide variety of groups have drawn from different periods in Pink Floyd's evolution, the Flaming Lips have emerged as one of the most influential bands of their generation, inspiring some groups with their psychedelic rock efforts (Modest Mouse, Grandaddy, the Secret Machines, Longwave, Apples in Stereo, Super Furry Animals, Earlimart), others with their orchestral pop (the Polyphonic Spree, the Olivia Tremor Control, Neutral Milk Hotel, the Arcade Fire), and others still via mutual admiration and the more general example of how they conduct their career (Radiohead, the White Stripes, Wilco, Tool, Deathcab for Cutie, Sparklehorse). But unlike

Pink Floyd, which eventually split into two acrimonious camps, devolved into mediocrity, and lapsed into inactivity, or even some of the bands the Flaming Lips have spawned, they remain a vital and vibrant concern, poised to reach an even larger audience in 2006 with their new album, *At War with the Mystics,* and their first feature film, *Christmas on Mars.*

Following the sudden twists and turns and unexpected highs and lows of this roller-coaster career has been enough to give any longtime fan whiplash. I first interviewed Wayne and Michael in 1989, before the release of *In a Priest Driven Ambulance.* In the years since, I've praised the group as one of the most inventive bands to emerge from the American underground, and I've sharply criticized its occasional missteps; Wayne still loves to debate me about the merits of the Boom Box Experiments. I've seen the band perform fifty times in five different cities; been a fly on the wall in the recording studio during the making of *Clouds Taste Metallic* and *At War with the Mystics;* participated in its biggest and best Parking Lot Experiment (like the Boom Box Experiments, this is impossible to explain briefly; see Chapter Eight); and dressed as the giant inflatable sun to introduce Wayne during a speech at the South by Southwest Music and Media Conference in 2004.

Because of this history, Wayne didn't hesitate for a moment when I called in late 2003 to say that I intended to write this book. "Well, sure, Jim, whatever you wanna do—it will be *your* version of the Flaming Lips' story." He knew what he was letting himself in for: that we'd spend countless hours talking about issues large and small; that I'd rifle through family photo albums and track down former girlfriends and bandmates he hadn't spoken to in years; that I'd pin down contracts, recover embarrassing articles from the past, and recount unflattering incidents he sometimes excluded from his own otherwise frank histories of the group. Wayne once wrote of my work: "Jim has always taken the 'investigative reporter' approach to any area of exaggerated hype in music culture—which usually means the bigger the egos of those being critiqued, the more fun he has pointing out their blunders. If only he could've been around for the birth of Christ."

To their credit and my gratitude, Wayne, Michael, Steven, Booker, Fridmann, and their spouses and family members never failed to cooperate fully and graciously with my intrusive efforts, allowing me to probe wherever I saw fit, and answering any and every question I posed without once asking to review, revise, or rescind their comments, much less see the manuscript before publication—a rare gift for any journalist in these days of omnipresent media manipulation. So Wayne is right: This is *my* version of the Flaming Lips' bizarre odyssey, but I hope that it is also the most thorough, insightful, and honest one, and that it is as inspiring and entertaining as their music. They deserve no less.

"I'd like to see the Lips in twenty years be kinda like the Grateful Dead—not their music, but this group that still goes around and people come see 'em and it's like this big party that never ends, although hopefully we'll keep making good records," Wayne told me in 1993. "We could do this for a hundred more albums, as long as Warner Bros. wants to keep giving us money." Thirteen years later, the Flaming Lips show no signs of slowing down, and that vision of the future seems more attainable than ever. I hope that they'll greet me with the same enthusiasm when I call in 2026 to begin working on Volume Two.

STARING

AT

SOUND

I WANT MY OWN PLANET

FRUSTRATED by the lack of opportunity in southwestern Pennsylvania and drawn by the promise of a new job and a better life in Oklahoma—"Brand new state, gonna treat you great," to quote the title tune of the Broadway musical, the official state song—Tom and Dolly Coyne loaded up the family car and set out on the seventeen-hour drive from Pittsburgh in the spring of 1961. Ranging in age from one to six, their four older children—Tommy, Kenny, Linda, and Marty—crammed into the backseat of the station wagon. Only a few months old, Dolly's youngest son sat on her lap or perched on the dashboard, watching U.S. Route 66 un-

"BY THE TIME I GOT INTO THE PICTURE, IT WAS LIKE TARZAN BEING RAISED BY THE APES." THE COYNE FAMILY IN 1965: FROM LEFT, MARTY, KENNY, TOM, DOLLY, MARK, WAYNE, LINDA, AND TOMMY.

fold before them. "Maybe that is where I got my love of the highway," Wayne joked forty-four years later.

Raised in working-class families of Scots-Irish, German, and Hungarian descent, Thomas Coyne and Dolores "Dolly" Jackson met and married in Pittsburgh's Troy Hill neighborhood in the early fifties, and Dolly gave birth to their first son a short time later, at age seventeen. The family continued to grow after Tom returned from serving in Germany during the tail end of the Korean War. The couple's fifth child, Wayne Michael Coyne, was born on January 13, 1961; their sixth and last, Wayne's younger brother, Mark, arrived two years later, after the family had settled in its new home on the North Side of Oklahoma City.

Tom and Dolly both had watched their fathers work backbreaking jobs and die at relatively young ages. "My dad said that he didn't want his kids growing up in the coal mines and steel mills of Pittsburgh, and that's all there was in the fifties and sixties," Tom's son Marty said. "He wanted his kids to have a future, and he didn't know what Oklahoma would bring, but he knew it would be better than Pittsburgh." As is his style, Wayne put a more romantic spin on his parents' decision to uproot their lives, leave their extended families, and move across the country: "They were going to go out and have this adventure."

A skilled cabinet maker, Tom had been offered a position with an office supply company, but he arrived in Oklahoma City to find that the managerial position he'd been promised had been eliminated, and he wound up loading trucks. "He had given up everything for this dream," Wayne said. "I always asked my mother, 'Why didn't you guys regroup and go back to Pittsburgh?' If things don't work out, so many people don't have the courage to face up to it, but she said, 'It sucked back there, too.' The struggle wasn't going to be any better anywhere else, so they stayed."

Seventy years after the land run that attracted the "boomers" and "sooners" who settled the state, and two decades after the Dust Bowl migration of the Great Depression, Oklahoma City rapidly expanded in the late fifties, flush with money from the thriving oil industry. Between 1958 and 1961, its population increased by nearly a third, to four hundred thousand residents, according to the U.S. Census Bureau, but outside the capital, agriculture continued to form the backbone of the state's economy, and rural attitudes and a striking homogeneity prevailed. According to the 1960 census, despite sizable populations of blacks and Native Americans, 90 percent of Oklahomans were white. Many were also poor—the median income traditionally is 75 percent of the national average—prompting a derisive nickname that lingers even today, when strip malls and office parks far outnumber family farms.

"Okie use'ta mean you was from Oklahoma," an itinerant farmer says in John Steinbeck's 1939 novel, *The Grapes of Wrath.* "Now it means you're a dirty son-of-a-bitch. Okie means you're scum. Don't mean nothing itself, it's the way they say it."

As Roman Catholics, the Coyne family was a minority in what is often called "the Buckle of the Bible Belt." To date, 77 percent of Oklahomans identify as conservative Christians, with the majority worshiping as Southern Baptists. The religious influence accounts for the fact that Oklahoma continued to ban liquor sales until 1959, a quarter-century after Prohibition ended in most of the country. State statutes still list blasphemy and failing to honor the Sabbath as misdemeanors, with penalties of one hundred dollars and twenty-five dollars per offense, respectively, though these are rarely enforced.

To a northerner who has made three week-long visits in the last decade, Oklahoma seems exotic only for its unrelentingly flat landscape and its pervasive blandness. It isn't exactly *nowhere,* as one longtime resident told me; it's just that it could be *anywhere.* There are strains of southern conservatism, midwestern tolerance, and the western frontier spirit, but none of the distinguishing eccentricities that characterize those regions. Residents can be suspect of new arrivals—"If you're an outsider, you're either a thief, someone else's relative, or a bum," another Oklahoman told me—but a strong work ethic is valued above everything besides God and family; the state motto, "Labor Omnia Vincit," can be translated as "Work Conquers All." Individual differences are tolerated with a quiet reserve, providing people work hard and keep to themselves, and the tight-knit Coyne family did exactly that.

"Because all of our relatives were in Pittsburgh, we didn't have cousins and aunts and uncles, and we didn't branch off into all these separate lives like a lot of families do," Linda, the family's only daughter, said. "We did everything together." Life revolved around sports, family dinners, and big holiday celebrations, with Dolly as the warm, outgoing, and eternally upbeat cheerleader and organizer. "She was always optimistic and always curious," Wayne said of his mom. "You never knew anything about her life, because she was always asking you, 'Now, what is happening in *your* life?'"

Dolly not only doted on her own children and encouraged their diverse interests—Kenny's running, Marty's motorcycle racing, and Wayne's drawing and painting—she became a mother figure for many of their friends. "Her house could never be too full, and Christmas celebrations and birthday parties regularly exceeded twenty-five to thirty people," Wayne wrote in her obituary in July 2004. "She saw happiness as a situation one must create, not as something to be longed for." To a greater degree than any of his siblings, he inherited this trait.

As reserved and determined as Dolly was gregarious and bubbly, Tom instilled in his children a respect for the virtues of hard work. "Coming from a family of six, if you wanted something, Santa wasn't necessarily going to bring it," his daughter, Linda, said. "When you were old enough, you went to work, doing paper routes or serving fast food at the Sonic. All of us always worked." Her brother Marty agreed. "If you weren't sweating your ass off, you weren't working hard enough. Wayne said to me several times that Dad just thought that if you worked hard, everything would be all right in the end. That is not really the way it is, but that is how he lived his life."

Unfailingly loyal to family, friends, and coworkers, Tom believed that a man's word was his bond, and he trusted people to behave as ethically as he did, but nine years after the family arrived in Oklahoma, his faith was shaken when he became the subject of a scandal that made front-page news in the *Daily Oklahoman*. Through his unrelenting labors, Tom had moved from the loading docks to become president of the Fields–Down Randolph office supply company when, on January 30, 1970, he was arrested by the FBI for embezzlement. The federal complaint alleged that he had conspired with Roy Meier, an assistant cashier and purchasing agent for the Oklahoma City Bank, to steal $1,660.50, a sum worth roughly four and a half times that amount in 2005 dollars.

The FBI claimed that Tom had submitted a phony invoice for bank deposit envelopes to Meier, who authorized the payment, then split the money with his alleged

"WE ALL DID WEIRD THINGS."
WAYNE, AGE SEVEN, WITH
HIS NAUGAHYDE "NAUGA
MONSTER," STILL ONE OF THE
RECURRING CHARACTERS IN
MANY OF HIS DRAWINGS.

co-conspirator. Tom maintained his innocence, but Meier, who had been the target of the investigation, pleaded guilty to misappropriating seventy-five thousand dollars during a six-year period, and he agreed to testify for the prosecution against Tom. The trial began in June 1970, when Wayne was nine. The school year had just ended, and the defendant's six children sat in the front row of the courtroom throughout the proceedings.

"Things will be in the newspaper, but they're all wrong: I didn't do it, and we are going to get through this," Tom told his family. His daughter, Linda, recalled his attorney arranging them in a line from oldest to youngest. "We didn't really know what the trial was all about, we just knew our dad was in trouble," she said. When neighboring kids taunted that their father was going to jail, the Coyne children had a ready response: "No, he's not, be-cause he *said* he's not." For Tom, the betrayal of a trusted customer was as hurtful as being falsely accused of a crime. According to a report in the *Daily Oklahoman*, the thirty-six-year-old father of six sat brooding as Meier testi-fied about their alleged fraud. The jury didn't believe Meier, and after four days, Tom was acquitted. But he paid a price.

"Our family changed through that," Linda said. "Our mom had to go to work, and our dad lost his job, which really rubbed him raw—he had been so devoted to that company. Up until then, he would go golfing with these guys he worked with; they had breakfast every Friday or Sunday, they would go bowling, and he belonged to all these groups. Once all that happened, he didn't do any of that anymore."

"I guess I was just so young and life was so good that it never dawned on me that he could go to jail," Wayne said of his father's ordeal. "I never felt like you could see a change in him the way Kenny and Linda talked about it. They said that before then, my mother and father were of the same [opti-mistic] ilk—the sunny day and the sunny day—and after that, it turned. She became even more resilient—like, 'Look, we know bad things happen all the time, but life is still good'—and he became very much like, 'Fuck 'em.' But it wasn't something that a nine-year-old could see." Nevertheless, an abiding respect for loyalty and a devotion to honesty were two more traits that Wayne would inherit from his parents and carry into later life.

Shortly before Wayne started his freshman year in high school, the Coyne family moved from the North Side to a slightly larger, though still over-crowded, four-bedroom house with tan aluminum siding near NW Twelfth

Street and N. Klein Avenue, one of a row of single-family homes in Oklahoma City's Classen-Ten-Penn neighborhood. In the years since, Wayne has often called the area "the ghetto," though he notes, "It's really lower-middle-class interspersed with desperate people. The truth about all ghettoes is there's always a mix of people who are trying to work and people who don't work and do illegal things or whatever. I say 'ghetto' just because in Oklahoma City, it's one of the worst areas."

Classen High School was one of the two oldest and poorest schools in the city, and it ranked among the least academically distinguished, with a faculty that cared more about coaching football than teaching class, and who viewed the Classen Comets as the only viable path for students who wanted to go to college. ("The law requires every citizen to be vitally interested in football," *The New Yorker* wrote in a brief profile of the team in December 1983. "Have your car safety-inspected, be home by nine-thirty, always know the score—those are the rules.") While enrollment was declining in the mid-seventies, the number of minority students was rising—about a third were African-American, and another third came from Oklahoma's growing population of immigrants from Cambodia, Vietnam, and Laos—and amid considerable controversy, city officials would close the school in the mid-eighties. When Wayne arrived in 1975, he found little to motivate him.

"We had come from the schools on the North Side, which at the time were the bigger and better schools in town, and we were used to things being a little more accelerated. I think if I had stayed in school on the North Side, I would have done better, but here, they were working at such a lower level that you could just zip through. I had some teachers who were really great—there was the occasional English teacher who'd really see when people had a curiosity about them—but the art teachers were for the most part a waste of time. I was like, 'I can do this work in five minutes. I can do better on my own.'"

The Coynes had already pegged Wayne as the artist in their midst, and in his early teens, he sometimes earned money by drawing pictures of the children of his father's coworkers. The siblings could tease each other about their ambitions, but ultimately they supported one another's dreams. "By the time I got into the picture, it was like Tarzan being raised by the apes," Wayne said. "We all did weird things—somebody was going to join the Hell's Angels, and somebody else wanted to be Evel Knievel—but they allowed me to do whatever I wanted without being beat up, which is a big deal when you are younger. Everyone thought I'd be an artist, and when you can view the possibilities, you think, 'Well, I guess I really could do that. Maybe I *could* be an artist.'"

Wayne could often be found sitting alone for hours, drawing or painting pictures in the bedroom he shared with his younger brother, Mark. Occasionally he worked on the dining-room table beside Tommy, six years his elder and a skillful artist himself, sketching comic-book heroes such as the Silver Surfer and the Hulk. At first Wayne tried to imitate his older brother. "I was still a really little kid, and I remember that I got stuck once on a picture and asked Tommy to help me," he said. Tommy refused and told his younger brother to do it on his own. "So I went ahead and did the drawing and found out that I *was* able to do it by myself. I came to see that whether it was with writing, drawing, or playing guitar, if you could remove yourself from all this exciting shit that was going on around you, and sit there by yourself and focus, you could figure things out on your own."

As a freshman at Classen High School, Wayne played on the football team, but he quickly discovered that organized sports didn't suit him. "I wasn't that good, and while the guys on the team liked me, the coaches hated me because I had long hair and I thought that they were kind of stupid. Plus, I didn't react well to this authority figure yelling at me." He preferred the rough-and-tumble free-for-alls arranged by his brothers and their friends, who had formed a sandlot football team called the Fearless Freaks.

"We'd listen to Pink Floyd, smoke a joint in the car, then go out and play football; it was awesome," Wayne said. "We had seen these factions: There were the jocks, but they didn't listen to Pink Floyd or smoke pot, and there were the freaks, but they didn't play football. My brothers believed that we could live our own lives in whatever way we wanted, and I think they looked at football as a way of being in a fight, but without guns or knives. They really did despise the jocks we played against, and I swear, they would murder these guys who were really good athletes."

Though he got along well with everyone at Classen, thanks to his gregarious personality, Wayne didn't fit into any of the established cliques, and he didn't have a big crowd of high-school friends. He didn't attend his junior or senior prom, and he skipped his graduation ceremony. "There was something about the camaraderie of being in high school that wasn't for me. I felt like, 'These are just a bunch of kids here.' Even though I was one of them, I was already feeling kind of superior," he said, laughing. "I wanted to be an adult more than the people I was surrounded by. Then, once I got the job at Long John Silver's, I was making money, dealing with the real world, and hanging out every night with the assistant managers, smoking pot."

"THAT WAS A REAL SHIT-BREATHER
GIG THAT NOBODY WANTS,
BUT I THOUGHT I HAD THE EASIEST,
BEST JOB IN THE WORLD." WAYNE'S
SELF-PORTRAIT FROM THE LONG JOHN
SILVER'S NEWSLETTER *Gangplank*, 1980.

**Artist-in-residence
and without a single lesson**

Wayne started working as a part-time fry cook at Long John Silver's in the spring of 1977, during his sophomore year at Classen High School. He would spend the next eleven years sporadically cooking at "America's largest quick-service seafood chain," returning to the job even after the harrowing night when three armed robbers forced him to lie on the floor of the restaurant, and the time a drunk driver crashed through the front window. "That was a real shit-breather gig that nobody wants, but I thought I had the easiest, best job in the world," he said. "I liked the idea of it being mindless work. It was like, 'While I am here earning money, I can think about my life, and when I work and make more money, I can do what I want.'" He won distinguished-service pins at the five- and ten-year marks, and the chain tried to promote him to assistant manager several times, but he declined, insisting on remaining what the company called a "third mate."

Like his siblings, Wayne never considered going to college, and his parents didn't push him to further his education. "I just don't think my mom saw any value in that. She had been around so many poor people all her life that she just thought, 'You make your life what it is. Be whatever you want to be, no judgments.'" This attitude rubbed off on all of Dolly's children, yet while they shared her philosophy of never looking down on one another or on anyone else, they didn't agree on many other issues, and family dinners could be as competitive and brutal as the Fearless Freaks' football games.

"We don't call it arguing, we call it debating," Linda said. "That's always been there, and it's still like that when we get together today. We probably all should have been on the debate team in school." Contentious conversations between the five brothers and their sister sometimes lasted hours. "We would all sit around the table at Christmas dinner and kick around the big themes—love and death, elections, football games, gay people, black people—anything to keep the ideas going," Wayne said. But he always probed harder than his brothers or sister, honing his own intense version of the Socratic method by firing off an insistent string of ever more challenging questions. "I always feel there's something I can dig out of people."

Years later, Wayne's cohorts would dub him "the Buzzard," because he was always pecking away at them, and they would coin a term for his relentlessly inquisitive talks—"confronsations." But his siblings took it in stride. "I never thought Wayne was confrontational," his brother Marty said. "It's just that when he finds something he doesn't agree with, he will push it. If he thinks he is right, he will go and go. It's not that he can't see the other side; it's just that he likes advocating the opposite position."

Religion, philosophy, science, and odd natural phenomena always fascinated Wayne, but by his own admission, he never read deeply about any of these subjects, merely flipping through magazine articles or quickly skimming books for the parts that interested him. He preferred to learn by picking people's brains, talking for hours with his family members and their friends, and soaking up knowledge like a sponge. He also watched as they began to experiment with drugs. "I remember being seven years old and hearing one of my brothers tell my other brother that he was on LSD. I thought, 'No way; that is what the Beatles are taking! That's what's on *Dragnet!*'"

"With all of us around the same age in the seventies, there were always a lot of drugs around, but Wayne never really did all that," Linda said. "He watched and observed and learned, and he saw how stupid we were." Through the seventies and into the early eighties, several of Wayne's siblings had brushes with the law and spent the occasional night in jail, and his oldest brother and fellow artist, Tommy, struggled with addiction for years, serving several extended prison terms and attending their mother's funeral in leg irons while doing time for possession. "As I got older, I saw a lot of people who were just destroyed by drugs," Wayne said. "I never looked down on them because of that, but I never thought it was cool or wanted to have anything to do with it, either."

During his late teens, Wayne admitted that he occasionally smoked pot or "got drunk with the fellows," and he eventually took three or four acid trips himself, but he disliked what he called these "unpleasant death trips." He described one of these experiences in the liner notes to the Flaming Lips' 2002 compilation, *Finally the Punk Rockers Are Taking Acid*. At age seventeen, he made a psychedelically enhanced early-morning trip to Jack in the Box shortly after a robber broke the drive-through window in an attempt to grab the cash drawer. The register had been bolted down, and the thief only succeeded in slashing his wrists.

"THERE IS A LOT OF BLOOD!!!! And it's all over everything— bright red fresh thick blood," Wayne wrote, but the clerk was still serving food nonetheless. "An order of greasy French fries was on top of the cheeseburgers . . . TIME STOPS . . . and the fries are wiggling! I try to change my doomed perception—shaking my head—the fries becoming white worms . . . FUCK NO!!"

Ultimately Wayne decided that he hated the feeling of losing control, and from his early twenties on, he never did drugs and rarely drank again. "I really trust and like my senses," he said. "I love seeing stuff, I love hearing stuff, I love smelling and touching stuff, and that really makes me who I am. When I did drugs, I wasn't able to think and perceive, and I'm nothing if I can't see, if I can't listen." He eventually would espouse the mantra "Don't do drugs, *be* a drug." Nevertheless, in his late teens, he had no problem dealing drugs, and for several years he exponentially built his income from Long John Silver's by selling pot.

"You could buy reasonably by the pound, and my brothers knew all these guys who sold it," Wayne said. "I don't know what kind of scales they were using, but I could spend a hundred bucks and make five hundred in a week. I knew it was illegal, I knew people who had gone to jail, and I knew I was taking chances, but I just didn't want to have to work until I was thirty before I got something."

Thanks to his entrepreneurial skills, wads of ten- and twenty-dollar bills piled up in Wayne's desk drawer. He sometimes granted his siblings loans, but he denied their requests for gifts. "Can I get a dollar for a Coke?" Linda would ask, but Wayne's reply would resemble his father's: "You have a job; buy it yourself!" Still, no one in the family ever raided his drawer. "We all knew the money was there, and in some families, that would have been an issue," Linda said. "But we knew Wayne probably knew exactly how much he had."

Eventually Wayne saved enough to buy a Yamaha 600 motorcycle, which he cautiously drove everywhere for the next few years—"He was like

"HE WAS A COMBINATION OF LEIF GARRETT AND PETER FRAMPTON—JUST MY TYPE." WAYNE AND HIS GIRLFRIEND HALI NEYLAND AT OKLAHOMA'S LAKE TENKILLER, 1980.

an old lady on that bike," his brother Marty joked—and at age seventeen, at the start of his senior year in high school, he rented an apartment of his own. He loved living with his family, but selling pot required privacy. And he had fallen in love.

Wayne hadn't shown much interest in the opposite sex during his first few years at Classen High School. "Girls always sort of liked me—not like they liked Johnny Depp or anything, but I never struggled with that," he claimed. Nevertheless, he didn't have a steady girlfriend until Hali Neyland summoned the courage to ask him out. "He's a good-looking guy, and when I saw him, I just about lost my breath," she said. "He was a combination of Leif Garrett and Peter Frampton—just my type."

Half Mexican, half Irish, and five months older than Wayne, Hali grew up surrounded by hippies and musicians. She was raised by her father's aunt, whose oldest son is Michael Brewer; in 1971, his folk duo Brewer & Shipley recorded the druggy anthem "One Toke Over the Line," a Top Ten hit (which the Flaming Lips later covered). "We knew everyone, and people were always coming and going, just like Wayne's family," Hali said. She first saw her future boyfriend during eighth grade at Central Junior High School, though they never spoke until they moved on to Classen High School the following year.

"We had one class together, math, and he sat right in front of me. He usually drew or slept, but when he did do his work, he did it really quickly, and I thought, 'Wow, he's really smart.' He wasn't a big talker with the girls;

he seemed kind of shy." During ninth grade Hali switched to another school, but she and her father sometimes ate at Long John Silver's, and when she saw Wayne at the restaurant, "something clicked. One day I phoned him out of the blue, and I made the first move."

The couple started dating, and they moved in together in October 1978, shortly after Hali's father died in a car accident. They lived together for five years. "It was fun, but it was reckless; it wasn't necessarily like a serious re-lationship," Wayne said. "There were always people there getting high—she and her friends did a lot of drugs—and I remember one of her friends com-mitted suicide and her dad was in an accident. There was always an element of drama around."

Wayne continued to augment his income from Long John Silver's by selling pot until he got a wakeup call shortly after his eighteenth birthday.

"MAYBE I *could* BE AN ARTIST." ONE OF WAYNE'S
FRANK FRAZETTA–INSPIRED PAINTINGS, CIRCA 1980.

He and Hali had just picked up a pound of marijuana and were driving home with his brother Mark when a police car started following them. "Don't swerve!" Hali said, but the squad car turned on its lights and pulled them over. As the cop questioned Mark on the curb, Wayne turned to his girlfriend. "Please, God, just let us out of this and I promise I'll never do it ever again!" he whispered. "I'll quit now!"

"Thank God the cop let Mark go, but it was a very close call, and that was when we stopped selling pot," Hali said.

Wayne still spent hours painting, sometimes creating surreal fantasy scenes in the style of Frank Frazetta—"You'll see some of the girls in those paintings with long black hair that look just like me, except he always drew gigantic boobs on them," Hali said—as well as using himself for a canvas. "He'd paint his shoes, he'd paint his pants, he'd paint his T-shirt, he was like walking graffiti, and everywhere we went, whether it was Roy Rogers or anywhere, the old people would just shake their heads."

The Coyne family continued to encourage Wayne's ambitions, and it welcomed Hali as one of its own. "His parents were really good people, accepting and very open-minded," she said, and she accompanied Wayne to dinner every Sunday. "His mom loved to cook for us, and every holiday she'd do it up: Every Valentine's Day we got a heart full of candy, and every Easter we got an Easter basket, and here we were in our twenties!" Occasionally Wayne's brothers chided him that he should make an honest woman of Hali, but he vowed that he'd never get married: He had a plan, and he didn't want anything to distract him from becoming an artist.

"Wayne knows what he wants and he gets it," Hali said, but one of the most inspiring things about her former boyfriend was that he believed that anyone could do the same. "One day we were painting together, and I thought, 'Gosh, I wish I could paint like you,'" she said. "He said, 'You can, if you want to.' That's just the way he thought: You can do anything, and nothing can stop you."

Wayne's longest collaborator, Michael Lee Ivins, was born on Saint Patrick's Day, 1963, in Omaha, Nebraska, though a month later, his family moved to Saigon, just as the Vietnam War started to escalate. "This was right when the shit was about to hit the fan," Michael said. "My mom would go down to the market with me in the stroller, and she could hear the explosions not too many blocks away."

Born William Robert De Fretes, Michael's father grew up as an orphan uncertain of his heritage. When he was adopted at age three, his foster parents renamed him Peter Ivins; later on he visited a Shinto priest who used a form of numerology to divine that his name should have been Padraic, the moniker he used from that point on. Following the path of his adoptive father, he joined the military, and rose to the rank of captain in the Air Force Intelligence Agency, specializing in Communist relations. Stationed in Florida, Padraic took a course at the University of Miami, and there he met Linda Greer, an independent, free-spirited woman who had been raised by a Scots-Irish father and a Jewish mother.

Linda wanted to be an actress, and she studied drama. "I realized that I didn't have what it took—going hungry, taking waitress jobs, waiting for a break—plus my mother was very much against it," she said. "Her idea of a good life is you find a good man. I got to a point where it was easier to do what my mother wanted than to do what I wanted." In 1960, she and Padraic married, and a short time later, the Air Force transferred him, first to Hawaii, then to Vietnam. The military generally forbade personnel from taking dependents into the country, but Padraic nevertheless brought Linda and his infant son, Michael, with him.

By the spring of 1965, Vietcong activity had made Saigon increasingly dangerous, and Linda and Michael relocated to Thailand for several months, before Padraic secured a transfer to Japan and moved his family there. His second son, Michael's brother, Charles, was born in a military hospital in Tokyo in November 1965.

As a two-year-old in Japan, Michael was stricken with spinal meningitis. "He didn't feel well, and I touched his head and he was burning up," his mother said. "We were very fortunate that we were living in military housing and there was a doctor near us. He put Michael in a tub of ice water and made arrangements for an ambulance. This doctor had seen meningitis before. Michael was in isolation for two weeks, and at the beginning, I don't think they expected him to live, but the doctor said he had never seen a child with such a will. Most children go peacefully, but he wanted to survive."

Disillusioned with the course of the war, Padraic resigned his commission in 1966. "I had a lot of problems with how the war was being run in Vietnam, and I came into conflict with the upper echelons," he said. "This happened to a lot of officers over there. It wasn't so much the war itself, it was the way it was being conducted: free-fire zones and such. You just don't do that in the military." A trained parachutist, he started a new career teaching skydiving and using his aerial skills to film television commercials for Kirin beer and Seiko watches, among other companies. The work continued after the family returned to Hawaii, settling in Honolulu in 1967.

Five years later, when Michael was ten, Padraic and Linda divorced, and she eventually remarried in October 1973. Linda had taken a job with the YWCA and was working toward a degree in human resources at the University of Hawaii when she met Chris Nuthall, a flamboyant, fun-loving New Zealander who had tried several careers, including a stint in the nickel mines of the Australian outback, before deciding to give college in Honolulu a shot.

"I wasn't getting laid at the University of Hawaii, so my buddy and I found a home economics class where they were teaching cooking," Chris said. "It was us and twenty-six women, and that is where I met Linda. I wasn't doing very well in school because I liked to party too much, so I thought, 'Let's get married so I can stay in the country.' Linda has been a feminist for years—she started the first free women's health clinic in Hawaii at the university—and when we got married, she wanted a marriage contract drawn up. We had one of the first in the United States—in fact, a TV station wanted to speak to us—and it said that if we got divorced, we'd just split everything fifty-fifty. But we're still married after thirty-three years."

Michael attended private schools in Hawaii, where he did well, and he loved to read on his own, devouring L. Frank Baum's stories about the Land of Oz before moving on to the work of Jules Verne. Wherever he went, he carried a book. "I have to have something in front of me at all times, and I have to finish it, because I want to know how the story ends," he said, and for a time he considered becoming a writer. "When I was about thirteen, I went to sort of a weird writing workshop. At the very end, we were supposed to look at a picture and then write a short story about it. I was sitting in the back, and I just could not tell what the picture

was about, so I started writing some kind of stream-of-consciousness bullshit. The teachers were just baffled. When I saw what the picture was"—an old-fashioned ice cream vendor—"I was like, 'Oh, man! If I had just known.' I guess I just didn't have the guts to get up and say, 'I can't

WHEREVER HE WENT, HE CARRIED
A BOOK: MICHAEL IVINS, AGE ELEVEN.

see it; I need to get glasses, I guess,' but that seemed to shoot down any sort of real writing career."

During junior high school Michael started to grow a huge Afro. Native Hawaiians had a bitter racial slur for Caucasian immigrants—"haoles"—and incidents of antiwhite violence often made the news, but Michael's hair won him a measure of acceptance. "The Samoan kids had never seen a white boy with hair like this," his mother said. "He'd always show his individualism through his hair or clothing."

For a few years after his parents divorced, Michael and his brother, Charles, visited their father on weekends, but they saw less of Padraic after he moved to Denver and then returned to government service as a civilian contractor at Wright-Patterson Air Force Base in Ohio, developing programs to manage weapons systems—though Michael suspected he worked for the CIA. The last time he spent an extended period with his father was in 1976, when he was thirteen and he stayed for the summer. "There was some kind of meltdown. I don't really remember what happened, but something made me think, 'I need to go home,'" Michael said.

Michael participated on the swim and track teams, but his father valued a more macho kind of athleticism. "We never really connected as parent and child, as friends, or as anything else," Padraic said. "Maybe it was my upbringing, or his upbringing, or some combination of both." Linda believed that her elder son and her ex-husband simply differed too much to ever really bond. "Padraic has a controlling kind of personality, and Michael was not one to be controlled, even as a child. Michael has always been his own person. It's not that he was not a good child, but if Padraic wanted him to do something, and Michael didn't want to do it, he wouldn't do it."

In 2005, at age seventy, Padraic was still skydiving, with eight thousand jumps to his credit. While his father was a daredevil, and his stepfather was a self-described "character"—"Michael would just shake his head whenever I did something outrageous," Chris said—Michael took after his mom, who was quiet and introspective, avoiding confrontations. "I was painfully, maybe even clinically shy," Michael said, but like Linda, who had studied acting, he also had a desire to express himself. "There is a part of Michael that has always surprised me," his mother said. "When he was twelve, at summer camp, he got up at the talent show and did an impersonation of Elvis Presley, and I was floored, because I had never seen that side of him."

During one of his weekend visits with his father, Michael had discovered Padraic's reel-to-reel recorder, and he remembered hearing tapes of

Tom Jones and Dave Brubeck. He became obsessed with music and started listening to the radio constantly. The first single he bought was by Elvis Presley; the first album, by Elton John; and soon his bedroom walls were covered with posters of other heroes. "Around 1976 or '77, I actually tried to build a guitar, but that didn't work out because no one had clued me in on the electronic end of things. I just really loved music and everything about it, and I remember that once I started seeing clips of the Beatles on TV, I thought, 'Boy, that would be pretty cool to actually be doing that.'"

In 1979, when Michael was sixteen, his mother received an offer to serve as the executive director of the YWCA in Oklahoma City, and the family moved to the mainland. "I had grown up on the eighth floor of a high-rise apartment building in Honolulu, facing the ocean, and there was always more sea than land," Michael said. "Then we came to this place where there was just land for as far as you could see." Other differences awaited when he enrolled as a junior in Classen High School, where he felt as if he knew more than many of his teachers. "That was a big cultural adjustment. The coaches would be teaching classes, and they'd be like, 'Whoever—come up here and start reading chapter five.' I'd be sitting there going, 'My God, man, what's going on here?' Half of them could barely read, and it was really strange to me." His parents regretted that they hadn't let Michael finish at the private high school in Hawaii, but he made the best of things.

"I was part of the Latin club, and I remember organizing a toga party, but it wasn't like an *Animal House* toga party. I went to the library, found an actual pattern, and made a real toga, wrapping it up the real way a Roman senator would, with the purple band to show that I was high up in the ranks. I was pretty much a geek. I would be interested in Babylonian culture for a week, and I would do stuff like go to the library, find all the books I could that mentioned Babylonia, and then start to assemble, with the copy machine, my own Babylonian book. The next week it would be Sumeria. I would just have these masses of binders and books."

Wayne had left Classen High School the year before Michael arrived, so they never encountered one another there, but Michael's family did frequent the Long John Silver's at Classen Avenue and NW Thirtieth Street, "and I do remember this weird guy who had long hair and a ponytail," Michael said. "I'm sure in the same way he noticed me."

◎   ◎   ◎

Eventually Wayne's parents would pull away from the Catholic Church—"Little by little, as we got older, if pressed on it, my mother would say, 'Oh, it's all bullshit,'" Wayne said—but in the late sixties the family still attended Mass regularly.

"I'm sure some of that is why I liked being in a band," Wayne said. "There was a lot of gospel going on in rock music at the time, and there were a lot of Sundays when there was a rock band playing, with a live drummer playing shit like you heard on the radio and a couple of guitar players with cool-looking clothes on. I remember sitting in this concrete-and-stone church and being startled when this guy started to sing."

Wayne didn't mind attending Mass as long as there was a band playing, but he never embraced his parents' religion, and at age seventeen, he would come to consider himself an atheist, with an outlook he summarized in an untitled poem that he wrote a few years later after an argument with a man he called "a Jesus freak."

> *His logic is one of simple opposite perception:*
> *"If you believe in Hell, you must believe in Heaven."*
> *My unspoken reply I thought was quite funny:*
> *"It's like sayin' if you believe in Santa Claus,*
> *   you must believe in the Easter Bunny."*

Other gods held more allure for Wayne. His earliest musical memory is of his brothers playing "The Pusher" by Steppenwolf—"You remember that song: 'I said God damn!/God damn the pusher man'"—and at age seven it held him spellbound. Another song that held endless fascination and sparked a thrill about dark, forbidden mysteries was "D.O.A.," the 1970 FM-radio hit by the grungy Texas hard-rock band Bloodrock, which portrayed the victim of a car crash lying on a stretcher pondering his imminent death. Led Zeppelin, Pink Floyd, the Who, and the rest of the seventies' classic-rock canon always blared from one of his siblings' bedrooms, but one group towered above the others in their pantheon. "There was a Mount Rushmore to us, and that was the Beatles," Wayne said. "We all collectively embraced the idea of rock as our religion: That was the way we lived, and that is all we ever did. We'd listen to things like the first John Lennon and Yoko Ono record, and I didn't know that this was supposed to be weird, and then there was this other stuff called pop music. To me it was all just music. My brothers were never critical of any of it—they were just stoners listening to the music of the time—but as I got to be more interested in it, I wanted to know: 'What is a guitar? What is a bass?'"

Wayne's fandom soon eclipsed that of his brothers and sister. In early 1977, when tickets went on sale for a performance by Led Zeppelin at the Oklahoma State Fair Grandstand, he camped out for three days in zero-degree weather to secure front-row seats. A young reporter named Gene Triplett surveyed the diehards living in the parking lot for a story in the *Oklahoma Journal,* describing the "ramshackle village built out of plywood and cardboard, where they huddled in sleeping bags and electric blankets like longhaired, thermal-wrapped mummies." Wayne's mother clipped the article, and years later, when Triplett had become the entertainment editor of the *Daily Oklahoman,* Dolly mailed it to him. ("The big difference now is that people stand in line for him," Triplett wrote of Wayne, who had just won a Grammy.)

Wayne had started toying with an acoustic guitar at age fourteen. His oldest brother, Tommy, lived in an apartment over the garage behind the family's house, and he frequently hosted parties where his friends jammed. They showed Wayne how to play the intro to "Stairway to Heaven," fingering the chords he couldn't figure out on his own. "Some of them were good musicians—there was a guy who could play Gentle Giant, Eric Clapton, and Steve Howe, all of those tough chords—but they were always these dorky, geeky guys," Wayne said. "I was like, 'I wanna rock! I don't want to be a dorky, geeky guy. I want to be *the* guy!'"

As he did when he was learning to draw, Wayne sequestered himself and worked at mastering the guitar. "My brothers would go to concerts or parties, but I would stay home alone in my room, the same way I would sit there and paint. Even though I didn't know how to play this Led Zeppelin song, I would sit there and make up some shit, so when they would come home, I could play this riff that I couldn't play that morning. I found some way with that solitude—because that really is the most boring thing about all art; it really is just you and your ideas—where I could force things out of myself."

After his first eight months dealing pot and working at Long John Silver's, Wayne bought a new Gibson Les Paul and a small amplifier. "To me, it all really started to get fun when I bought the electric guitar and I could get loud and run it through wah-wah pedals and distortions and echo. Playing an acoustic guitar is fun, but it's very James Taylor or something. I wanted to be like Jimmy Page and Frank Zappa, that freaky shit. After about a year of

"TO ME, IT ALL REALLY STARTED TO GET FUN WHEN I BOUGHT THE ELECTRIC GUITAR." WAYNE WITH HIS LES PAUL, CIRCA 1979.

playing that sort of guitar, people started to be like, 'I don't know what the fuck you're playing, but it sounds great.'"

Immersing himself in rock magazines, Wayne began to read about a new sound called punk in 1977, and he wrote about the debut album by the Sex Pistols for his high school newspaper, in one of several reviews he contributed after he befriended some of the staffers in typing class. "The editor knew I was into music, so I'd just go buy *Creem* magazine and steal the review out of there and rewrite it. I think I said, 'The Sex Pistols are fun, but Led Zeppelin is still the shit.'" In January 1978, during their only American tour, the Sex Pistols performed at Cain's Ballroom in Tulsa, their penultimate gig before disbanding. Wayne didn't make the hundred-mile trip to see them, but their celebration of passion over virtuosity inspired him, and he became convinced that the Sex Pistols were on to something when he turned eighteen and started to see New Wave cover bands playing at the local bars.

At the same time, while his family still lived in Hawaii, Michael also became fascinated with punk and New Wave via the articles he read from England, and he began buying records by the Sex Pistols, the Buzzcocks, and XTC. The punks decreed that anybody could play rock 'n' roll, with no training necessary, and he decided to give it a try. "I think there was a guitar lying around, but, oh gosh, it just seemed really complicated. Then I listened to an interview with the bass player from the Psychedelic Furs, and he said he actually picked up the bass because it only had four strings."

Pawn shops proliferated along Pennsylvania Avenue in Oklahoma City, and when the family relocated, Michael bought his first bass during his junior year at Classen High School. "I had this really, really crappy all-in-one stereo set with a turntable and a cassette player built into it, and I ended up rigging a cable so I could actually hear it. I didn't know you were supposed to tune it to D–A–G–B. I don't know if it's because I never had anyone to sit there and point things out to me, or I just didn't actually get it, but I could never quite grasp music theory on my own. After a while, it kind of didn't matter that I didn't know what makes a seventh chord, or why you would go from this chord to that chord. It was just like, 'Hey, that sounds cool! Why don't I do that.'"

After graduating as the high-school valedictorian, Michael enrolled at Oklahoma University in nearby Norman with the vague ambition of studying linguistics. He had always been interested in languages—Padraic said his son spoke Chinese before he spoke English—and had excelled in Latin, but while he earned good grades, he found the social scene in the college dormitories alienating. "I didn't have a lot of friends. I'm not a social retard, but for a long time I just wasn't comfortable around people. I didn't have a crew, and I didn't have any pals that I hung around with."

Michael embraced his individualism and expressed it on campus through fashion, sporting what some later described as "an albino Goth look," clad head to foot in black, wearing black eyeliner, and teasing his sizable Afro into an outlandish New Wave hairdo à la A Flock of Seagulls. "I just thought it was oddly, inherently cool, but it wasn't like I was trying to impress anyone. That's the weird thing: I don't know what I would have done if anyone *did* pay attention. Looking back, it seemed like it was this weird, personal, individual journey that really didn't have anything to do with the outside world—the dressing up, the music—because I never knew anyone that actually liked that kind of music until I met Wayne. It was like I was living out this weird fantasy, hoping to be a part of something."

In 1981, Wayne started jamming with a group of his brother's friends, playing variations of tunes such as Oklahoman Eddie Cochran's "Summertime Blues" as rendered by the Who on *Live at Leeds*, but he yearned to try something more ambitious. "These guys only wanted to play cover songs, so by the time I met Michael, who was also not interested in playing cover songs, we just thought we would make up our own tunes, and it would be even cooler."

During the Christmas break in 1982, Michael's parents went on vacation. As wild and outgoing as Michael was reserved and introverted, his younger brother, Charles, hosted a party at the family's house on NW Seventeenth Street. "He was throwing it and I was enduring it—it was with all these people, and I didn't know who they were—and basically, Mark Coyne crashed my brother's party." Although they were in the same class at Classen High School, Michael didn't know Mark, "but I knew of him, because he was the quarterback of the football team, and I always hated going to those pep rallies."

Wayne's jam sessions had morphed into a nebulous band with Mark on vocals and a friend of his older brothers, Dave Kostka, on drums, but they

"WE WERE ALWAYS LOOKING FOR SOMEONE MORE PUNK ROCK."
WAYNE (LEFT), AND MICHAEL (WITH HIS STEPFATHER, CHRIS NUTHALL,
AND HIS MOTHER, LINDA) AROUND THE TIME THEY MET, 1983.

needed a bass player. Mark had seen the quiet weirdo with silver pants and a New Wave hairdo at Charles Ivins's party, and he had asked Michael if he played an instrument. "No, but I own a bass guitar," Michael said. A few days later, Wayne rang the doorbell.

"We were always looking for someone more punk rock," Wayne said. "Michael came to the door, and I said, 'I heard you play bass. Do you have a bass?' He said yes. I said, 'Do you have an amp?' He said no. I said, 'Well, I have an amp, do you want to come play with us?' And he said, 'Sure, whatever.'"

After his acquittal on the embezzlement charge, Tom Coyne started his own business, Tomco, selling office supplies and furniture and building cubicles in the new office buildings springing up downtown and in the suburbs. He looked at it "like a family farm," Wayne said, expecting his sons to help him out, but keeping pace with Tomco's boss could be difficult. When they'd complain about being hungry during a job moving furniture or setting up cubicles, their father would press them to continue until they finished the tasks at hand. "Finally, it would be about ten o'clock at night, we'd be driving home, and he'd say, 'Now we can stop at McDonald's,'" Wayne said. "But by then we'd be too tired to care."

Tom ran his new company out of a former grocery store at NW Twenty-fourth Street and Robinson Avenue. Mismatched chairs, battered desks, used filing cabinets, and boxes of paper were piled up everywhere, but his sons Wayne and Mark claimed an old meat locker at the back as their rehearsal space. The walls had been thick to begin with, but they hung padding and partitions to make the place even more isolated so they could play as loudly as they wanted any time of the day or night. Oklahoma City is located near the heart of Tornado Alley, and sirens warning residents to take shelter from potentially deadly twisters are a frequent occurrence there. The aspiring musicians never would have heard them while ensconced at Tomco, but they joked that if a tornado *did* hit while they were jamming, the bunkerlike freezer would probably be the only thing in the neighborhood left standing.

Mark passed around a gallon jug of Chianti when Michael arrived at the space, and Wayne helped him tune his bass, which he had adorned with Sex Pistols stickers. The group ran through raucous covers of the theme from *Batman*, "Summertime Blues," and songs by the Monkees as Michael plunked along, trying to keep up. "I thought it was kind of weird, because it was almost, sort of like a punk-rock outfit, but here was this guy with this long hair tied up in a ponytail, almost like a hippie," he said of Wayne.

After Michael left, the other band members compared notes. Mark and Dave observed that Michael couldn't really play. "Well, neither can we," Wayne said. "Let's keep at it."

"So many people have good ideas, but they don't do them," Wayne added years later. "A mediocre guy who works all the time gets more done than the super genius who hides in his glass castle. You gotta do stuff; you can't just sit around and think about it."

CHAPTER 2

FINALLY THE PUNK ROCKERS ARE TAKING ACID

THE <u>FLAMING LIPS</u> EP (1984)
AND <u>HEAR IT IS</u> (1986)

MORE animated than his bandmates, Wayne Coyne careered across the small, cramped stage, his curly brown hair flying behind him as he rang squalls of feedback from his Les Paul. On lead vocals, his younger brother, Mark, stood riveted to the microphone, alternating between the extremes of screaming and whispering; with his quarterback's muscles bulging out of the tank top under his overalls and an impressive mullet atop his head, one fanzine would later evoke the ghost of Lynyrd Skynyrd to describe him as "a low-rent Ronnie Van Zant . . . lost in a truck stop somewhere."

Determined to hold things together, drummer Dave Kostka kept the rhythms spare and steady on February 22, 1983, during the band's first gig, at an Oklahoma City bar called the Blue Note Lounge. As stoic as John Entwistle, the bassist for the Who, Michael Ivins hid behind his outrageous Afro. Midway through the show, his amplifier died, prompting calls from the crowd of "Let the bass man have some!"

"We just soldiered on," Michael said. "I'm sure it sounded like absolute hell." Added Wayne: "It was amateur clownishness, but it sure was fun."

Located next door to Tomco, the Blue Note was a rough-and-tumble dive that usually booked blues bands. "It was almost exclusively black, but my dad and the owner of the club knew each other, so we didn't seem like outsiders," Wayne said. The band had learned a generic twelve-bar blues, and it invited the bar owner to come by the meat locker so that it could audition for him. The quartet had been practicing for about eight weeks, honing its chaotic covers as well as noisy originals that drew equal inspiration from the lush psychedelia of Pink Floyd and the more aggressive, stripped-down, sped-up sounds of hardcore punk. Whether the club owner liked what he heard or felt a sense of neighborly obligation, he gave the group a gig.

The band had never come up with a name, and on the eve of its first show, it needed one. Wayne suggested two meaningless monikers. "Almost from the get-go, we had come up with some kind of identity, and that is the key part of being in a rock 'n' roll band, because you get to invent yourselves. The name is what you make it." He favored the Tijuana Toads, but his bandmates preferred his second choice, and the group made its debut as the Flaming Lips.

In the years to come, the band would encourage a number of myths about the origins of its moniker: It was the title of a porn flick; it referred to burning your mouth while smoking a roach; it had come to Wayne as a vision from the Virgin Mary. None of these was true; nor was the name inspired by the 1964 comedy *What a Way to Go!*, starring Shirley MacLaine, Dean Martin, Dick Van Dyke, and Gene Kelly as a director making a film called *Flaming Lips*. It simply appealed to Wayne as a bit of psychedelic surrealism, and a distinct alternative to names such as Reagan Youth and the Dicks, or the many hardcore bands known by their initials, such as AOD (Adrenaline Overdose), MDC (Millions of Dead Cops), or JFA (Jodie Foster's Army).

"I think in the big picture just keeping the name 'the Flaming Lips' over the years feels like the hardest thing we ever did," Michael said. "We were supposed to change it after the first night, 'cause nobody liked us, but it was just too much trouble to come up with another one."

Wayne had drawn several weird fliers publicizing the gig, with outlandish R. Crumb–inspired characters proudly announcing the debut of "Oklahoma's Boldest New Band," and he and his bandmates plastered them around Oklahoma City. Forty or fifty friends and family members showed up, including Michael's mother and stepfather; Wayne's girlfriend, Hali Neyland; and all of Wayne and Mark's family. "There were definitely a lot of Coynes there," Michael said. "There might have been a couple of punk rockers, and there were definitely a lot of guys there just innocently trying to have a beer, and then of course we came on and assaulted them."

The group impressed the audience less for its music than for the fact that it had mustered the courage to perform in public. "Is that really Wayne on stage?" his sister, Linda, asked, while Chris Nuthall couldn't believe that his shy stepson Michael had transformed himself into a punk rocker. "I didn't think too much of it," Wayne's brother Marty said. "What I saw was

"OKLAHOMA'S BOLDEST NEW BAND."
ONE OF WAYNE'S FLIERS FOR THE FLAMING LIPS' FIRST GIG,
FEBRUARY 1983.

that these guys were having a good time, and I liked it because they were enjoying themselves, not because I really enjoyed it."

From the beginning, Wayne and Michael treated the group more seriously than Dave and Mark. A few years older than the others and a solid
drummer with progressive-rock chops, Dave seemed to be biding his time
until a better gig came along, while Mark just wanted to party and have fun.
In retrospect, Wayne always had been the more likely front man. "Wayne
sort of wrote the songs, with all of the lyrics, and he showed Mark how to
sing them," Michael said. "I think Mark had no real desire to do that." But
Wayne had taken the Who as his model for the group, and with himself in
the role of Pete Townshend, he needed someone to be Roger Daltrey. "It's always been Wayne's band," Hali Neyland said. "He always had to be in charge
of everything, every little detail, but he's just that kind of guy."

Wayne constantly pushed the group to rehearse. "I've gotta practice,"
he said when Hali asked what he had planned for her birthday. "It's not like
they had a gig coming up at the time, but he had to practice all the time, and
I started to get pretty lonely," she said. Mark and Dave didn't complain, because they didn't have anything better to do, but Michael embraced the reg-
imen because it provided a sense of purpose. "I think some of the reason
why you get in a band is so you can actually say, 'Hey, I'm in a band.' For the
longest time, that's really all we did: We practiced all the time, and after we
were done practicing, we'd hang out in the practice space and talk."

Oklahoma City was hardly a musical hotbed in the early eighties, with
country cover bands and generic blues groups predominating at most of the
bars that booked live music. The coolest rock club in town was called the
Bowery, but it favored rockabilly bands, faux-R.E.M. heartland rockers such
as the Wickers, funky New Wave dance bands like the Fortune Tellers, and
sub–Minor Threat hardcore groups such as No Direction and Diet of Worms.
The downtown venue showed no interest the first few times Wayne tried to
book a gig: The Flaming Lips straddled several genres, and they didn't fit
easily into any of them. Wayne admired elements of hardcore, including the
energetic drumming, distorted guitars, and screamed vocals, but he made no
apologies for loving the melodies of classic rock or the freaky experimentation of psychedelia.

When the Flaming Lips played a show in a friend's basement, a hardcore punk fan approached Michael, who had cut his hair into a Mohawk, and
asked how he felt about being exploited. "It was like I was on the wrong
team or something, and I just thought that was kind of weird. I'd come to

find out that these so-called punk rockers were actually the sons and daughters of lawyers and doctors from the suburbs."

"The punks hated the hippies, and hippies took acid, so the punks hated acid, and in turn rejected the whole acid-rock approach," Wayne wrote in the liner notes to the Flaming Lips' 2002 compilation, *Finally the Punk Rockers Are Taking Acid.* "The hardcore kids even hated the Beatles, and especially the psychedelic stuff, and in a way that's where the line was drawn." He also had a basic philosophical difference with the rigid mindset of the hardcore bands. "Everybody came across in their music as pissed-off and hating everything . . . which isn't necessarily bad, but mostly it seemed artistically limiting, and I didn't want limits. I wanted to explore and experiment."

Shut out of the hipper venues, the Flaming Lips played wherever they could, including house parties and backyard barbecues. They also formed an alliance with another group of outsiders called the Hostages—"Two gay guys and a girl, with distorted bass, amateur drums, and Yoko Ono screaming," as Wayne described them—and the two groups scored a double bill at another neighborhood bar called the Maze, which catered to transvestites. "My brother [Charles] came to that one," Michael said. "He told our folks that he was upset that no one picked up on him."

The band's drummer, Dave Kostka, didn't like the idea of playing at "a gay bar," however, and he was so uncomfortable that he refused to come inside until the band took the stage. In the first of a half-dozen defections in the years to come, he quit a short time later, but within a few weeks, the group had found a replacement.

Born in Oklahoma City in 1963, Richard English had been a friend and classmate of Mark Coyne's from the sixth grade through Classen High School. In the seventh grade, Richard played viola in the school orchestra, but he switched instruments after being wowed by an African-American student who wailed on the trap set. "I said, 'Damn, that's pretty cool, I want to do that!' So I started taking drum lessons at Jacob's Music and playing to the Bee Gees and anything that had a simple 2/4 beat."

Just as the older Coyne brothers had opened Wayne's ears, Mark inspired Richard to turn away from his David Cassidy and Sonny and Cher records in favor of the Beatles and the Who. "Then, in about 1977, Mark told me that his brother was camped out at the fairgrounds, waiting in line for Led Zeppelin tickets a week before they were going on sale," Richard said. The day of the concert, he scored a ticket himself, and from his seat in the grandstand he looked down at the front row. "I saw this guy with this wild

THE FLAMING LIPS' FIRST DRUMMER, DAVE KOSTKA, "WAS A COOL GUY
INTO PROGRESSIVE ROCK AND SHIT," BUT HE DIDN'T LIKE THE IDEA OF
PLAYING FOR A CROWD OF TRANSVESTITES.

hair, and then I saw that he was sitting next to Mark. So I ran down and Mark introduced me to Wayne, his older brother. There I was at my first concert—and it was huge, with Frisbees flying everywhere—and I met this guy with curly hair who looked like Robert Plant. It was just too cool, and I had this aura about Wayne set in my mind from that point on."

Richard saw the Flaming Lips perform with Dave Kostka on drums at a party in a friend's backyard. "I was wasted, and I was like, 'Oh, Wayne is doing this!' It made perfect sense." A few days later Richard strolled into Long John Silver's. "Our drummer is flaking out," Wayne said as he manned the fry vats. "Do you want to be in a band?"

"From then on we were practicing at the furniture warehouse," Richard said. "At the time, Mark was a heavy smoker and drinker, and I was, too, so we were pretty much the druggies in the band, but Wayne and Mike were crystal clear."

"Richard was an alcoholic that Mark knew; they all partied together," Wayne said when asked how the band had found its second drummer. "He was drunk and fun-loving, and he wasn't that good, but he played like a freak, and we embraced that. Dave had been very stiff and reserved; he kept it steady so we could follow him. Once Richard came along, you couldn't hide the amateurism, so we got lights and smoke, and it all just became a big freak-out."

Shortly after Michael joined the band, in between their frequent rehearsals and sporadic gigs, the Flaming Lips started recording at Benson Sound, an Oklahoma City studio that specialized in taping gospel bands and commercial jingles.

In the early eighties, Oklahoma's oil industry went bust, prompting the failure of Penn Square Bank, the seventh-largest financial institution in the state, and taking a devastating toll on the local economy. From a peak of twenty-nine thousand in 1982, the number of oil-related jobs fell to about seven thousand in 1985, according to industry reports, causing a ripple effect as other businesses failed and real-estate values plummeted. Oil workers who had pulled up to Long John Silver's in their Cadillacs a year earlier now walked in looking for jobs. As a result, some businesses, including Tomco, tried to organize under the barter system to trade for goods and services they could no longer afford to purchase.

"Basically, the local guys tried to help each other," Wayne said. "My dad, being the believer in hard work and keeping your word, always kept his, but some of the other guys didn't. He'd given this recording studio a bunch of chairs or something, and they owed him. One day, he sort of begrudgingly said, 'Wayne, either you use up this time, or I lose it.' So every couple of weeks, when the old man was in a good mood, we'd go into the studio."

Over a period of several months, the group recorded a handful of songs to use as a demo cassette for booking gigs, including its raucous versions of the *Batman* theme, "Anyway, Anyhow, Anywhere" by the Who, "Handsome Johnny" by Richie Havens, and a pissed-off, pseudo-hardcore original called "Killer on the Radio," all rendered with a minimum of overdubs. "I remember even then being pretty fascinated with the whole recording process, but coming out of it with no better idea of how it was actually done," Michael said. "Then, after we'd made that tape and had been playing for a little bit, we saw other people coming through town, and we learned a lot just from watching these bands like the Replacements or Black Flag, who all had records out."

"I REMEMBER BEING PRETTY FASCINATED WITH THE WHOLE
RECORDING PROCESS, BUT COMING OUT OF IT WITH NO BETTER IDEA
OF HOW IT WAS ACTUALLY DONE." WAYNE, MICHAEL, RICHARD ENGLISH,
AND MARK COYNE WORKING WITH AN UNIDENTIFIED HOUSE ENGINEER
AT BENSON SOUND IN OKLAHOMA CITY, 1984.

The early eighties witnessed the birth of an indie rock network that
flourished across the United States in the wake of punk. Intrepid young promoters arranged shows at VFW halls, student unions, and small basement
clubs for punk and college-rock bands that crossed the country in battered
old vans, augmenting their take at the door by selling homemade T-shirts
and vinyl records that they either pressed themselves or released on small independent labels. College-radio DJs promoted the shows and played these
do-it-yourself recordings, and aspiring critics reviewed them in underground
fanzines, which they printed in the middle of the night courtesy of friends
who worked at copy shops.

Hotbeds of independent music sprang up across the country—in New
York, Hoboken, Boston, Minneapolis, San Francisco, and Washington, D.C.—
producing bands such as Sonic Youth, Black Flag, the Feelies, Minor Threat,
Flipper, the Gun Club, the Replacements, Hüsker Dü, Redd Kross, and the
Minutemen. By 1983, Norman, twenty miles south of Oklahoma City and
the home of Oklahoma University, had become one of three dozen stops on
the cross-country underground circuit, thanks in part to David Fallis, a jour-

nalism major who played in the punk band No Direction, wrote for the college newspaper, and worked as a DJ at the college radio station. Wayne and Michael often listened to Fallis's show, and it further exposed them to the burgeoning indie rock scene.

"He usually played what is thought of by some today as white supremacist music, then known as skinhead rock, and for a little while, I thought it was exhilarating, but a lot of it sounded, after a while, very much the same," Wayne wrote in 2002. "[But] one night, after not hearing him for a couple of weeks, I turned on his show and suddenly he was playing a different kind of American underground music—Redd Kross, R.E.M., Black Flag, Meat Puppets, Butthole Surfers—and I thought, 'Wow, this stuff is great!' It was melodic, intense without being one-dimensional, and some of it sounded very fucked-up. And then he played a track by Hüsker Dü, who I always thought of as 'just another hardcore band,' doing a cover of the Byrds' 'Eight Miles High,' and fuck! . . . It was a forceful, searing, religious spasm of melody and energy so out of control that the music is overwhelming even those who are playing it . . . It shook me up, and it transcended . . . and I thought, 'Finally, the punk rockers are taking acid!'"

Fallis met the Flaming Lips a short time later, after he began booking some of these bands at Oklahoma University. "We just started calling people and saying, 'Hey, we'll book a hall and do shows,'" Fallis said. "At that point, it was still very informal, all on a handshake. The turnout was usually pathetic, but we did shows at the National Guard Armory and the American Legion Hall, and that's how I met Wayne. He was just an optimistic guy working at Long John Silver's in Oklahoma City, with a wild, wiry mane of hair, and he wanted the Lips to play." Like every underground promoter, Fallis constantly wrestled with the problem of renting a decent sound system. "And Wayne was like, 'Dude, I've got this PA!'"

Word on the scene held that the powerful public-address system the Flaming Lips used in their rehearsal space had been liberated from a cowboy bar. "We knew a lot of guys from the dope-dealing days, and I told a couple of people I was looking for a PA," Wayne said. "Suddenly there were some guys from the neighborhood who wanted to sell one. They were criminals stealing from other criminals; it really was as simple as that."

Whenever Fallis needed it, Wayne and Michael fetched the PA from the meat locker and hauled it to Norman. "The deal was that Wayne brought his PA along—whether the Lips were opening up or not, I can't ever remember him saying no—and this went on all through '83, '84, and '85. They were always the odd band out, at least at the shows I was booking, with thrash bands, maybe a noise band like No Trend, and then the Lips. I remember Mike sitting around reading *The Electric Kool-Aid Acid Test,* but I don't remember them being partiers at all. They would throw parties, and it would always be like a mental institution—there would be this insane cast of alcoholics, drug addicts, sober guys, a religious guy handing out hemp—and Wayne and Mike were always just stone sober and very hospitable. They were ambitious, but it wasn't articulated. It was just clear that they were coming from somewhere else."

During the summer of 1983, with the barter system showing signs of collapsing, the Flaming Lips decided to use Tom Coyne's remaining credit with Benson Sound by following the indie-rock example of making their own record. The resulting self-titled five-song EP featured the group's latest originals recorded in the order they were written. Wayne recalled that the staid Baptist engineer didn't quite know what to make of the band, "but we did our best to get along with these people. It wasn't like we went in there and said, 'Fuck you, we know everything.'" The group employed as many studio frills as it could during its limited time, running the snare drum through an amplifier drenched in reverb to achieve a strange slapping sound, fading "Scratchin' the Door" in and out no fewer than four times, and dropping in "samples"—actually predigital taped snippets—of outer-space noise and an orchestral fanfare. "But basically the EP is just us playing," Wayne said. "This is the only one of our records that is about a performance—a performance of amateurs, without the strobe lights and the smoke."

The record opens with "Bag Full of Thoughts," a hypnotic drone with a dark and mysterious vibe. The song is driven by a massive drumbeat and a fuzz-drenched guitar riff, with Mark's whispered vocals—"Put your thoughts into a bag/If it becomes a drag/Throw it up into the air"—sitting behind the mix, nearly inaudible. "It was this sludgy, trippy song that we thought of as early Joy Division," Wayne said, though the chord progression is more reminiscent of "About a Girl" by Nirvana, which would follow six years later.

More dynamic and even more foreboding, with a sound that recalls the psychedelic garage bands compiled on *Nuggets,* "Out for a Walk" finds Mark delivering a spirited vocal about an ominous event—the specifics are never spelled out—that happened during a walk in the park. Its dominant feature is a distinctive underwater bass sound. During the preceding six months, Michael had grown considerably as a musician. "A lot of it was because there ended up being this freedom: It wasn't like, 'Oh, we have this song, it's in the key of A, you have to do these things this way,'" he said. Instead the material was crafted around the band members' abilities. "I guess that's why some of the stuff is truly weird."

It is also ambitious. "Garden of Eyes/Forever Is a Long Time" and "Scratchin' the Door" are both epic, multipart suites with waves of crescendos, bizarre-sounding guitar solos, distinctive melodic shifts, and an ambience that hints of Wayne and Michael's fondness for the neo-psychedelia of the Chameleons and Echo and the Bunnymen and the gothic "death rock" of Bauhaus, but the standout is the last track to have come together, and it closes the EP. In memorably cosmic terms, Wayne's lyrics for "My Own Planet" pay tribute to creating your own reality: "Ain't talkin' about no Hitler kind of trip/Just want a place where things can be just as we wish . . . I want my own planet, 'cause this one here is a drag."

"'My Own Planet' is cosmic, and it's punk rock; it's melodic, and it's noisy," Wayne said. "It was kind of rebellious, but it wasn't rebelling against this Reagan power thing, like the hardcore bands. It was rebelling by creating yourself. We didn't come up with another one like that for ten years." Added Michael, "That was sort of our Jesus and Mary Chain, balls-out rock song."

In fact, Scotland's Jesus and Mary Chain wouldn't release its debut single—a slice of feedback-drenched dementia called "Upside Down" paired with a warped cover of "Vegetable Man" by Pink Floyd founder Syd Barrett—until the fall of 1984. The Flaming Lips first heard "Upside Down" one night when they went to the Bowery while their friend Jon Mooneyham was spinning records. When he played the 45, Wayne and Michael descended on the DJ booth from opposite ends of the club. "This is the best thing we've heard, ever!" Wayne said, but his band had arrived at a similar sound entirely on its own, and it resisted easy pigeonholing.

On the East Coast, groups such as the Chesterfield Kings, the Lyres, and the Fuzztones had spurred a resurgence of the trippy garage rock of the mid-sixties, while in California, a scene called the Paisley Underground had produced more polished psychedelic pop by the Dream Syndicate, the Three O'Clock, and the Rain Parade. The Flaming Lips' influences ranged too far for them to be tagged as garage revivalists, and they were too raw and aggressive to fit with the Paisley popsters. In the coming years their closest peers would be acid-damaged Texas noise rockers the Butthole Surfers and avant-garde New Yorkers Sonic Youth, though at the time they hadn't heard either.

With the recording finished, Wayne called a pressing plant that advertised in the punk-rock bible *Maximumrocknroll*. Michael's maternal grandmother loaned him fifteen hundred dollars, the group mailed out the master tape along with a check, and a few weeks later it received a thousand copies of its first EP on green vinyl, an indulgence that had seemed well worth the extra cost. Wayne designed the cover, which featured a gothic photo of Richard peering out from behind a curtain in the Tomco meat locker while holding a skull covered in dripping candle wax. Wayne also designed and paid for a fancy four-color poster. "He got a loan—I'm not sure if it was from a loan shark or what—and did this painting of a weird, Jimi Hendrix–after-the-Apocalypse-looking guy playing the guitar," Michael said. A photo of the band appeared as an inset.

"I just did it all right there in the kitchen, and you can actually see the Magic Marker on the cover," Wayne said. "People who are graphic designers know; they say, 'What is that, Magic Marker?' If any graphics guy had come along to help me, I would have gladly accepted, but I didn't know anybody, so I just said, 'Fuck it, that is pretty good as it is.' The homemadeness is really what the Flaming Lips were about."

The group called its DIY record label Lovely Sorts of Death, after the tag line from Roger Corman's 1967 psychedelic exploitation film, *The Trip*. "I had actually seen that poster a long time ago, but I didn't know it was for *The Trip*," Wayne told *Forced Exposure* fanzine. "We just did it so we could be like John Lennon with 'Lucy in the Sky with Diamonds' and say, 'We didn't know the initials were LSD.' But nobody even asked us."

The record impressed the band's friends in the small Norman punk scene. "It seemed like such a huge deal, because they were actually on vinyl," Fallis said. The group finally started getting good gigs at the Bowery, and the EP won the Flaming Lips their first fans outside Oklahoma. By reading *Maximumrocknroll* and chatting up the touring musicians who borrowed his PA, Wayne had compiled a list of college radio stations, underground rock clubs, and fanzines, and in early 1984 the band mailed out half of its initial pressing of a thousand records in an effort to spread the word. The remainder went to the independent distributor Systematic, which shipped them to punk-friendly record stores across the country. (Eventually the band paid for a second pressing of another thousand records, this time on red vinyl.) The promotional push paid off.

"Just to have the poster and the record seemed like a big deal, and then when we got our first review in *Maximumrocknroll*, all of the sudden we were basically *in*," Michael said. Emulating the gonzo, amphetamine-fueled prose of pioneering rock critics Lester Bangs, Richard Meltzer, and Nick Tosches, who had helped inspire the punk movement a decade earlier, the fanzine

THE FLAMING LIPS

writers of the mid-eighties wrote in a wildly colorful and often hyperbolic style. "Hold the phone, Jesus is back! Mannnnn . . . This be a hot-shit record," *Maximumrocknroll* raved. Even more effusive was a review in *Forced Exposure* by its editor, Byron Coley, a Meltzer acolyte with a corresponding love of invented contractions. "As's been conclusively proven by the likes o' Black Oak Arkansas & the Thirteenth Floor Elevators, there's nothin' quite so invigorating as hillbillies who've sensed that there IS a better way," Coley wrote. "Wow. What we've got here's a fat brick o' sockodelic design that owes not one plugged hoof t' the revobilly hysterics that seem t' grip most musicians w/any sorta altered perception . . . A true gasser of absolute real McCoy design."

"When Byron Coley wrote those things, it changed everything," Wayne said. "Within a day, people reading it who thought we were clowns had changed their minds, and I saw the power of this perceived coolness. Whatever he said in the article—'These drug-damaged hillbillies who were one part Black Oak Arkansas, one part Black Flag'—if we had said that a day earlier, people would've been like, 'Fuck you, you're a poseur!' But now that Byron Coley said it, it was real, and they bought it. That was awesome."

As U.S. Route 40 stretched through the deserts of New Mexico and Arizona, Wayne and Michael passed the twenty-hour drive from Oklahoma City to Los Angeles deep in conversation. In the future, some members of the Flaming Lips' camp would come to dread sitting in the "hot seat" next to Wayne, but Michael didn't mind.

"Talking during these endless drives passes the time, and I get to find out what people are like," Wayne said. "They'll be cool for like the first hour, and then in the second hour you can start to break stuff down: 'Wait, what did you mean by that? Because if you mean *that*, how can *this* be?' After about the fourth hour you get to know what people really think. When people tell you the honest truth, it is always going to be fascinating. Sometimes, when we arrive, they're like, 'Are we already here?,' and it would have been like nine hours. It's rare that people can sit there for that long a time keeping that one thing going and going and going. By the end of it, someone is either revealing themselves, or they are lying."

Despite his innate shyness, Michael relished these talks. While their personalities differed dramatically, the introverted Michael and the outgoing Wayne held similar views about the band, the world, and philosophical issues such as God, love, and the meaning of life. "That's why a lot of times I didn't talk much in interviews, because when someone would turn the microphone over to me and say, 'And what do you think?,' I'd be like, 'Well, he just said it,'" Michael said. "We'd end up saying the same stuff, because that's what we both believe. Maybe we have different ways of saying it, but a lot of our beliefs about the world, why we're in a band, and what a band should do are basically the same."

Thanks to college radio station KUSF-FM's embrace of their first EP, the Flaming Lips had landed a prestigious gig in December 1985 opening for the Jesus and Mary Chain when its first American tour stopped at the I-Beam in San Francisco. Wayne and Michael had planned to drive to Los Angeles for a live interview with a supportive college radio station there before heading north for the gig. Wayne's brother Mark had gotten married, and he and his wife were flying to San Francisco with Richard, who wanted to minimize the time away from his job at an Oklahoma City law firm. Wayne had borrowed his father's Ford Impala and hitched it to a trailer hauling the band's equipment, and Michael had been driving through the night of intense conversation when the highway suddenly narrowed to one lane.

"Somewhere out in the desert it had rained a few days before, and it washed away part of the road," Michael recalled. "These orange barrels had been put down the middle of the passing lane—the slow lane had washed away, and there was no shoulder or anything—and I was trying to avoid the barrels when all of a sudden Wayne said, 'Look out!'" Michael swerved to avoid a hole that had opened in the highway in front of them, but the trailer's tire clipped the edge of the broken pavement, the car spun around and flew off the road, one of its tires blew out, and the trailer tipped over.

"Weirdly enough, we actually ended up pointing in the right direction, but off the side of the road," Michael said. "We opened up the trailer, saw that everything was still in one piece, tipped it back over, dragged it back up onto the highway, got the car out of the ditch, and fixed the flat. It was sort of like, 'Wow, that was weird. We're alive, but we're going to miss this radio show.' We were talking about it as we were driving home afterwards, and we said that maybe other bands in the same situation would have said, 'Fuck it,' and we didn't. It was like, 'If it didn't kill us, then we're going to keep going.'"

Two decades later, when everyone would compare their friendship to "an old married couple that doesn't even have to talk," Michael would cite the drive, the conversation, and the accident as the incidents that cemented his bond with Wayne. "I don't think there was any sense of 'Oh my God, you're my best friend now.' It was just, 'Well, here we go.' We had looked down the hill, and instead of walking along the top of it, we found ourselves at the bottom but just kept going."

A few months after the gig in San Francisco, Michael dropped out of college to devote himself to the Flaming Lips. The decision disappointed his mother and infuriated his stepfather. They expected him to become a lawyer or a professor, but Michael figured he could always return to Oklahoma University if the band didn't work out. Meanwhile he worked part-time as a line cook at Harry Bear's, and he would eventually log as many years at the more upscale hamburger restaurant as Wayne did at Long John Silver's.

The *Flaming Lips* EP paved the way for more gigs out of town, and from the middle of 1984 through the end of 1985, the quartet made several road trips of four or five days each to small clubs in Texas, Minnesota, Wisconsin, Iowa, and Kansas. Wayne connected with a punk-rock booking agent in Minneapolis, and Dolly Coyne plotted the course of her son's tours on flip-over TripTik maps that she collected as a member of AAA. "She'd mark all the rest stops and write notes about construction and stuff, all these little things that would get you there and get you back, and it was always an adventure," Wayne said.

In the fifties, Jack Kerouac had documented the cross-country odyssey of his quest for kicks in the classic novel *On the Road*. In the sixties, the Beat Generation ideal had morphed into the hippie backpackers hitchhiking to giant music festivals near Monterey, California, and Woodstock, New York.

Despite the cultural conservatism of the Reagan era, with its yuppie materialism, the growing gap between the haves and have-nots, and the looming threat of AIDS, this spirit of wanderlust thrived in the underground rock scene of the eighties. At the end of day-long drives, small communities waited to greet indie rockers with college radio stations that would play their records, fans who'd feed, house, and sleep with them, and promoters who'd pay them a few hundred dollars if people came out to their shows.

"Occasionally you'd get these super gigs out of nowhere, and if you had one of those in a city, you'd love that city forever," Wayne said. "There were other times when the gig was just a gig—nobody was there and nobody cared—but we were like pirates crossing the country, and we didn't care. It's like any job that you end up being good at: You like the job. If we didn't like driving, seeing the countryside, playing music and talking, loading in equipment, sleeping on floors, and meeting people, we would never have been able to be the Flaming Lips."

Life on the road didn't hold the same allure for all of the band members, however. "Mark liked it at first, but he changed," Wayne said of his brother. "It seemed like he never liked writing the songs and singing in front of people, but there was this thing about being a weird, confrontational guy that could sing some fucked-up stuff that appealed to him. But after you've done that for a while, it's like, 'I've had that kick. Now what do we do?'"

By late 1985, Mark had a wife, a house, a car payment, and steady work with his father at Tomco. "He flatly didn't like being on tour and being away from his job," Wayne said. "He didn't like not making any money, and he didn't like sleeping on strangers' floors. He was never into talking about music and art and ideas. We'd drive to Minneapolis, play with some of the guys in Soul Asylum, and stay at their house. Me and Michael would stay up all night and find out about different bands and scenes, but Mark never cared about that."

Mark also got pressure from home. One road trip north included gigs in Madison and Milwaukee with a day off before the next show in Minneapolis. According to Richard, Mark's wife forced the band to make the twelve-hour drive back to Oklahoma from Wisconsin so he could spend the night at home before returning to perform in Minnesota. "It was just brutal for all of us," the drummer said. Another trip ended with a disastrous gig in Lawrence, Kansas, that netted the band seven dollars. "I thought we were going to get rich," Mark groused. Wayne assured his brother that if they persevered, they might reach the level of indie icons the Minutemen or Hüsker

Dü. "Hüsker Dü? What the fuck is that?" Mark said. "I want to be like Led Zeppelin!"

Awkward and self-conscious onstage, Mark always had been the band's weakest link. "There were a lot of people early on who thought Mark just sucked," Richard said. "He basically screamed, and no one felt like he had talent. I don't know if Mark heard those critiques or not, but I don't think he ever felt totally sure of himself, even though Wayne encouraged him and worked hard to write songs that Mark could sing." Like his father, Wayne believed in loyalty, and he never considered firing Mark, until his younger brother made it obvious that he wanted to go. "When you're sitting there reading *Rolling Stone*, you think that is what a band is supposed to be," Wayne said. "The more we faced what life would really be like, even though Mark didn't want to quit, he didn't like it, and it just made it miserable for everyone else, until one day I said, 'You know, Mark, we aren't going to do this anymore.'"

"He's a true artist, where I'm just a jock that's having fun," Mark told Bradley Beesley in his 2005 documentary, *The Fearless Freaks*. "It was better that I got out when I did, which forced him into other types of music." Over the next few years, whenever Mark didn't have work at home, he'd climb into the van again to tour as the band's roadie, but some members of the family said he came to resent the group's success. "For the first few years, he made the right decision," Wayne said. "For a long time, there wasn't any bitterness about what could've been, but as we got successful, I think he started thinking, 'Man, I wish I was in the band,' and it was like, 'Well, that is never going to happen.'"

Wayne quickly settled into his new role as front man. "I looked at other bands I liked and said, 'You know, there is always a guy that makes it happen, a guy who stands up and takes the punches. Everyone else has this; why don't we?' I was always singing the songs to everyone anyways, since I was writing them, and we always had songs where Mark and I would sing together. He was such an unpredictable singer that if I hadn't been there singing with him, he would've forgotten what he was singing. So I just said, 'Fuck it. It's time.'"

The Flaming Lips played their first show with Wayne on lead vocals as well as guitar in Dallas in early 1986, and they had no problem making the transition from a quartet to a trio. "It was just another case of 'Here we go. Let's see what happens,'" Michael said. But Mark wasn't the only casualty of the band's constant touring. "That was a big part of what broke us up, because that is all Wayne thought about," Hali Neyland said. "He told me, 'I'm gonna be gone and you can't come with me; I'm gonna be sleeping in the van and this is how it's gonna be.' I was glad he was doing something he enjoyed, but I became very lonely, and I ended up leaving. We loved each other, but I wanted to experience having a baby and getting married. I was going down that road, and he was going down another road."

When Richard English joined the band, he brought a more frenzied style of drumming inspired by the Who's Keith Moon, and the Flaming Lips started to build their shows into sensory assaults complete with strobe lights, a mirror ball, and machines that filled the club with fog or bubbles. They had also written several strong new tunes, including "Jesus Shootin' Heroin," which they demoed with Mark before he left the band, and they were itching to make another record. "Almost immediately after we made the EP, we didn't like it," Wayne said. "We were already moving on." The group approached several indie record labels, but only Enigma Records showed interest.

Music lover and aspiring entrepreneur Bill Hein founded Enigma with his brother and another partner in Southern California in the early eighties. By 1986, the label ranked beside SST, Twin/Tone, and Homestead as one of the most successful indie-rock record companies. Best-selling acts such as the hair metal band Poison and the Christian metal group Stryper funded releases by cooler underground artists such as the Dead Milkmen and Ben Vaughn, which were issued on Enigma's Restless imprint. Another sublabel, Pink Dust, concentrated on albums by psychedelic legends such as Roky Erickson of the Thirteenth Floor Elevators and garage revival bands such as the Pandoras and Plasticland.

"I remember the Flaming Lips walking into our lobby when they were coming through L.A. with their self-released EP," Bill Hein said. "I recall a couple of us playing this record on colored vinyl and really liking it. There wasn't much debate: We sent them a contract, signed them, and had them start making another record all pretty rapidly."

From the band's perspective, finalizing the deal took forever, so it decided to speed things up by driving to California to sign the papers and start recording. The label had planned to pair the group with Helios Creed, the guitarist and producer of noise rockers Chrome, but when the Flaming Lips just showed up, their new label scrambled to book a studio and turned to producer Randy Burns, who had a break between sessions with Megadeth, the group Dave Mustaine formed after leaving Metallica. Utilizing a five-thousand-dollar advance at a time when Wayne earned seven thousand a year at Long John Silver's, the Flaming Lips spent two days recording with Burns at one Hollywood studio and two days mixing at another, sleeping on the floor throughout.

The group had honed half an album's worth of songs at rehearsal and in live performance, and it improvised the rest on the spot. Stubborn, opinionated, and used to working with more polished musicians, Burns imposed a lot of his own ideas, adding handclaps to the end of one tune, putting reverb on the drums, and goading Wayne and Michael to perfect the harmonies in the backing vocals. He also spent four hundred dollars of the budget on the extravagance of hiring a "drum doctor" to tune the drums Richard had purchased at a garage sale and adorned with X-rated centerfolds.

"The producer was real pushy, but he did have fun with it," Wayne said. "We admitted that we didn't know the chords we were playing, and he had a laugh and showed us." When the Flaming Lips criticized some of his sounds, however, Burns ignored their suggestions and snapped, "I've been in the business for twenty years."

"Twenty years later, I would never say that to anyone," Michael said. "I wouldn't dismiss somebody's idea. This guy didn't make it very enjoyable, but he did make us do a few overdubs, which I'm glad that we ended up doing. When we were a three-piece, I think we had some sort of misguided idea like, 'How can we have more instruments on the record? That's not real.' We obvi-

"THERE WAS SOMEBODY DOING WHAT I WAS DOING IN EVERY TOWN IN AMERICA." THE FLAMING LIPS' FIRST MANAGER, MICHELE VLASIMSKY, IN 1987.

ously got over that really quick and decided that live is one thing and the studio is another."

When a dispute with Burns arose during the mixing, Wayne finally stood his ground. "It was a hell of a fight for a while, and I just watched Wayne stand there and say, 'We're going to have to agree to disagree,'" Richard recalled. "Wayne got what he wanted, and I thought, 'Wow, that's pretty cool.'" The band returned home carrying a cassette of its first full album. "As we drove from L.A. to Oklahoma City, we listened to it a thousand times," Wayne said, "and by the time we got home, we were like, 'Okay, we won't do it *that* way again.'"

The woman who would become the Flaming Lips' first manager and Wayne's second girlfriend was born in Germany in 1966 to well-educated, upper-middle-class parents who had emigrated from Czechoslovakia. Michele Vlasimsky's father had been involved in the underground during World War II, escaped from prison twice, and served as an American spy before working as an executive in the oil industry. The family moved to the United States and spent several years in Kansas City during Michele's childhood before finally settling in Tulsa.

Michele enrolled at Oklahoma University in 1983 as a film student, and she became a regular at David Fallis's punk shows, one of the few alternatives for anyone seeking culture beyond Sooner football. "At the time, Norman was basically a sleazy little college town, with the old town tavern, a twenty-four-hour diner that was almost like a Socialist place where all the dissidents went, Shadowplay Records, and that was about it," Michele said. The fast-talking, hyperenergetic brunette started helping Fallis promote gigs. "I was kind of like Dave's female gofer and gal Friday, and that's how I met Wayne, who was the PA guy."

When Fallis burned out on hosting shows in late 1985, he passed the mantle to Michele, who took over booking bands such as Sonic Youth and Scratch Acid at the American Legion Hall. "She took it to the next level right when things were starting to break nationally," Fallis said. "Little networks were starting to come together in a more organized fashion; bands were actually getting record deals, and they were starting to come through with more regularity."

"There was somebody doing what I was doing in every town in America," Michele said. "The benefit of being in a place like Norman—which is a total cultural void where nothing is going on—is that it gives you the oppor-tunity to start something. You had to create your own fun, because there was very little to do."

Like Fallis before her, Michele called Wayne whenever she needed a PA, and if the Flaming Lips weren't touring, Wayne and Michael made the trek to Norman. "Because Wayne was the more personable guy compared to Mike, I always wound up talking to him, and we became friends," Michele said. "At that time, Wayne was amazing: He was the nicest, kindest, sweet-est, most generous guy, who would do anything for anyone. He was com-pletely sacrificial, obviously; you don't drive sixty miles round-trip with the PA just to do it. He wasn't doing it for the money, he wasn't doing it as a job; he was just doing it to do it, and because he wanted to be part of the scene and help make shows happen and help bands play. He was a super-, super-wide-eyed, nice guy, and a little . . . I don't want to say hippie-ish, but he had his own personal style."

One night as Michele lay in bed in her apartment, she heard a knock on the window: Wayne and Michael had come bearing a copy of the *Flaming Lips* EP. "To this day, I love that record," she said. "I don't listen to it, and as far as their catalog, it's not their best recording. I'm sure it's because I'm emo-tionally tied to it: Wayne told me he recorded it so that I would fall in love with him. It was a romantic thing."

Wayne and Michele started dating, and he soon moved in with her in Norman. "Wayne was a guy from Oklahoma City from a very poor family in the ghetto who got a job at Long John Silver's, moved out at sixteen, and supported himself because he so badly wanted to get away from that," Michele said. "He had much bigger dreams and goals than what that life was and where his other brothers were going." Every bit as eager as Wayne to make her mark on the world, Michele matched her boyfriend's passion for music, his boundless energy, and his love of talking. As the indie-rock scene blossomed and she booked bigger and more successful shows, they became the power couple of the Oklahoma underground. Eventually she launched her own club, called Subterranea, on Main Street in Norman, and shortly af-ter the Flaming Lips recorded their first album, she began working as their manager.

"It's all professionally and personally intertwined. I don't know how it came about, except that Wayne must have said, 'Do you want to book some shows for us?' One thing led to another, and the next thing you know, I was not only booking all their shows, but doing all the radio, press, retail promo-tions, and micro-marketing with the Restless deal. Before that they were just patching things together. It wasn't until *Hear It Is* that they learned, 'This is what a national record release is.'"

The band's first full album issued on Enigma/Pink Dust is a mixed bag. Some of the songs are genre exercises that fall flat, such as the garage rocker "Man from Pakistan," the gothic drone "She Is Death," and the Who-style romp "Trains, Brains & Rain," with lyrics Wayne seemed to have tossed off at the mike ("This is the last song ever written/About trains and brains and rain/Ain't it a sin?"). Others are overly derivative: "Just Like Before" and "Charlie Manson Blues" both owe obvious debts to Sonic Youth. (The New York quartet had sung about Manson in its 1984 single "Death Valley '69," which the Flaming Lips often covered live.) Yet while the musicians were disappointed that they hadn't written another anthem as memorable as "My Own Planet," *Hear It Is* showed impressive growth since their first EP.

"Wayne will level the charge that we were just making record-collection music," Michael said, but the album's finest moments display the origins of a unique sound, more dynamic and textured than the group's earlier recordings. Despite the disagreements in the studio, *Hear It Is* also benefits from Burns's slightly slicker production.

The album opens with an unabashed love song called "With You." Wayne strums an acoustic guitar and offers the heartfelt declaration "When I walk with you, I feel weird," before the band kicks into rollicking noise-rock mode. "I don't think I ever wrote songs that were specifically just about me," Wayne said when asked if he'd penned the tune about his new girlfriend, Michele. "It was really just about pairing the simple, pop, Phil Spector thing with the demented, noisy, apocalyptic thing."

"Unplugged" is a hard groove with a memorable fuzz-guitar riff and lyrics inspired by some drug-damaged fans the band met in Houston. "Thinking they're great, some new kind of drug/They got their wires pulled out/Tell ya, man, they're unplugged," Wayne sings, delivering a warning more in tune with Nancy Reagan's "Just Say No" than the underground's prevailing pro-drug ethos. "As far as drugs go, we want to have a good time," Wayne told *Forced Exposure*, "but we're not out to destroy ourselves."

"Jesus Shootin' Heroin" also utilizes druggy imagery, evoking "Heroin" by the Velvet Underground as rendered by the Birthday Party. The title came from a favorite phrase of the Flaming Lips' pal Jon Mooneyham. "It was a line that he would say, like, 'I'll be dipped in shit,'" Wayne recalled. "It didn't matter what the song was about, as long as it was druggy and unpredictable and heavy." In fact, as the group builds tension via a monolithic rhythm, eruptions of noise guitar, and bloodcurdling screams, Wayne delivers some of the most memorable lyrics of the band's early career, summarizing the sort of philosophical conversations he had with Michael while driving: "Well, I never really understood religion, except it seems a good reason to kill / Everybody's got their own conceptions / And you know, they always will."

The deceptively spare lyrics of "Godzilla Flick" seem to be about killing time watching a Japanese monster movie and a Clint Eastwood film, though they actually chronicle the nerve-wracking night Wayne spent sitting with his oldest brother in front of the television during a bad drug trip when Tommy kept talking about suicide. The acoustic guitar melody and Wayne's homely vocals evoke a slacker version of legendary Oklahoma folkie Woody Guthrie, until the song abruptly ends with a giant, echoed crash—presumably Godzilla's foot stomping down upon the studio.

Just as powerful is the album's final track, which segues into a reprise of "With You." The title "Staring at Sound" brings to mind the phenomenon of synesthesia—the sensation of "seeing" sound waves as colors or images, sometimes prompted by a psychedelic trip—and Wayne sings about finding a band that plays "a song that sounds just like you look," then following this group like a stalker. "The goal was taking the hippieness out of psychedelia, being more psycho than psychedelic, and, like Sonic Youth, trying to show that you could be noisy and freaky and not be sixties," he said. In another of the song's memorable couplets, he sings, "I want to be a movie star / And play the part of a man from outer space"—a goal he'd realize fifteen years later, when the Flaming Lips began filming their first movie, *Christmas on Mars*.

Once again Wayne designed the album cover, choosing a slightly blurry photo of the band with Michael sitting out front, smiling beneath the mushrooming Afro that inspired some Oklahoma fans to wear buttons heralding "the Church of Michael Ivins's Hair." For the back cover, Wayne chose an enlarged photo of an eyeball, one of his favorite artistic motifs.

Released in the fall of 1986, *Hear It Is* garnered an even more enthusiastic reception from college radio—it reached number 20 on the *College Music Journal*'s Top 100 radio chart, behind albums by R.E.M., the Smiths, Love and Rockets, and Nick Cave—and it was once again lauded by the underground press. "With screaming guitars, deranged vocals, and a drum set haunted by the ghost of Keith Moon, the Lips are staking out a weird terrain somewhere between *Meaty Beaty Big and Bouncy* and vintage Blue Öyster Cult," *Creem* magazine gushed. In *Away from the Pulsebeat*, Art Black wrote that "the Flaming Lips are so fucking neighborly, they don't even bother to disguise the riffs they steal, yet they're so completely fucking *wired* that their original 'sources' compare like aspirin to acid." And their first critical champion, By-ron Coley, returned to applaud what he called "a jumbled, beautiful mess of guitar squack, post-logical finesse, and overall tongue beauty."

At first, the Flaming Lips didn't notice much of a difference between re-leasing the EP themselves and issuing *Hear It Is* on a bona fide record label. "I remember working one night at Long John's and one of the guys from the label called me and said, 'I'm sorry I'm just now hearing the record you made two months ago, but this is going to be one of the best releases we've had all year,'" Wayne said. "They were shysters." But the company did its part to distribute the album, and the band began to see evidence of its music reach-ing a much broader audience. Wayne had just dumped another batch of french fries into the oil at Long John Silver's another night in the spring of 1987 when the restaurant's manager told him he had a call from Europe: "Some guy who wants the band to play there or something."

A few months later, in July 1987, the Flaming Lips flew to Copenhagen, Denmark—the first time Wayne or Richard left the United States—to appear at the sixteenth annual Roskilde Festival on a twenty-four-band bill topped by Iggy Pop, Rickie Lee Jones, the Pretenders, and Van Morrison. One of the promoters had heard "With You" playing in a record store, and he booked the band to perform on the smaller second stage before fifteen hundred peo-ple, just as the sun was beginning to set on the middle of the three-day rock fest, following Sonic Youth and preceding Australian garage rockers the Hoodoo Gurus. "We were totally psyched," Wayne told *Contrast* fanzine in 1988. "It was like Woodstock or something. The crowd liked us—people knew our songs and everything—and we were like, 'Are you *sure* you got the right band?'"

Richard had worried that the trio wouldn't come across in such a big setting, and he had to cope with a lightweight rented kit instead of his own pinups-enhanced drums. "But our fearless leader's Pete Townshend–esque jumping and stomping seemed to convey the energy we usually had. We got the total VIP treatment—I still have a Roskilde towel from the hotel—and all in all it was a whirlwind trip that took some Okie boys across the ocean and made us heroes . . . at least in our own minds."

CHAPTER **3**

EVERYTHING'S EXPLODIN'

OH MY GAWD!!! . . . THE FLAMING LIPS (1987) AND
TELEPATHIC SURGERY (1988)

AS WAYNE COYNE watched from the control room of Goodnight Audio, a recording studio set up in a former church in Dallas, Michael Ivins, Richard English, and Mark Coyne (who had come along on a lark) enthusiastically attacked the old upright piano with the tools they'd brought expressly for the task. "I remember working up a big sweat over that thing: Swinging sledgehammers is not so easy after about thirty seconds," Richard said. "We started out strong, whimpered for a second, realized we were still recording, and went back at it again."

Eventually, the trio smashed through the casing and keyboard, pounded the hammers and strings in the piano's innards, and finally left a pile of shattered wood on the floor of what had once been the church's altar, though the sound didn't prove to be as massive as Wayne had hoped, and the group had to overdub some other destructive noises to achieve the results it sought. The band wanted to end its second album with a bang, literally, after the final song, one of several standout tracks and stylistic departures.

"Love Yer Brain" is a ballad driven by Richard's piano playing but focusing on Wayne's lyrics, which champion the power of imagination to transcend violent or depressing realities, and his understated vocals, the most self-assured and musical performance he'd delivered since replacing Mark as vocalist. While he didn't take drugs himself, Wayne didn't look down on people who thought they needed them—"If your choice is to do drugs or kill yourself, I'd say that you should do some drugs," he said—and he wrote "Love Yer Brain" after the night a druggie friend came to visit him at Long John Silver's. He usually could slip away for a few minutes to chat, but this evening the restaurant was hopping, so his friend sat forlornly drinking a Coke before leaving. The next day, Wayne learned that the man had killed himself a few hours later in his garage with the car exhaust running. "You can love yer brain, even if it slips down the drain," Wayne sings. "Man, I'm not no drug addict, but a person's gotta have something/To keep him from going insane."

The song ends with a minute and a half of the piano meeting its demise. The group had purchased the old upright for three hundred dollars outside Ardmore, Oklahoma, with the sole intention of destroying it. "I think we got a pretty weird reaction from the people selling it," Richard said. "They wanted to know if it was going to a nice home." In fanzine interviews, the group didn't discourage the rumor that it actually had demolished a white baby grand that Elton John gave Stevie Nicks, the vocalist and "White Witch" of Fleetwood Mac, who once owned the Dallas recording studio.

Dissatisfied with the experience of working with Randy Burns in Los Angeles on *Hear It Is*, the Flaming Lips vowed to maintain more control over their second album, which would be issued on Enigma/Restless. "We had so many people tell us, 'You're gonna sign with the company, they're gonna treat you like shit, and you'll just be lost in the shuffle. Whatever anybody liked about you on your first record will be totally lost,'" Wayne told Fred Mills in a long interview with *The Bob*, another fanzine, in early 1988. "We had all these warnings, and a lot of that does go on. Bands can have a certain charm about them, and they don't really know what it is, then they'll go do a record and it won't even be what you thought you liked about them. So we just figured, 'Fuck that, we're gonna make a lot of records!' We just went for it."

In a fourteen-month blur of activity, Restless released *Oh My Gawd!!! . . . The Flaming Lips* in mid-1987 and the band's third album, *Telepathic Surgery*, a year later, in late 1988. Dallas had been the first city outside Oklahoma to embrace the band—"They were like the nonlocal local band," said Robert Wilonsky, then the rock critic at the *Dallas Observer*—and the Flaming Lips recorded both albums there, a three-hour drive from home, but fourteen hundred miles from potential interference by its label. Goodnight Audio paired the band with one of its staffers, Ruben Ayala, an accomplished musician and an easygoing, open-minded engineer who provided the technical knowhow the group lacked without imposing his own views about how records "should" be made.

Ayala met the Flaming Lips at the studio the night before they started work on *Oh My Gawd!!!* "My first impression of them, after seeing some of their artwork and stuff, was, 'This is some kind of really out-there rock 'n' roll band; these are going to be some weird, drugged-out sessions,'" he recalled. After the musicians unpacked their van, Ayala asked where they intended to spend the night, and they told him they planned to sleep in the parking lot. "I don't know who it was, but one of them piped up, 'Do you think we could crash inside the studio?' I was going, 'I don't even know these guys; what will the owners think?' I had to make a judgment without even knowing them, but I trusted them, and they turned out to be like the most straightest, hard-working band I'd ever met. Obviously, they were not what my initial impression was."

The Flaming Lips were as pleasantly surprised as Ayala. "Ruben was a good engineer with a great ability to let the show go on around him without dabbling too much in the chemistry," Richard said. "He listened intensely, and he had good ideas, but they didn't disrupt what the band was about." Added Wayne, "At some point, Ruben always let us do what we wanted, for better or for worse. We learned a lot about how to record, though it wasn't very musical: A lot of it was just a barrage of sound."

One factor that distinguished the Flaming Lips from other indie-rock bands was that they always worked in relatively professional studios, instead of using cheap home-recording units. "It set us apart, because we were doing these stupid things in expensive studios, while most bands were just doing it on four-tracks and it sounded like hell," Wayne said. "We were ill prepared and amateur, so we sounded like the Shaggs anyway, but it seemed like we had intentionally decided to expose every flaw, and that stuck out."

Before returning to the studio, Wayne and Michael had spent weeks scrutinizing their favorite albums by Pink Floyd and the Beatles, as well as dozens of others. "We'd heard some records that sounded good, and some records that sounded like shit, but we didn't really know why," Michael told *The Bob* fanzine. "We ended up making little snippets of examples: Here's a bit of Poison, and here's a bit of our old record, and here's Poison again, and then the new Cult record, just to go, 'Okay, this sounds good, this doesn't.'" Added Wayne, "We'll listen to the Who records, and there's Keith Moon playing tons of stuff, and a lot of it gets totally lost. If Richard's gonna play a ton of stuff, we want you to be able to hear that, and it should be really loud. You'll put on some records that should be really heavy rock records, but they're really sort of thin. Soul Asylum is a good example: You see them live, and it's like, '*Kkrrrrhhhh!,*' but you hear their records, and there's nothing there. A lot of people are really into this 'independent sound'; it's like independents are supposed to sound like shit. We don't want to sound like shit, yet we don't want to sound slick."

Oh My Gawd!!! made more use of dramatic dynamic shifts and subtle textures to color the music, with Wayne alternating acoustic guitar and bursts of electric noise, Richard overdubbing piano, and the group adding more taped samples lifted from other recordings. "It wasn't so much experimental as it was, 'Let's have raucous fun with the music we love,'" Richard said. But once again, the trio couldn't stretch the six-thousand-dollar advance from Restless far enough to try everything it wanted, and it had to make do with five days total to record and mix.

"We tried to get as much bang for our buck as we could," Wayne said. "We camped out at the studio and never left. We'd wake up at nine a.m. and stop working at four; crash for five hours, then do it again. You lay down the drum tracks, then the bass tracks, then a day later for the same songs you're doing guitar tracks, and at the end you're doing vocal tracks. That leaves a day to mix, but we were like, 'We need a week!' So it was 'No sleep! No sleep!' Everything went until the last possible second, with all the money and all the time we had." The band finished assembling the master tape at six in the morning the day another group was scheduled to arrive, leaving an exhausted Ayala two hours to nap at the recording console before starting his next work day.

In the midst of recording, the Flaming Lips got a call from Enigma/Restless saying that its catalog was going to print, and if the band didn't settle on a title by the morning, the new record would simply be called *The Flaming Lips*. "Oh my God, *The Flaming Lips?*" Wayne asked. "Then we thought about it and decided just to go with that. The 'Gawd' bit is kind of like when people think you're a hick: We thought that maybe we'd been getting a little too arty, so we should offset that with a kind of goofy name."

Wayne often played the "hillbilly"/Okie role to the band's advantage. The only other Oklahomans to make an impact on the national indie-rock scene were hardcore punks Defenestration; the group would follow the Flaming Lips in recording its 1987 debut with Randy Burns, and its leader, Tyson Meade, would go on to form the more glam-rock-influenced Chainsaw Kittens. Fanzine writers in Boston, New York, or Los Angeles imagined that both groups came from a rural backwater, the epitome of what critic Greil Marcus would call "the old, weird America." Many of the Flaming Lips' early reviews mentioned the only thing writers knew about Oklahoma: In August 1986, letter carrier Patrick Henry Sherrill shot twenty-one of his coworkers at a post office in Edmond, killing fourteen before shooting himself; the first in a rash of such incidents, it inspired the phrase "going postal." Wayne didn't mind channeling a bit of "Crazy Pat"—exaggerating his drawl and his eccentricities—if it gave reviewers an angle.

While its creators came to hate the name *Oh My Gawd!!! . . . The Flaming Lips*—"That truly is a shitty title," Wayne said—they took justifiable pride in the cover art. They convinced Restless to spring for the extra expense of a full-color gatefold sleeve, and the trio collaborated on an elaborate collage inspired by Salvador Dalí (who is name-checked in the lyrics for "The Ceiling Is Bendin'"). Wayne painted a weird phallic creature and two melting skulls

"SALVADOR DALÍ WATCHES FROM HIS WINDOW IN A DREAM."
THE SURREAL COVER OF *Oh My Gawd!!!* . . . *The Flaming Lips,* 1987.

with bulging eyeballs, and Michael and Richard pasted up photos of the Beatles, Marilyn Monroe, the crowd at Woodstock, the first moon walk, the explosion of the space shuttle *Challenger,* the shark from *Jaws,* fields of poppies,
and scenes from the Vietnam War.

Both albums the band recorded in Dallas contain moments of inspiration
as well as self-indulgent clatter and failed experiments, but *Oh My Gawd!!!* is
the stronger effort, and it opens with two diverse but equally memorable
tunes. In "Everything's Explodin'" the band congratulates itself for rocking
so hard and playing loud enough to wake the dead, before launching into a
tuneful but raucous chorus about explosions and car wrecks. "It's kind of
the last song that we had with that balls-out, straightforward, *Hear It Is* atti-

tude," Wayne told *The Bob*. It is also a succinct summation of the group's psychedelic-punk philosophy: "When I look in my mirror and my brains are fallin' out of my head/Well, there's nothing wrong, it's just the way I feel/And if you don't like it, write your own song."

More than nine minutes long, "One Million Billionth of a Millisecond on a Sunday Morning" explores a completely different vibe, bringing to mind slow and creepy Pink Floyd epics such as "Careful with That Axe, Eugene" and "One of These Days." It would become a live staple for the next six years. "It's part Velvet Underground, part Pink Floyd," Wayne said, and the recording thrilled the musicians so much that they cheered when they heard the playback. "'One Million Billionth' is the quintessential Lips song to me, because it's all about this huge universe in this tiny pinhead," Richard said. "We were all just standing on chairs in the studio and shouting, 'This is too good!'" Unfortunately, the rest of the album doesn't rise to the peaks of this track, "Love Yer Brain," and "Everything's Explodin'," and it stands as a collection of interesting ideas that don't quite gel.

"Prescription: Love" is marred by an overly long introduction and the lack of a strong hook, though the lyrics pursue another of Wayne's favorite themes, pairing the hippie notion that people fill their lives with empty materialism to make up for a lack of love with the cynical punk observation that perhaps love just needs a stronger ad campaign: "Let's give love the marketing scam."

"Ode to C.C. (Part I)" is a bit of studio tomfoolery that provides a sarcastic comment on backwards masking, the allegedly subversive practice of embedding messages that only become apparent when listeners spin the vinyl LP in the opposite direction. In September 1985, the U.S. Senate had held a series of hearings instigated by the so-called "Washington wives," concerned mothers who had formed the Parents Music Resource Center to combat what they called "pornographic" rock lyrics and supposedly hidden messages on albums by artists such as Judas Priest, Iron Maiden, and AC/DC. Spinning "Ode to C.C. (Part I)" backward reveals Richard screaming, "Mom, you fucked up when you raised me!" and a lick from "Talk Dirty to Me" by C. C. DeVille and the hair-metal band Poison. "We used some special effects to make the voice really low," Richard said, "like what they use in movies for when the devil talks"—a sound that would become a hallmark of Flaming Lips records thereafter. "We just needed another song for that side; that's why it's on there," Wayne said. "But maybe we also thought we could land on the censorship panel with [Dead Kennedys leader and free-speech activist] Jello Biafra at the next New Music Seminar."

The site of three mental hospitals, Norman was notorious in the eighties for the number of patients who'd been turned out on the streets by Reagan-era deinstitutionalization. "This in turn attracted a lot of Jesus freaks who wanted to preach to these desperate, homeless folks," Wayne said, and he wrote the acoustic ballad "Ode to C.C. (Part II)" after being accosted about the state of his soul while waiting at a bus stop. When asked if he wants to be born again, Wayne responds in the lyrics that heaven rejected him, "but I think hell's got all the good bands anyway." Musically the song attempts "this real cheesy, Woody Guthrie, fifties type of thing," Wayne said, and it could have been a gem if he had treated it as more than a one-take toss-off.

Despite Wayne's assertion that the band had left straight-ahead psychedelic garage rock behind, several of the other songs on *Oh My Gawd!!!* could have fit neatly on *Hear It Is*. "Maximum Dream for Evel Knievel" is "our idea of what [Led Zeppelin's] 'Black Dog' would be if someone tried to write a song like that today," Michael said; "The Ceiling Is Bendin'" borrows one of Wayne's favorite Alice Cooper riffs while employing the gimmicky effect of the rhythm section fading in and out throughout the tune, and "Can't Stop the Spring" is a generic rocker memorable only for including a fantastic orchestral sample.

The remaining tracks, "Can't Exist" and "Thanks to You," are lyrically heartfelt but musically unremarkable love songs written by the band's drummer. "That really tells you how open Wayne can be," Richard said, "because looking back, I don't think they're the greatest songs, and they don't fit in with the style of the band. But he was willing to say, 'Hey, man, it's all shit; let's just throw your songs at the wall with everything else.'" Wayne downplayed his bandmate's contributions when asked about them in *The Bob*—"Richard played them on guitar, but he can't play guitar any good"—though he later came to appreciate their sincerity. "At the time, Richard's songs were very embarrassing to me and Michael," Wayne wrote in the liner notes to the 2002 compilation *Finally the Punk Rockers Are Taking Acid*. "We were so convinced that to 'shock' or 'teach' listeners was more important than being real. What fools we were. Richard showed us it's better to be honest even at the risk of humiliation than to be (with shame) a poser."

With their new manager (and Wayne's girlfriend), Michele Vlasimsky, booking their tours, the Flaming Lips spent much of 1987 and 1988 performing at small clubs across the United States. "They were definitely building it one fan at a time," Michele said, and at some shows they now earned as much as five hundred dollars. "They played a lot, and we were very strategic about having them go back to these cities every two to three months to keep building their audience. We had them go anywhere that was driving distance; and for them, Buffalo, New York"—twenty hours and thirteen hundred miles away—"was driving distance. They were road warriors."

"For a long time, being on the road was better than living at home," Michael said. "You always had money. You always had a place to stay. It never became overly uncivilized." The musicians would leave on a five- or six-week tour, return to work at their day jobs in Oklahoma City for two months, save up enough money to cover their expenses for another trip, then head back out again. "Touring costs a lot of money: You make a lot of money, but you spend a lot of money, so we have to work in between," Wayne told *The Bob* in 1988. Added Michael, "There'll be times when we'll drive back from L.A.—thirty hours straight—get home, take a shower, and go to work."

By aggressively working the phones and building relationships with club bookers across the country, Michele brought the band to another level as a national underground act while at the same time honing skills and contacts that would pay off when she started working with other groups through her new booking agency, Bulging Eye—a name that reflected one of her boyfriend's favorite images. Wayne appreciated Michele's efforts, but he missed the days when his mother, Dolly, mapped out the tours with help from AAA. "The first tour we did after Michele started with us, she refused to let my mother help, and there were no directions. There were no directions ever." The musicians joked that in routing its tours, Michele used a map six inches square. She'd measure a distance the size of her thumbnail and assume that the drive would be a snap, when it fact it would be a sixteen-hour haul.

"THEY WERE ROAD WARRIORS." THE FLAMING LIPS ON TOUR IN CHICAGO, 1987.

By late 1986, the Flaming Lips had graduated from borrowing their parents' cars to buying a van of their own, a two-year-old blue Ford Econoline with two massive gas tanks, which they purchased for $8,900 and paid off in installments. "Old Blue" had 27,000 miles on it when the band bought it; as it entered retirement eight years later, the odometer stood at 485,000. Cracked insulation around the windows made it unbearably hot in the summer, ridiculously cold in the winter, and noisy and breezy all year round, but the band made things as comfortable as possible by building bunks in the rear, over a storage bin for the guitars, amplifiers, and drums, and upgrading the all-important stereo system four times. "We were lucky with that damn blue van; it fucking worked forever," Wayne said. "We'd sleep on top of the equipment, but still, to this day, it was some of the best sleep I've ever gotten, because you'd be so damn tired. We'd pull up to some rest stop outside of North Dakota, and you might as well have been in the middle of the ocean or the desert."

If the group could spare the expense, it stayed at a Motel 6 or a Super 8, filling a thirty-dollar room with three musicians plus a friend or two who'd come along as roadies, carrying equipment, tuning guitars, and setting up the lights and the fog and bubble machines. Other times, the band crashed with appreciative fans, promoters, or fellow musicians, which could be problematic. Richard recalled an unsettling night when they accepted an offer from a fan to stay at a comfortable house in Atlanta. He and Michael were sleeping

"WE WERE LUCKY WITH THAT DAMN BLUE VAN; IT FUCKING WORKED FOREVER." WAYNE AT THE WHEEL OF OLD BLUE, CIRCA 1987.

on the floor when the owner stormed in. "What the hell are you doing in my house?" the man asked. "All we could say was, 'I swear there was someone here a while ago; I don't know where they went,' and get out of there as fast as we could."

The indie-rock code required reciprocation: If a band put you up or got you a gig, you did the same when it came to your city, and the Flaming Lips forged a number of enduring friendships. Tim Rutili loved *Oh My Gawd!!!,* and when the group played at Batteries Not Included in Chicago, his band, Friends of Betty, opened. The Flaming Lips stayed at his apartment, and the next time they came to Chicago they covered a Friends of Betty song. Seven years later, when Rutili's group had morphed into Red Red Meat and signed to Sub Pop, it got the opening slot for a tour the Flaming Lips headlined. "Wayne is a hero of mine, and he was really sweet and kind to us," Rutili said, "though at times it was kind of like dealing with Foghorn Leghorn. He was always asking a lot of questions and not giving me time to answer."

Food was not a priority on tour, and the musicians invariably returned weighing less than they had when they left. "It's a big contest of who weighs less," Ricky Rollin, who worked as a roadie in the early nineties, told *Cake* fanzine. Wayne also has an aversion to eating in front of people he doesn't know well, and from time to time, he experimented with seeing if he could achieve a natural hallucinatory state by fasting. "If he's not eating at all, which comes around every now and then, he just drinks orange and tomato juice, because he figures it's just like eating a bunch of oranges or a tomato," Rollin said. "He's a very pleasant man when he doesn't eat . . . he's very nice to us all."

Showers might be a twice-weekly luxury, but the band rarely did its laundry on the road. "The first time I went out with them as a roadie, I took a lot more clothes than Mike and Wayne," said their friend Ted Drake, who played in an Oklahoma group called Captain Eyeball and roadied with the Flaming Lips in the late eighties. "They were into wearing the black pants back then, and they would just wear one pair through the whole tour. The second time I went out with them, they were all making fun of me because I brought a pair of leather pants. Then they opened for the Jesus and Mary Chain, who explained that the good thing about leather pants is that if you have the really nice ones, you can pull out the nylon liner, rinse it out, put them back on, and be ready to go."

The touring-band cliché of nonstop sex, drugs, and rock 'n' roll never applied with the Flaming Lips, as it did even with many indie-rock bands. "I met some fine women along the way, and some of them were fairly aggressive,"

Richard said. "If I had been one of those kinds of guys, there would have been some notches on the belt, but I'm not one of those kinds of guys. None of us were." The three musicians said they usually declined the proffered joint or line of cocaine, though as they spent hours sitting in smoky bars waiting to perform, Richard and Michael liked to drink. "Wayne gets drunk every now and then," Ricky Rollin told *Cake*. "He drinks a lot of tequila—José Cuervo Gold; don't buy him any of that clear shit, 'cause he won't drink it—and then says he's not drunk."

Of rock's unholy trinity, this left only the music. Club soundmen who worked with the band contended that it was one of the loudest they ever mixed, as well as one of the most visually outrageous. "They used to do the deal where they threw the confetti into a fan and turned on the strobe lights and it would look crazy, with all of these little particles floating in the air," Ted Drake said. "Sometimes there'd be so much smoke in the club from the fog machine that you couldn't see your hand in front of your face, or the guys on-stage. People were always hopped up and excited, even at the smaller venues, and it just seemed like they were getting bigger and bigger as time went on."

One night, a soundman threatened to beat up the musicians because their strobe lights had nearly caused him to have an epileptic fit. "We hardly ever notice the strobes anymore," Wayne told *The Bob*. "The first time we used them, they fucked with us, and we were throwing up and stuff, but after a while, you don't even notice that they're there." The bubbles could be more troublesome. "They're weird: You follow one bubble, and you get lost, then you go, 'Oh, we need to change chords!'" Michael said. Onstage in Raleigh, North Carolina, Wayne attempted one of Pete Townshend's famous flying scissor kicks, but he slipped on the bubble-slick floor and landed flat on his back.

Michael controlled the low-budget special effects via a tangle of duct-taped extension cords, switches, and foot pedals near his bass amp. After a stop at a Florida store that sold fireworks, he rigged some homemade flash pots, and the group began to employ these mini-explosions whenever it thought the club owner wouldn't summon the fire marshals. "The first time I worked with them, the effect was stunning," Todd Nelson, a former sound-man at Kansas City's three-hundred-capacity Grand Emporium, wrote on the Flaming Lips' Web site. "It assaulted every sense of the human body and scared the hell out of a lot of people. No one had heard or seen anything like it before."

Midway through a show at the Grand Emporium in 1988, Michael set off the flash pots, then turned his back to fiddle with his amp. At first he didn't understand why fans were shouting about something burning, Nelson wrote. Then, when Michael realized he'd set his sprawling Afro on fire, "he wouldn't drop the bass in the middle of a song to put himself out. Finally someone rushed up on stage, beer still in hand," and extinguished the flaming bassist.

"We were always trying to fit a bigger show into the space that we were actually playing," Michael said, and the group would do almost anything to get a reaction from a sullen crowd. "I've played in the nude before onstage, and I wasn't embarrassed," Wayne told the Oklahoma City music magazine *Stage Left* in 1988. "It was funny, and no one really cared. There were some girls in front that were sort of watching me for a while. They just sort of looked down after that, like, [whistling aimlessly]." For a trio of themed shows in 1987 at the University of Oklahoma, the band celebrated drugs, devil worship, and sex. On the middle evening it screened *The Exorcist,* and Michael dressed as a priest, Richard portrayed the devil, and Wayne donned a nightgown to evoke Linda Blair's possessed twelve-year-old. For the "sex" show, all three musicians wore drag, "and Michael was actually sexy," Wayne said.

When the band members grew bored with their regular set, they turned to covers. They often played "Communication Breakdown" and "Thank You" by Led Zeppelin and the title track from *Wish You Were Here* and "Wots . . . Uh the Deal" from *Obscured by Clouds* by Pink Floyd. The Who also remained high on their hit parade, and on several occasions they covered Pete Townshend's epic rock opera *Tommy.* "Not the whole thing, just the good songs," Wayne told *The Bob.* "We went from the beginning where they find out he's deaf and dumb and blind, then we did the 'Pinball Wizard' bit." Wayne played the role of wicked Uncle Ernie in "Fiddle About," while Michael was Cousin Kevin.

"We've played some real fucking wild shows," Wayne told fanzine writer Fred Mills, "and some to next to nobody." On a Monday night in Portland, Maine, the group arrived to find the club empty except for six hardcore fans. "They bought T-shirts and records and stuff, and they were like, 'Are you guys gonna play good like you would if there were a bunch of people here?' We said, 'Fuck yeah!' We just act like, 'This could be it; this could be our last gig ever! Let's go for it!'" But as all touring rock musicians learn, the downside can be the twenty-three hours a day when they aren't onstage.

In late 1988, the Flaming Lips made their second trip to Europe. The Dutch booking agency Paperclip organized tours for American indie-rock bands, providing a van, a driver, and rented equipment, and working with individual promoters in each country to organize shows on their home turf. A Paperclip agent had been impressed with the band's performance at Roskilde a year earlier, and he loved *Hear It Is,* which had been picked up for distribution by a small German label. The agency flew the trio to London, where it was scheduled to perform at the end of the six-week tour. As longtime fans of the Who, Pink Floyd, and Led Zeppelin, the musicians looked forward to that gig as the highlight of the trip.

The tour started off well, with energetic shows before enthusiastic crowds at clubs in Denmark, Germany, Switzerland, and Austria, but things ground to a halt with several days off during the Christmas holidays. The Flaming Lips' Dutch hosts packed Richard off to stay with one Paperclip employee in Utrecht, while Wayne and Michael crashed with another in his cold and barren attic, à la Anne Frank. "It all sounds very bohemian and sort of exciting and exotic," Michael said, but in fact the pair was stranded with no money in a country where they didn't speak the language, confined to a room with two mattresses on the floor and no diversions. "We couldn't come down and hang out in the house with this guy—I don't know if it was because his parents were coming over or what—but he did lead us down into his living room for about forty-five minutes. We had a Christmas toast, and then it was like, 'Back into the attic.'"

The tour resumed with four gigs in Italy, but an incident at the border proved to be an omen of things to come. The Dutch driver got out of the van to talk to the border guards, and a uniformed Italian officer climbed in, cradling a machine gun in his lap. "How is going for you?" the guard asked in broken English. "You have drugs?"

"He was all happy and smiling, like he wanted us to share," Michael said. "We kept telling him, 'We don't do drugs,' but I had never been that close to a firearm before, and it all just seemed surreal." The band eventually arrived in the coastal resort of Rimini, the first stop on its Italian itinerary, and the local fans treated it royally. "We were staying in this beautiful building facing a piazza, and it was really awesome," Michael said. "They took us out to eat, and we had this incredible five-course meal: real Italian food, for the first time ever, not just spaghetti. The people were all really nice, the wine was flowing, and I can't remember if it was that night or the next day when the whole thing unraveled into, 'Okay, now we're going to let you know what's actually going on.'"

The local promoter responsible for booking the Italian gigs had disappeared. The band drove to several of the cities where it had been scheduled to play to see if the shows had been arranged before he skipped town—"I think one of the clubs was nice enough to pay us two hundred thousand lire, which was like a hundred bucks or something," Michael said—but it never performed in Italy. Dispirited, the trio set out for London and the last show of the tour, but two weeks earlier, on December 21, 1988, Pan Am Flight 103 had exploded over Lockerbie, Scotland, an act of Libyan terrorism that killed two hundred fifty-nine people on board and eleven on the ground, and English customs agents had been placed on high alert.

"This was back in the days when the promoters would say, 'Working papers? Just tell them you're visiting or in transit,'" Michael said. "So we got to England and the driver and Richard got through, no problem. Then somebody let it slip that we were actually playing a show. All of a sudden it was like, 'Wait a minute, do you have any working papers?'" When the three grungy, long-haired Americans couldn't produce the documents, customs agents ushered them into a holding cell. "This begins the long international nightmare."

British officials marked the Flaming Lips' passports with an X and refused them entry into the country. They spent the night in detention. "We were herded with the other undesirables, waiting and watching TV, and we took watches—'Okay, if you guys go to sleep, I'll stay up'—because it was all so weird," Michael said. In the morning, agents led them to a ferry back across the English Channel. "Even the cop that was escorting everyone to the boat was like, 'What are you chaps doing here?' We said, 'Well, we don't have working papers.' They were laughing at us, but they decided to stick the letter of the law to us. By this point we had missed the show in London, and we just wanted to go home."

The musicians wound up in Brussels, but the X's on their passports prompted Belgian officials to deny them entry. After another tense day in another holding area, Paperclip formulated an escape plan: The three Americans could return to Amsterdam to book a flight from there to London and then on to the United States, but they would be segregated at the airports, and customs officials would hold their passports until they boarded the plane home. "I had actually been given an American Express card by my folks for emergencies, and in a very short time we ran up like ten grand, with four ferry trips and two train rides in three days, three flights from Amsterdam, and the changes on our tickets back to the United States," Michael said.

"I can honestly say that for Wayne and me, it was just this weird sort of adventure, and we really didn't let it get to us. For us, the worst thing was that we had to field questions for years afterwards because we had those X's on our passports; whenever we got to England, it always seemed as if everyone needed to know where we were staying, how long we'd be there, when we'd be leaving, what the hotel was, what clubs we were playing at, and what we'd be doing on our days off. There'd always be that tense moment before they stamped us, and then the relief when they finally let us in. But that first time was the sort of pivotal experience where if you let it get under your skin, it had some potential to really change you, and I think it really did change Richard and sour him on the whole thing. You could see why someone would look at this and go, 'Damn, this just isn't any fun at all.'"

Between tours and less than a year after completing *Oh My Gawd!!!*, the Flaming Lips returned to Goodnight Audio in Dallas to record their third album. Restless gave the band its biggest advance yet, ten thousand dollars, but the group still couldn't afford as much time as it wanted in the studio. Once again the musicians worked for as many hours as possible without sleep, and Wayne and Michael actually tried to make going without rest another adventure, experimenting to see if they could achieve a hallucinatory state without taking drugs.

The group had barely had time to write or rehearse. "Wayne couldn't write material when he was on the road, at least not good material," said Michele Vlasimsky. "I did not want him to be in the studio to record that album after months and months of touring; I felt strongly that he should have time to stay home and write." The group set out to record nonetheless, armed with solid ideas for only two tracks. "We knew we were going to do 'U.F.O. Story' and 'Hell's Angels Cracker Factory,'" Wayne said, "but some of the other songs were just made up on the spot. We got into this groove of making another record because we said we were going to."

The band believed, correctly, that it had made progress on *Oh My Gawd!!!* by incorporating other instruments and different textures, and, less convincingly, that tape-collage experiments such as "Ode to C.C. (Part I)" could be pushed further. "You make a leap, and then you spend the next record playing with those leaps," Wayne said. But with one exception, none of the songs on *Telepathic Surgery* betters those on its predecessor.

The album's best track, "Chrome Plated Suicide," follows "My Own Planet" and "Everything's Explodin'" as the band's next great anthem, though the melody is hardly distinctive. "I think somebody showed me the chords to 'Sweet Child O' Mine' by Guns N' Roses," Wayne said. The lyrics are more original, providing another strong synopsis of the songwriter's optimistic existentialist worldview as he sings about the power of love over the sort of primal, stripped-down drumbeat favored by the Jesus and Mary Chain and layers of distorted guitar that alternate with more chiming melodies. "If all my dreams were a tidal wave and every day was Christmas/We could spend our lives in the drip at the edge of the world/'Cause love does something that you can't see, it's like telepathic surgery."

The phrase "telepathic surgery," Wayne explained, refers to "anything you can't see or hear or touch, but it gets in your head and just fucks with you." The classic example is an annoyingly catchy hook that you can't stop humming, though the Flaming Lips themselves didn't deliver another melody as strong as "Chrome Plated Suicide" anywhere else on the album. While some of the experiments with feedback and ambient noise point toward a new sound that would come to fruition two years later, *Telepathic Surgery* too often seems like a derivative and less inspired version of records by Sonic Youth and another band of fellow travelers in the indie underground. "There was definitely a Butthole Surfers hangover," Wayne confessed. That band's frontman put it more bluntly. "I'm really bitter about the Flaming Lips stealing my shtick," Gibby Haynes said, laughing.

Heirs to the twisted Texas tradition of the Thirteenth Floor Elevators, the Butthole Surfers came together at Trinity College in San Antonio in 1981, as unlikely a musical hotbed as Oklahoma City. Living a nomadic lifestyle, shifting personnel frequently, and recording prolifically, the group explored a dark, psychedelic style of noise rock, full of crude humor and obsessed with the aesthetics of ugliness. Onstage, Haynes and his bandmates revived Hawkwind's nude go-go dancers and disorienting light show, adding smoke, fire, and autopsy films checked out of the college library, while on album, they created dense musical pastiches with tape loops, samples, two drummers, feedback, distorted vocals, and the occasional classic rock cover of Black Sabbath or Donovan.

Wayne and Michael didn't hear much to get excited about on the Butthole Surfers' recordings—they remained more enamored of Sonic Youth—but when the Flaming Lips shared a bill with the Texas band in 1986, something clicked. "We saw the freakiness and the sheer attitude of holding nothing back, and it was loud and scary and just so wonderful," Wayne said. "The Buttholes were guys we could relate to, where we couldn't relate to Thurston [Moore of Sonic Youth]. They were nice people, but there was a New York artiness about them, and we were just a bunch of hillbillies. When we hung out with the Surfers, we were brothers, and they became the living embodiment for us of 'Being in a band is what you do because that is who you are.'"

In the past, the Flaming Lips' finest recordings had struck the perfect mix of weird noises and indelible melodies, but their third album suffers from going too far in the direction of the former. Of the two tracks the group planned to record when it entered the studio, neither can be considered an actual song. "Hell's Angels Cracker Factory" is a twenty-three-minute tape experiment that starts with the sound of a revving motorcycle, then shifts through several bouts of free-form jamming. "It was our attempt to do an 'Alan's Psychedelic Breakfast,'" Wayne said, but the Pink Floyd track on *Atom Heart Mother* is only half as long, and it combines sound effects and music to tell a story, albeit the slight one of roadie Alan Stiles frying up his morning eggs.

"After the first two albums, bands kept coming up to us and asking us how we did things, and I think that encouraged us to keep exploring; that's why most of our energy on *Telepathic Surgery* was spent on 'Hell's Angels Cracker Factory,'" Wayne said. At one point, the group intended to fill an entire vinyl album side with the track, but it ultimately appeared only on the CD. "I still felt like we were trying new things in the studio, and we didn't care if the songs didn't make sense."

"U.F.O. Story" is exactly that: Wayne recounting two occasions when he and his brother Mark saw six objects hovering in the sky over Oklahoma City. Though he hoped it sounded spontaneous, Wayne actually had rehearsed the tale quite a bit. As with all comedy records, it loses its impact after the first few listens, and the spoken-word section is followed by more pointless jamming. It ends with a pretty piano melody written by Richard, which is wasted as a coda when it could have powered its own song.

In "The Last Drop of Morning Dew" and the regal ending of "Begs and Achin'," the Flaming Lips take a stab at the catchier style of psychedelic pop favored by Paisley Underground bands such as the Rain Parade and the Dream Syndicate, but the harsh production values fight against their intention. The lyrics seem slapdash, though the former does contain a line pointing to a key theme on the next album: "God fucked up when he made us."

The remainder of *Telepathic Surgery* is filled with Sonic Youth and Butthole Surfers–style noise rockers ("Shaved Gorilla," "Redneck School of Technology") and more of the garage rock the band claimed to have left behind ("Right Now"). The best thing about "Hari-Krishna Stomp Wagon (Fuck Led Zeppelin)" is the title; the song ends with a flailing, Keith Moon–style drum solo, a seventies staple that had long since become a sign of a band with no better ideas. "Michael, Time to Wake Up" is simply a frantic burst of noise guitar. Michael had been sleeping with his head next to a guitar amp when Wayne decided to wake him up with a wailing solo in the style of the Butthole Surfers' Paul Leary. "Wayne was just going crazy, and I swear to God, it was so loud, but Michael did not even move," recording engineer Ruben Ayala said. "He just flipped over onto his other side and went back to sleep."

Richard contributed one song, "The Spontaneous Combustion of John," a vignette marked by some lovely finger-picked acoustic guitar. "I started to write more songs for *Telepathic Surgery,* but I don't think that's what I really wanted to do," the drummer said. "Part of me was competing with Wayne to see if I could do it. It wasn't a big focus of mine, but it made it harder and not easier. *Telepathic Surgery* was a difficult album: It was a lot of hard work, and it just seemed to be too overanalyzed. Michele made some downright ugly critiques, and I think it hurt Wayne a lot."

Inseparable whenever the band wasn't on tour, Wayne and Michele had been living together for three years. They shared an old Datsun that people called "the Shark Car" because Wayne had adorned the hood with a painting of a great white, and Michele said they talked about starting a family. On the professional front, while the Flaming Lips remained her favorite band, an increasing amount of her energy went into other projects with Bulging Eye, which had started doing publicity and marketing for bands as well as booking their tours. Its growing roster included groups such as Mudhoney, Tad, and Nirvana, which recorded for Sub Pop, indie rock's hottest new label, and the key proselytizer for the burgeoning Seattle music scene.

In late 1988, Sub Pop issued the first two offerings from its "Single of the Month Club," Nirvana's first recording, "Love Buzz"/"Big Cheese," and a split 45 by Mudhoney and Sonic Youth. The third single in its celebrated series followed in January 1989 and included a different version of "Drug Machine in Heaven" from *Telepathic Surgery* and the Flaming Lips' medley of "Strychnine" by Seattle garage rockers the Sonics and "(What's So Funny 'Bout) Peace, Love and Understanding," which Nick Lowe had written for Elvis Costello. The band had hit upon the idea of combining the songs because they followed one another on a mix tape that its friend Jon Mooneyham made for the van.

Michele believed that Wayne was "insanely jealous" about the attention she paid the Sub Pop groups. "Suddenly I was like, 'Who is this bitter guy I'm dealing with?' He was always happy for other bands and supportive of other bands, but he really, really had issues with their rise to fame. And it wasn't just that: He was in some bizarre way blaming me for their success and the Flaming Lips not doing the same thing." Wayne disagreed. "I don't know if I was jealous as much as I was annoyed that she was booking Soundgarden, because she hated all these bands that took their shirts off and sang about fucking. To her that would be sexist, classic-rock bullshit, and here she dug that Chris Cornell guy more than anything else."

Still, others did notice what they considered a jealous streak in Wayne. "We got to stay at Michele's house, which was a nice (air-conditioned!) condo in a development with a swimming pool," Dean Clean, the drummer for the Dead Milkmen, wrote in his band's tour diary in July 1985. "Her boyfriend Wayne was in this band called the Flaming Lips. He was crazy jealous of us being there, worried that we were taking 'advantage' of his girlfriend (we were not!), and calling her on the phone constantly."

Wayne and Michele agreed that their professional and personal relationships had become so tangled that arguments from one realm often spilled into the other. One long-simmering disagreement involved the Flaming Lips' use of druggy imagery. For Wayne, it provided a license to let his imagination roam free, but for Michele, it seemed hypocritical to refer to LSD or heroin when he didn't take drugs. "It used to piss me off, to say the least. I'm very honest, and I believe in honesty in advertising: If you aren't a heroin addict, and you put that or [some reference to] acid on your T-shirt, that's bullshit, and I would call him out on that every time it came up during the time I was their manager. He'd say, 'Oh, come on, have a sense of humor,' and I'd be like, 'What, are you fucking afraid that somebody is going to make fun of you because you are too fucking straight?' I just think it was insecurity, to be honest."

A more dramatic argument stemmed from Michele's dislike of *Telepathic Surgery*. Wayne had been calling his girlfriend from Dallas with enthusiastic reports from the recording sessions. "He'd say, 'Just wait till you hear this stuff, hon. It's so amazing; we're experimenting big time on this record!' But their idea of experimenting big time was that they had become obsessed with this [stereo] panning idea of hard left and hard right. They thought that this was just going to be the most amazing fucking sound they'd ever heard. Basically, when they were down in the studio, they would go with no sleep for however many days straight that they were recording. It would get demented—sleep deprivation makes people lose objectivity—and they had been up far too long."

Midway through the sessions, Wayne drove home to appear in court to contest a speeding ticket. He brought a cassette of rough mixes of some of the new songs, and he proudly played it for Michele. "I had the flu and was lying in bed in the middle of the night when he got home. He put on this tape and I started crying; I just wept and said, 'What *is* this?' He totally freaked out.

First he was screaming—and he was not someone who screamed—and then he was crying, and it was a very emotional scene. I was just like, 'This is horrible! This doesn't even sound like the instruments are on the same record.' He was tearing me apart—'How could you say that? You're destroying me!'— but it's not like I felt happy saying it. Whether it was as his manager or his girlfriend, I wanted to love it, and I wanted to be able to say something nice about it, but I couldn't. I had to tell him, 'You've *got* to redo some of this and make this right.'"

"She never liked the 'Hell's Angels' trip," Wayne said, "and I remember we did go back into the studio to try to fix some things," eliminating the more extreme stereo mixing. While Wayne and Michael defend *Telepathic Surgery* as a learning experience necessary for the band's progress, it remains their least favorite recording. "Basically it was a lot of experiments that really didn't come off too well," Michael said. Even the cover art, a photo of Michael preparing to toss a hubcap into the sky like a UFO, proved to be a disappointment. "I sent them a mockup, but we wanted someone to do graphic lettering for us, and I had just drawn what I sent them in ten minutes," Wayne said. "They sent it back and said, 'We finished it for you.' It was such a disaster, but it's not like we could change it at that point."

Telepathic Surgery didn't garner as many enthusiastic fanzine reviews or as much college-radio play as the earlier releases, and the mainstream attention that started to be accorded some of the Seattle bands still eluded the Flaming Lips. The group's contract with Enigma/Restless had expired, and so far no other label had shown interest. The musicians began to wonder if their adventure was coming to an end, but Michele had booked them through 1988, and on their next tour, they had a new companion in the van.

Five years younger than Wayne, Jonathan Donahue grew up outside the Hudson River town of Kingston in New York's Catskill Mountains, and he enrolled at the State University of New York at Buffalo in 1984. Daunted by higher mathematics, he abandoned the goal of becoming an engineer and changed his major to literature, and he took several courses taught by poet Robert Creeley. Like many artistically inclined misfits in college at the time, Jonathan gravitated toward the indie-rock scene—"Literally, these incredible records were coming out every three weeks," he said—and in the fall of 1987, he secured a spot on the student union's activities board. "They said, 'We need someone to book bands,' and I said, 'Well, I know a lot of bands, not personally, but I have their records.' They gave me a blank check, and I basically called all of my favorite bands."

Jonathan already had promoted shows by Sonic Youth and the Butthole Surfers when he phoned Michele Vlasimsky at Bulging Eye to see if she had any acts traveling through western New York. "I'm loaded: I've got a check for five hundred dollars. Who have you got?" he asked. Michele suggested her boyfriend's band, the Flaming Lips. "Okay, I know what they're doing," Jonathan said. "I liked *Hear It Is*. Bring 'em on up!"

"A lot of it was Michele V. back then," Jonathan said. "She was more the face and the mouth than Wayne ever was at that time, in terms of promoting the band. Wayne, Michael, and Richard just had this paisley, bubble-driven backdrop; they went up and they did their thing, but it was Michele that would be in your face. Whether it was T-shirts, money, or buying the records, the idea of self-salesmanship started with Michele."

The Flaming Lips performed at SUNY Buffalo in November 1987, opening for Throwing Muses. Afterward they crashed with Jonathan at his dorm and hung out with his friends David Baker and Sean "Grasshopper" Mackowiak, members of his nascent band, Mercury Rev. "They were all living somewhere on campus there," Wayne said. "Jonathan's folks had enough money, and he could live however he wanted, but he wanted to legitimize who he was and what he was. He wanted to have an adventure."

"College was going nowhere, and I just wanted to be a part of something external," Jonathan said. A few months after meeting the Flaming Lips, he called Michele again and asked if any of her bands needed a roadie. "I can drive a car and put strings on a guitar," he said. Once again Michele suggested the Flaming Lips, and Jonathan joined the group for several jaunts in early 1988. "He was sort of the road manager, soundman, T-shirt dude, help-drive-the-van guy; whatever we needed," Wayne said. "He was just this cool guy who liked us and liked our music."

Weeks of touring with the same people can wear on the most solid friendships, and the Flaming Lips greeted the slyly fun-loving Jonathan as a welcome addition to their traveling circus. "He was a real road kind of guy, a lot of fun, and sort of a wild man," Richard said. One night, the band stopped at a roadside tavern with an all-you-can-eat buffet when, apropos of nothing, Jonathan announced, "Extravagance breeds memories," and began hurling spoonfuls of mashed potatoes at Richard and Michael. "We started throwing stuff back at him—I think Wayne got up immediately and ran out—and we made a real mess and then left," Richard said. Unfortunately, the drummer forgot his jacket. "I got out of the van to go get it, and of course, Mike and

Wayne were not going to come with me, but Donahue did. The guys at the bar were pissed as hell, and they'd thrown my jacket in the trash, but we rescued it and got out of there, and I thought it was cool that Jonathan had got my back. He was that kind of guy."

"It was just the four of us in the van," Jonathan said. "Richard was a very down-to-earth, straight-shooting person, and not what you would consider the eccentric rock 'n' roller at all; he was interested just as often in baseball as rock. Michael was very insular, within himself most of the time. I knew that there was something special between Wayne and Michael right away, but I'm very hesitant to say what it is. Don Quixote and Sancho Panza—let's leave it at that." But Jonathan did witness one epic blowup between the pair.

"For the record, the biggest argument Wayne and I have ever had was about cabbage," Michael said. Wayne couldn't understand how Michael could say that he liked cabbage but didn't like sauerkraut. "Usually, once the Wayne train got rolling, Michael would either hop on board or get out of the way," Jonathan said, but the founding members of the Flaming Lips debated this particular conundrum throughout an entire eight-hour drive.

Unlike Michael, the band's new roadie had yet to develop tactics for dealing with the Buzzard, and during a long drive at the end of a tour in the fall of 1988, Jonathan found himself pinned in the hot seat bearing the brunt of one of Wayne's confronsations. The experience rattled Jonathan so much that he quit and went back to Buffalo. "Me and him got into a stupid fight, which I regret more than him," Wayne said. "Jonathan really, really loved Neil Young, and I said, 'I like some of Neil Young's music, the hits or whatever, but I'd never sit around listening to a whole album.' People think we do, since there is so much Neil Young in my voice, but I never really listened to him, and Jonathan was offended."

"I *know* you listen to him, you just won't *say* you listen to him," Jonathan said.

"No, man, I am telling you the truth," Wayne insisted. "You are not going to dig something up someday."

"That is where the split came," Wayne said, "because there were a lot of things that Jonathan never wanted people to find out about him, and when we would have these truth sessions, we would really learn something about one another without faking or lying or trying to sound cool. You either go for that or you don't. After that, we parted ways." The Flaming Lips thought they had seen the last of Jonathan; on subsequent tours in early 1989, their old friend Ted Drake climbed back into the van. But the group soon suffered another defection.

Wayne and Richard had their share of musical differences. "Richard would just play constant fills," Jonathan said, "and Wayne would be begging him for more John Bonham while Richard would be a sort of Keith Moon man." The drummer's desire to write more songs also caused tension. Incidents such as the ordeal of escaping from Europe at the end of the Paperclip tour prompted Richard to question whether he wanted to continue living as a destitute nomad; the band had been on tour while his parents divorced; and life on the road had become less enticing since he had quit drinking.

"Back in the good old days, Richard was a drunk, and that was good, because he would be happy all the time," Wayne said. "Then he wrecked his car up and he couldn't drink, and they sent him to a therapist—the kiss of death. He was a young guy, he was confused, and then he had some therapist telling him [imitating Al Franken's self-help addict, Stuart Smalley], 'You're good enough, you're smart enough, and gosh darn it, Richard, people like you!' It really changed him, and he really became analytical about all kinds of shit."

Richard now spent much of his time in Old Blue reading self-help books or listening to inspirational tapes on his Walkman. "I was really learning and growing a lot, and therapy helped me increase my self-esteem and deal with conflict. The confrontations with Wayne were getting greater, and I was standing my ground more than ever before. When we had conflicts, I never looked to Mike to be a person who would side on my side; I wanted him to be at times, but he wasn't. When I look back at it, Wayne was like my playground to exercise these things and see, 'What does it mean to stand up and disagree with him?' The aura of Wayne had crumbled, and he was just a person with opinions and creative thoughts—a very interesting person, but so was I."

The situation came to a head after a show in Columbia, South Carolina, in March 1989. "This is back when if you got a hotel room, it was a big deal," Wayne said, and the three musicians and their roadie Ted Drake all piled in to share two double beds. Heavy smokers at the time, Michael and Wayne lit a couple of cigarettes before turning in, and Richard objected, saying that if they wanted to smoke, he wanted his own room. Wayne told the drummer he could sleep in the van. "We'd slept in the van a hundred nights before; what would it matter?" Wayne said. "But it wasn't about that; it had been brewing."

"So they fought about the smoking, and the next day they were still fighting," Drake said. "That morning, something happened as I was sleeping in the van: I heard them arguing, and I got up, and the next thing you know, Richard was saying, 'Take me to the bus station.' And I was like, 'Oh, man.'"

Richard had gone into a drugstore to buy some orange juice before the band drove off. "I had gotten the money from the show the night before, and I put it in my suitcase. Wayne asked me in some strange, accusatory way, 'What are you doing with the money?' It was so far out of character for him—we had this trust, and that had never been an issue—but we had been going through this crap the night before, and when he said that to me in the store, it was like, 'That's it.' I just walked out and got in the van. I told Mike what happened—I guess part of me was hoping he would remedy the situation and do something—but he didn't, so I just said, 'I quit.'"

After five years in the van, Richard got out at the nearest Greyhound bus station. Wayne told him that he and Michael would play "To Sir, With Love" in his honor; the drummer responded that they should perform their cover of Louis Armstrong's "What a Wonderful World" instead. "And that was it," Richard said. "I was out of the band."

Two shows remained on the itinerary, a club gig in Charlotte and a windfall thousand-dollar booking at Princeton University in New Jersey. Wayne and Michael drove on to North Carolina, and as they approached the Pterodactyl Club in Charlotte, they saw Jonathan, dressed all in brown, standing on the corner with his suitcase at his side. Jonathan didn't play the drums, but his appearance made Michael think of the story of Keith Moon materializing at an early Who show, attired in a ginger suit and with his hair dyed to match, announcing that he'd come to elevate the band from mediocrity. "He always had this weird, elfin quality, Donahue did, and when we saw him there, it was sort of like the apparition of Keith Moon all in ginger. I don't believe in a preordained state or anything like that, but I'm definitely a big fan of synchronicity and things like the concept of luck. They're really just opportunities that you have to know how to take advantage of."

Jonathan had decided to forgive Wayne's heretical opinions about Neil Young and rejoin the road crew. When he discovered that the group had just lost its drummer, he started pumping change into a nearby pay phone. He tracked Richard down at the bus station in Atlanta, but the drummer refused to return. "When I left the band, it was very cathartic to say, 'Okay, I'm going to go on without this,' and I never looked back," Richard said.

Wayne and Michael had no choice but to perform as a duo, employing the usual arsenal of visual effects and hoping for the best. Wayne told funny, rambling stories before each song, and he learned a lesson that would prove valuable for the future: Even without a full-on rock assault, he could rely on his charisma to be an effective entertainer. "I remember being pretty petrified, but after that first show, we shook hands and were like, 'All right, we made it,'" Michael said. "Whether or not it was any good, I'm not sure, but we were proud just because of the fact that we pulled in and said, 'We're going to do this and take our lumps and see what happens.'" The club only paid the band two-thirds of its guarantee—"They figured there was only two of us, so they didn't owe us the whole amount"—but the group went on to perform in Princeton, and finally to limp back home with Jonathan in tow.

The lackluster reception of *Telepathic Surgery* combined with Michele's criticisms and Richard's departure to plant a seed of self-doubt with Wayne and Michael. "We were starting to wonder if maybe we wouldn't ever be able to make music the way we heard it in our heads," Wayne said. "We liked Led Zeppelin, but we couldn't sound like Led Zeppelin; we didn't know anything about music or songwriting. We would listen to Led Zeppelin and the Who and think, 'Man, those guys can sing. We really can't sing.' We weren't discouraged, but we thought, 'Maybe this is the limit of what we can do.' We were really lucky that Jonathan Donahue came along. He was able to see through some of that and say, 'Come on, guys, you can do this,' and we were like, 'Yeah, you're right!'"

CHAPTER 4

YOU'RE FUCKED IF YOU DO, AND YOU'RE FUCKED IF YOU DON'T (HAIL, FREDONIA!)

IN A PRIEST DRIVEN AMBULANCE (1990)

FIVE YEARS into their Flaming Lips odyssey, Wayne Coyne and Michael Ivins hit their lowest point when they returned to Oklahoma in the spring of 1989. Michele Vlasimsky had moved to San Francisco over the Christmas holidays in 1988; her club in Norman, Subterranea, had failed because of the usual problems with money and conservative city officials, but her booking agency, Bulging Eye, thrived, acquiring a number of new bands that all seemed to be doing better than her boyfriend's group. Distance and disagreements about the direction of the Flaming Lips strained Wayne's relationship with Michele; he and Michael were broke; they couldn't tour without a drummer; and their deal with Restless Records had expired.

At age twenty-eight, Wayne returned to the fry vats at Long John Silver's and moved back in with his parents, who'd sold the house where he'd spent most of his years growing up and bought a smaller place in the Classen-Ten-Penn neighborhood. All of Tom and Dolly's other children had flown the nest. Tom was still running his office-supply business, Tomco, with intermittent success and long, difficult lulls; when there was work, his sons Kenny and Mark helped him out. After several years of self-destructive drug use, Wayne's brother Marty was starting to straighten out and devote himself to his family and his work as a mechanic, but Tommy continued to struggle with drug addiction, and he served several terms in prison. "He's always been going to jail, for as long as I can remember," Wayne said. His sister, Linda, had married a troubled man who also had problems with drugs and the law; in 2002, a few years after they divorced, he would be stabbed to death in his home during a dispute with another man.

The family remained close and still gathered for Dolly's big holiday celebrations, and despite their individual troubles, as always, they never looked down on or judged one another.

Michael, twenty-six, returned to work in the kitchen at Harry Bear's. His mother and stepfather, who continued to hope he'd give up the band and return to college, had moved out of state and put their red-brick Tudor on NW Seventeenth Street up for sale, but the market was dead, and they allowed Michael to stay in the empty house until it sold. With nothing in particular pulling him back to Buffalo, Jonathan Donahue had accompanied the Flaming Lips home to Oklahoma City after the last tour, and now he crashed with Michael.

Wayne dealt with the difficulties and uncertainties of the time the way he handled any problem: He picked himself up and went to work, encouraging anyone who was willing to join him. Jonathan had brought a four-track cassette deck with him, and Wayne set the goal of writing and recording one new song per day in Michael's parents' house. The bassist had turned one room into a practice space, soundproofing the walls and lining them with aluminum foil à la Andy Warhol's Factory. "We took it as a task: 'This is work; this is serious,'" Wayne said. "You would look around and see these bands who thought they were the greatest thing ever, but they were just a bunch of lazy fucks who weren't doing anything. We knew that if we really worked at it, we could make something click, and Donahue definitely played into that."

Jonathan was coming into his own as a songwriter and an inventive guitarist, full of energy and bursting with ideas, and his attitude that the musicians "could all be our own George Martins" clicked with Wayne's own ambitions. The same scene played out every day through the spring of 1989: At about noon, Michael and Jonathan would be awakened by a knock at the door. "Louis, come in!" Jonathan would shout. Wayne often called Jonathan "Dingus," a childhood nickname bestowed by Jonathan's dad, while Jonathan called Wayne "Louis," the moniker on his Long John Silver's nametag. A cab driver Wayne knew from his days selling pot used to stop at the restaurant and call him "Luigi," as if he were in the Mafia, and Wayne's coworkers had turned that into "Louis."

"Well, what's it going to be today, boys?" Wayne/Louis would ask before promptly answering his own question. "Michael, set the snare over there in that corner and play the drum while triggering that bass thing with your other hand. I've got this little chord progression . . ."

"We'd record the chord progression, Michael would bang on the single snare drum, and I would get it all down on tape while doing these noise bits on my guitar in the background," Jonathan said. "Then we'd all go, 'Wow, that's something!' We'd take the cassette out, do a mix-down from the four-track, and say, 'Let's go for a ride.' We'd drive around later that night in the blue van, which was always at Michael's parents' house, and pop the tape in. We'd sit there and laugh and play the thing and say, 'God, that's great! It's the best thing ever!'"

While recording the demos that came to be called *The Mushroom Tapes,* the band didn't bother naming any of the new tunes, and they were all just sequentially marked as "Jesus Song No. 1," "Jesus Song No. 2," and so on. "God" made several appearances in the lyrics, and after the final versions of the songs were compiled on an album, Wayne appeared in a photo holding a painting of Christ, prompting some fans to ask if he had been born again. "Jesus was just part of the imagery that we used, like a literary character or a superhero," he maintained. "All of our songs, to us, are the greatest thing that ever happened. We think they're all masterpieces, so they were all 'Jesus Songs.'"

"ALL OF OUR SONGS, TO US, ARE THE GREATEST THING THAT EVER HAPPENED." THE NEW LINEUP OF THE FLAMING LIPS—FROM LEFT: NATHAN ROBERTS, MICHAEL, WAYNE, AND JONATHAN DONAHUE—AFTER RECORDING *The Mushroom Tapes.*

Wayne never returned to the Roman Catholic teachings he'd rejected at age seventeen, but his early exposure to religion had done its damage, and eleven years later, he struggled with a crisis of faith. "I began to understand and appreciate how useful and how genius this invention of God, Jesus, and any form of sacred submission truly was," he wrote in the liner notes for the Flaming Lips' 2002 compilation, *The Day They Shot a Hole in the Jesus Egg.* "The desire to believe is so instinctual and so pleasurable that for most people it's never challenged, but I had challenged it and decided to side with science. Easy for a seventeen-year-old; much tougher for a twenty-seven-year-old. The temptation to retreat to a world of angels and demons intensifies as one experiences the meaninglessness and evil of reality. The more one understands reality, the more one is consoled by this ingenious fabrication." Nevertheless, Wayne continued to reject religion, increasingly placing his faith in the ingenious fabrications people could build here on earth, providing they believed in themselves and worked hard.

In between the demo sessions, the Flaming Lips performed a few experimental noise-rock gigs under a number of different aliases. During a show as the Chrome Leeches, Wayne, Michael, and Jonathan unleashed Sonic Youth–like squalls of feedback while Wayne's brother Marty played motorcycle, taking his bike onstage, revving the engine full throttle, and filling the club with exhaust fumes. Then one day in mid-April, Wayne showed up on NW Seventeenth Street accompanied by the drummer who would solidify the Flaming Lips' new lineup.

A classically trained percussionist who had performed with the Oklahoma City Philharmonic, Nathan Roberts had lasted one semester at Bethany Nazarene College, thanks to cussing, carousing, and other conduct unbecoming a young Christian. "The dean called me into his office and said, 'It would be best for the university if you no longer attended,'" Nathan recalled. At twenty-one, he worked as a barber and played with a local band called Mauschovonian Love Beat. "It was kind of like fifties rockabilly with a free-form, Grateful Dead, psychedelic thing on top," Wayne said with disdain, but he loved Nathan's drumming, which was more straightforward and powerful than Richard's. "Wayne used to always come up to me and talk about my drum sounds," Nathan said. "To me, [Led Zeppelin's John] Bonham was the only rock drummer."

Before the band's old lineup had fallen apart, Michele had booked a West Coast tour around a prestigious gig opening for Jane's Addiction, which had released its second album, *Nothing's Shocking,* in the summer of 1988 and been hailed as a harbinger of a new alternative sound. Nathan agreed to fill in with the Flaming Lips for that trip, a temporary commitment that soon became permanent. "I was deadly nervous showing up for the first rehearsal," he said in an e-mail interview with Scott Bakal for the Flaming Lips Trading Post Web site. "We bashed through 'Unplugged,' and by the end of the song, I had broken all of my cymbals, sticks, and drumheads, but they liked me, so the next day we went and bought me some new gear, and we rehearsed two more times before leaving for Salt Lake City."

Jonathan had never felt entirely confident mixing the band's sound, so he recommended that the group use a friend of his from Buffalo. Dave Fridmann met the group shortly before it left Oklahoma, and he added an array of wild effects as well as an outlandish spectacle: Clad in a long hospital smock with no pants underneath, the "Mad Scientist" played the sound console as if it were an instrument, frantically turning knobs and pushing faders, and occasionally adding Fender Contempo organ. Meanwhile, in addition to acting as the road manager, Jonathan added second guitar, hiding behind a thick mop of black hair and sitting in back of the drums as he created odd atmospheric textures or dense walls of noise, making the group's sound bigger, louder, and more mysterious than it had ever been.

Ten days into the tour, on April 22, 1989, the band opened for Jane's Addiction at the Ford Amphitheater in Los Angeles. "I had dreamed of that point all my life; I got bad grades in high school dreaming of that," Nathan said. He got so carried away by the moment that he overturned his drum set at the end of a furious version of "Scratchin' the Door." The stage manager, concerned that Nathan might have damaged the house microphones, had two stagehands corner him after the show and hold him while he punched him in the face. "Luckily the guy hit like my grandmother," the drummer said.

"Nathan was the archetypical all-American Midwest boy in the best sense of that outlaw, greaser, devilish James Dean kind of character," Jonathan said. "He was our alter ego: When we would be talking late at night about Socrates or quantum physics or debating about music in some rhetorical way, he would be in the back talking about Jack Daniel's and getting laid, and that would put things in perspective whenever we got too serious."

Jonathan was never formally invited to join the group—"He'd just sort of been dicking around with us, and it was like, 'Oh, now you're in the band,'" Wayne said—but he had become an integral part of its new sound, even though the group's manager still didn't know it. Michele resented what she saw as Jonathan's attempts to insert himself into the band. "I can liken it to someone who, in a very interesting way, promoted himself through the company laterally and all over the place, and suddenly you were like, 'Wow, how did he end up here?'" she said.

"During the time that we were doing *The Mushroom Tapes,* I never mentioned to Michele that I was playing on them, and if I played a gig, it would have always been, 'Well, he'll just sit there' or 'We're just doing the Chrome Leeches thing,'" Jonathan said. "It wasn't to be mentioned, because Wayne felt that it might be disruptive. I never held it against him; he probably understood quite well that she would have flipped out. She was losing the band at that point." Wayne concurred. "She didn't like any of what was happening. I don't think it was because of the music; it was the way that we were going about it. It wasn't *her* way; it wasn't *her* ideas. She didn't see what we were doing as part of the plan that she wanted us to follow, so we were starting to bypass her."

On the personal front, Michele had expected Wayne to join her in relocating to San Francisco, but it soon became apparent that he didn't want to leave Oklahoma. "At the time I was very young and confused and thought, 'What the fuck is going on?'" Michele said. "I was working very hard to bring us together and find ways to have quality time, and that didn't work. He was living with his parents and working very strange hours that made communication difficult. The impression I got years later was that there was some kind of abandonment thing going on, which I never would've guessed before, but that could be reading too much into it; he could've just hated me all of a sudden. He became like a stone man, and I was like, 'I don't know this person at all.' And that was the beginning of the unraveling."

"Michele V. never wanted me to talk to my mother or get advice from her, and here was I living with my mother again," Wayne said. "To me it was no big deal, but I think she looked at it as 'My boyfriend lives with his mother; how white trash is this?' It was a standard that she couldn't tolerate. And I loved my brothers and my family, and she never liked them. It was like, 'You are different from them. You are an artist.' I was always arguing against that; to me, we are all the same."

After Michele moved to the West Coast, Wayne became increasingly close to a woman whose artistic temperament, aspirations, and family background more closely mirrored his own. People in the band's camp had begun to call Michele Vlasimsky "Michele V." or "Michele with one l" to distinguish her from Wayne's new friend, Janet Michelle Martin, a strikingly pretty blonde who went by her middle name, Michelle.

Almost eight years younger than Wayne, Michelle Martin grew up as the oldest of four girls in a working-class family in Oklahoma City that adhered to the strict tenets of the Assemblies of God, a Pentecostal Church. "My mom's mother and grandfather were sort of these pitch-a-tent revival preachers, with brimstone, damnation, and apocalyptic screaming, which is pretty scary when you are a little kid," Michelle said. "A lot of that scarred me growing up, but I got a driver's license and got out of there as soon as I could." At nineteen she enrolled in art school at the University of Oklahoma, studied drawing and painting, and worked part-time at a restaurant in Norman with Michele V.

"She was very wound up, very talkative, and the most intimidating woman in art school, but we always had a lot of fun together," Michelle Martin said of Michele Vlasimsky. "She got me interested in photography, and I took photos of some of the bands she booked, including the Flaming Lips. I would go to her house to borrow the camera, and she would always be on the phone, so I would end up sitting there talking to Wayne. She and Wayne were both very intense, and I think they fought a lot. Michele was pretty unhappy in the relationship; I don't know if he was, because I didn't talk to him about it."

Michelle M. sensed the growing distance between Wayne and Michele V. when she helped her girlfriend move to California. "Wayne was on tour at the time, and Michele V. wanted to leave, but I said, 'We should wait one more day; you should see him before we leave. It's just twelve more hours.' So we waited, but there was friction between them, just very awkward." Michele V.'s condo had long been the Flaming Lips' headquarters and hangout. When she moved, Wayne and Michael began spending time with Michelle Martin and her roommate, Jennifer Flygare, who shared an apartment in a duplex in Norman that everyone called the Hen House.

"We were all just friends," Michelle said. "Jen and I would feel bad for them and have them over for dinner or to watch a movie. We'd talk about philosophy and painting and music, and we'd eat. Wayne doesn't have a lot of friends; he has people that he works with, but he doesn't have friends that he pals around with to watch the game or whatever, and his family was always pretty insulated."

Despite Michael's well-intentioned warning—"He took me out to breakfast at Denny's once and told me, 'You know, Wayne is really *weird*'; Michael was always a good friend to me, very sweet and generous, and I think he was looking out for me"—Wayne and Michelle grew closer. "Wayne doesn't flirt; he never stuck his toe up my pant leg at dinner or any of that. I remember thinking, 'I need to find someone like Wayne,' but because of Michele V., it was too weird to think about the two of us getting together."

"MICHAEL WARNED ME, 'YOU KNOW, WAYNE IS REALLY *Weird*.' "
WAYNE AND MICHELLE MARTIN, 1990.

Then, at two a.m. one day in the winter of 1989, Michelle heard a knock at the door of the Hen House and swore at "Gordzilla," assuming it was her hard-partying upstairs neighbor, Gordon Holmes, but Wayne shouted a friendly hello. "He said that there was an ice storm and his car wouldn't start, so he asked if he could come in for a while; he'd been in Norman to record or hang out or whatever." Michelle made some coffee and played albums by Soul Asylum and Echo and the Bunnymen on the stereo. "He was all wound up, so I thought, 'I'll sit and talk to him for a while.' He seemed all weird."

Wayne plopped down on the couch and made a confession. "I'm not sure what the exact words were, but basically it was, 'I have been falling in love with you for a long time.' It had to have been an hour before either one of us said anything, and then I asked, 'Well, what are we going to do about that?'" The two started dating, but they kept their relationship discreet. "He would drop me off in his big blue '78 station wagon after we went out to eat or drove around, and we would just shake hands. We went to great lengths to not have a relationship until it was clear that Wayne and Michele V. weren't a thing."

But breaking up with his manager and girlfriend proved daunting to Wayne. "I was having that dilemma of Michelle Martin and Michele V., trying to decide which way is right. Sometimes you can say, 'I think this is right, and regardless of what happens, I'll be fine in my decision.' But sometimes, it's not good or bad or clear or confusing: You are fucked if you do, fucked if you don't. There were so many things in our creative life and professional life and personal life where there just was no path."

After several months of making demos at Michael's parents' house, Jonathan Donahue suggested that the Flaming Lips try recording their new material in Fredonia, New York, with his friend who had just accompanied them on their recent West Coast tour. "Dave Fridmann works at the college and can get us cheap studio time; what about recording this stuff there?" The ponytailed, twenty-one-year-old Fridmann had grown up in Williamsville, a suburb of Buffalo, listening to jazz fusion and progressive rock. He wanted to

"THE BEST WAY TO MEET LIKE-MINDED PEOPLE WAS GOING TO BE IN THE STUDIO." DAVE FRIDMANN DURING THE RECORDING OF *In a Priest Driven Ambulance*, 1989.

be a musician, but had decided to study audio engineering as a backup plan. "Also, the best way to meet like-minded people was going to be in the studio," Fridmann said, "and I came across the Mercury Rev people as a direct result."

A loose collective of outsiders who couldn't fit in with any other bands, Mercury Rev came together at the State University of New York in Buffalo. Jonathan and his friend Sean Mackowiak, aka Grasshopper, played guitar; Jonathan shared vocal duties with the wildly eccentric singer David Baker; and Fridmann played bass and recorded the group in the Fredonia School of Music's Sound Recording Technology studio, fifty miles southwest of Buffalo. The group had gone on temporary hiatus while Jonathan worked with the Flaming Lips, but he planned to continue recording with Fridmann whenever he returned to New York.

While his own tastes ran more toward Steely Dan, Fridmann welcomed the challenges presented by recording freaky indie rockers, and his willingness to experiment, his calm and implacable demeanor, and his strong work ethic made him a perfect foil for Wayne. "I have a retarded, German drive to work," Fridmann said. "If I'm gonna bother to do it, I'm gonna do the best I can, and I felt that way about being a busboy, too. Wayne seeks people like that out, but they also sort of naturally gravitate to him."

With or without explicit references to mind-altering drugs, much of the music the Flaming Lips loved most sprang from the two-decades-old genre of psychedelic rock and its goal of using the recording studio to take listeners on a mind-expanding trip to an imaginative world that existed only in the space between the headphones. Inspired by the creativity of the initial psychedelic explosion in the mid-sixties, seventies art rocker Brian Eno contended that the studio itself had become rock's ultimate instrument, and musicians could utilize overdubbing, multitrack technology, synthesizers, and an array of electronic effects to build orchestral waves of sound that would never have been possible in live performance with "real" instruments. As he prepped for his last year in SUNY's Recording Technology program, Fridmann offered the Flaming Lips a deal: They could record at the college studio for five dollars an hour at a time when similar facilities charged twenty times more. The sterile, white-walled hallways contrasted with the hip vibe most studios cultivated, but the gear was solid, and time limits wouldn't be a concern.

The band had so far spent a total of sixteen days and twenty-one thousand dollars recording its first three full albums. "We just didn't want to make a record again if we had to do it the old way," Wayne said. "We really wanted to break free of that whole thing where independent bands go in and spend fifty dollars making shitty records in a weekend." The Flaming Lips received an unexpected gift when Enigma/Restless opted to extend their contract for another album, and the label gave them ten thousand dollars for their publishing rights. Wayne and Michael decided to spend all of what they called their "ludicrous windfall" recording with Fridmann.

"We did the album thinking, 'This is the last record we're ever gonna do, let's go out in a blaze of glory,'" Wayne said, and the group camped out in Fredonia for three months during the summer of 1989. It finally had the time, the money, and the willing co-conspirators to craft its version of a psychedelic-rock classic such as *Revolver* by the Beatles or *The Dark Side of the Moon* by Pink Floyd. "Fridmann was working with all of these guys who wanted to be engineers, and we'd just give them challenges," Wayne said. "We'd ask, 'Could you set up an amp and a mike sixty feet down the hall?' And they'd say, 'Sure!'"

Their new working methods were best illustrated by the way the band recorded a striking track called "There You Are—Jesus Song No. 7." The tune sprang from an unsettling incident the Flaming Lips witnessed on their West Coast tour in April, during a six-hour drive from Santa Monica to San Francisco. The band occasionally pulled off the road to stage fake UFO photos: The musicians would stretch their legs, throw a hubcap in the air, and snap a few Polaroids. On one particularly disturbing evening, they had stopped in front of a tire factory with smokestacks belching fire when they spied an abandoned trailer park nearby. "We were all kind of amped up still from the gig, and we wandered into the place, but something about it really spooked the shit out of us," Wayne said. "We all turned to one another at the same time and said, 'Hey, let's get out of here.'"

As they pulled back onto the highway, the van's headlights suddenly died, but they continued the drive, propelled by a cassette of *Atom Heart Mother.* The title track of Pink Floyd's 1970 album is a lush but disquieting instrumental suite that finds the quartet augmented by an orchestra and choir, and it originally filled an entire side of a vinyl LP. By now it was three a.m. and the musicians were winding down, smoking, and listening to the music when they drove past a car smashed into the divider and facing the wrong way. "We wondered if we'd really even seen it," Wayne said, so they made a U-turn and doubled back. The driver had been thrown from the wreck and lay face down on the road, his belongings littering the highway. "We were already spooked, and then we saw this thing, and it was like, 'Fuck, he's truly dead.'"

The group sped to a rest stop to call for help—"These were the days before cell phones," Wayne said—but another driver had already called 911. "We were just a bunch of fucking punks who didn't know anything about saving anybody," but they headed back to the scene nonetheless. A light rain had started falling and the paramedics had arrived. "They had put those red flares out in the road, and just as we pulled up, they threw a sheet over this guy's destroyed head. It was really just like something you'd see in a David Lynch movie. The whole time that fucking Pink Floyd track was still playing. After all those years of driving around the country, Michael and me didn't have very many superstitions about the road, but from then on, it was, 'Hey, don't play that Pink Floyd song again!'"

In order to capture an appropriately eerie vibe, the Flaming Lips convinced Fridmann to record the basic tracks for "There You Are" outdoors in the middle of the night during a full eclipse. Even at midnight, convoys of tractor-trailers heading north to Buffalo on the New York State Thruway sporadically rocketed through the western outskirts of the sleepy college town of Fredonia. Wayne, Michael, and Jonathan cradled their acoustic guitars as they sat on the edge of a concrete retaining wall bordering the highway behind Tops Supermarket. The summer air hung hot and humid, its stillness interrupted only by the crickets and the rush of the trucks, and the musicians sweated as they waited for Fridmann to run half a dozen ambient microphones through the weeds and the trash in the ditch beside U.S. Route 90.

"It had a slight air of 'We're not really supposed to be doing this,' and there was the definite question of, 'What are we going to say if a cop shows up?'" Michael recalled. "But really the only thing they could have gotten us on was stealing electricity." Fridmann had unplugged the line of coin-activated motorized hobby horses in front of the supermarket to power the recording session. He hadn't needed a lot of prodding to pile a digital recorder and a small mixing board into the group's trusty blue van. "It was like, 'You wanna go record by the freeway? Great! Pick up some mikes and let's go do it. The sky's the limit!' " Fridmann said. "We kept trying to capture bigger and weirder sounds, and once we realized what we could do, it spiraled out of control."

The band had recorded a spare instrumental version of "There You Are" for *The Mushroom Tapes*. Heavily influenced by what Wayne called "Pink Floyd's gothic period," circa *Atom Heart Mother*, it sounded too much like a conventional acoustic singer-songwriter ditty once he had written lyrics and developed the vocal melody. "We were looking for something that took it out of being Dan Fogelberg," Wayne said, and Jonathan had suggested recording the album version on the median of the Thruway as the traffic whooshed past. That proved impractical—"The trucks kept running over the microphone cords," Jonathan said—but the modified plan succeeded in capturing the ominous mood that inspired the song. The crickets chirped obligingly at the beginning of the tune, and the tractor-trailers fortuitously punctuated the final verse recalling the fatal car wreck.

"There you are/And you drive in your car and you wish for the stars/ And you end up face down in the road, dead as fuck," sings Wayne in a plaintive but self-assured voice that marks a departure from his previous vocals. Ironically, given the fight that nearly ended his friendship with Jonathan, he had gained new confidence as a vocalist when the band recorded a cover of Neil Young's "After the Gold Rush" for the 1989 Young tribute album, *The Bridge*. "That Neil Young track really showed us the new vocal style that I was going to pursue, and that even if I wasn't a very good singer, I could still do something melodically."

"There You Are—Jesus Song No. 7" is an existential musing on a God indifferent to human suffering, with Wayne posing the question of whether, given the cruel twists of fate, there is any point to trying to accomplish something in life—to "work so goddamn hard to do anything at all." Wayne would provide an answer elsewhere on the new album in another song called "Five Stop Mother Superior Rain," inspired by his personal dilemma of being caught in the middle between Michele V. and Michelle M.: "You're fucked if you do, and you're fucked if you don't."

The title of the group's fourth album had emerged while recording *The Mushroom Tapes*, and it captured both the fatalism of the time and what Wayne called "the weird religiosity" of the new songs. The joke is that you know you're screwed when a rescue vehicle arrives driven by a clergyman ready to administer the last rites, but the full name, which appeared only on the vinyl release, includes a subtitle that hints at Wayne's unquenchable optimism: *In a Priest Driven Ambulance (With Silver Sunshine Stares)*.

The powerful new two-guitar attack, the more aggressive rhythms that contrast with the quiet acoustic interludes, and the imaginative psychedelic production are all part of the charm of *In a Priest Driven Ambulance*, but its real strength is the songwriting. The opening track alone boasts more hooks than all of the songs on *Telepathic Surgery* combined, and the disc features some of the band's most memorable lyrics. Michael, Jonathan, and Nathan all contributed key melodies and stray lines, but as always, Wayne drove the project and provided its conceptual core.

The album is divided into distinctive halves. The dark but perversely named "Smile Side" opens with "Shine On Sweet Jesus—Jesus Song No. 5," which kicks off with sounds evoking a calliope, as if to announce, "Welcome to the circus." Washes of backward reverb and frenzied noise jams connect the verses and choruses, and the dizzying swirl of the two guitars is almost overpowering, but in contrast to the band's previous efforts, the vocals occupy a proud position at the front of the mix. "Waitin' for my ride/Jesus is floatin' outside," Wayne sings in his new Neil Young vocal style. "Shine on, sweet Jesus, on me," responds a choir of odd backing voices, including a down-tuned vocal by Michael that sounds like Satan singing through a megaphone.

The album's most raucous rocker and its nominal single follows, and Wayne estimated that the band did two hundred mixes of "Unconsciously Screamin'" before it was satisfied. (The Flaming Lips also filmed their first

"WE'D WAKE UP IN THE MORNING AND IDEAS WOULD BE FLYING OUT OF OUR HEADS." MICHAEL, WAYNE, JONATHAN, AND NATHAN RECORDING *In a Priest Driven Ambulance* AT THE STATE UNIVERSITY OF NEW YORK FREDONIA SCHOOL OF MUSIC'S SOUND RECORDING TECHNOLOGY STUDIO, 1989.

"real" video for the song, a freaky black-and-white clip that found them in an abandoned biblical theme park called Holy Land.) Despite lyrics about paranoia, staring into the void, and "screaming 'til our lungs are full," it's a love song, albeit one that finds the narrator so overwhelmed with emotion that he can't express himself, except through "unconsciously screaming/And whispering at everything she brings."

"Rainin' Babies" pursues a similar theme, portraying a man in the midst of an assault so strange and apocalyptic ("It's rainin' babies from the sky down on me") that he's unable to move ("If I breathe, you know, I'm gonna lose it"), though he maintains that he still has something unique to offer ("This is my present to the world"). Slow, spare, and creepy, adorned with tinkling piano, tambourine, and ringing bells, the tune is driven by Michael's catchy walking bass line, as is the next track, the plodding "Take Me ta Mars." The melody, rhythm, and choppy vocal delivery here are borrowed from Can, the most celebrated band from Germany's early-seventies psychedelic-rock scene, which British critics dubbed Krautrock.

It's not the album's only case of a purloined hook. "For God's sake, 'Rainin' Babies' is almost exactly based on Juice Newton's version of 'Angel of the Morning,'" Nathan told the Flaming Lips Trading Post Web site, "and 'Shine On Sweet Jesus' is so close to 'Put a Little Love in Your Heart' that it's almost criminal." Wayne insisted that the imitation wasn't always intentional. The Flaming Lips first heard Can's "Mushroom" on tour in 1988 when they crashed with a fellow music lover in Cincinnati and sat up all night listening to records. "That guy only played it for us one time, so we didn't exactly set out to copy Can. We just had this riff in our heads, and we probably weren't even sure where it had come from." Nevertheless, Can's "Mushroom" had made enough of an impression to have inspired the name *The Mushroom Tapes.*

Side one ends with "Five Stop Mother Superior Rain," a regal ballad with a Dylanesque title, portentous horns, elegant acoustic and slide guitar parts, and an understated piano that recalls "Wild Horses" by the Rolling Stones. Once again the singer finds himself dwarfed by troubling events, each more surreal than the last. The first verse opens with Wayne announcing he was born the day J.F.K. was shot; the second with the declaration "I was born the day they shot John Lennon's brain"; and the last with, "I was born the day they shot a hole in the Jesus egg." He waves his hands in the air and tries to assert his humanity—"Somebody please tell this machine I'm not a machine"—but it seems as if no one is listening.

"We were just trying to connect these wicked things, and 'the Jesus egg' was such a perfect lyric," Wayne said. The phrase had come from the title of *Jesus Egg That Wept*, a 1984 EP by English art rocker Danielle Dax. "I don't know what it means, but it has great imagery. A song like 'Wild Horses' is this long epic, and we took that format and filled it with cosmic, existential shit. We wanted to sing about shit that we truly didn't understand, but then we would come up with these lines that would cut right to the heart of things: 'You're fucked if you do, and you're fucked if you don't.' I don't know what 'Five Stop Mother Superior Rain' means, but you have the hallucinations right next to the horrible realities of life, and I thought, 'Damn, I kinda like that.'"

The album's "Brain Side" begins with the quiet, dark, and mostly acoustic "Stand in Line." Unsettling images of babies are once again on Wayne's mind: "Ten moms stand in line at the maternity ward/They're not bringin' no babies out to play/Anytime today." The similarly low-key "There You Are" separates the album's other full-bore rockers, "God Walks Among Us Now—Jesus Song No. 6," where Nathan's pounding drums propel the rhythm, and "Mountain Side," the Flaming Lips' amped-up take on the rollicking "Mountain Song" by Jane's Addiction. "Mountain Side" once again merges images of love and death. Addressing the unnamed object of his affections, Wayne not only boasts of "Dyin' in your plane crash of love" and "Crashin' through your windshield of love"; he claims to be holding an electric toaster while "Standin' in your bathtub of love."

The lyrics of "God Walks Among Us Now" are even more striking. With distortion adding urgency to his vocals, Wayne the control freak asks how it feels to be falling apart. Rather than finding comfort in religion, it adds to his distress. "It used to be all right, but things got strange/Used to be uptight, but things've changed and God walks among us now."

The song stemmed from all-night talks in the van with Jonathan. "I think we liked each other because we could talk about God and outer space and really confront the idea of 'So, you don't believe in God? Well, we don't either,'" Wayne said. "But the other side of that is 'Well, what *do* you believe in?' For some people it really is devastating when they don't have this belief in the mysteries of the universe anymore. It's great to believe in unicorns and God and Jesus and all that."

With a mix of cynicism and optimism, the album's nine originals assert that there is nothing to believe in except for yourself and the power of love, requited or otherwise; no one is coming to save you, no ambulance, no priest, no divine power. But the final track insists that even if all our efforts are for naught, life is still a pretty wonderful trip.

A major force in the music industry for nearly six decades, the late Bob Thiele worked for ABC Records in 1968 when he presented a ballad called "What a Wonderful World" to Louis Armstrong. Thiele had written the impossibly cheerful anthem with George David Weiss as a deliberate contrast to the horrors of the war in Vietnam and the race riots on the streets of some of America's biggest cities. Armstrong needed a follow-up to his massive hit with "Hello, Dolly!," which had exposed him to a new audience unaware of his stature as a founding giant of jazz, and Thiele had produced his earlier, legendary recordings with Duke Ellington. Satchmo loved "What a Wonderful World" and recorded it with an orchestra, eschewing his trumpet and singing in his distinctive, gravelly voice, but ABC President Larry Newton hated the track and didn't promote it. Although it became a number-one hit in England, selling six hundred thousand copies, it sold fewer than a thousand 45s in the United States, and it never found a wide audience until Barry Levinson included it on the soundtrack of his 1987 film *Good Morning, Vietnam,* where the Flaming Lips first heard it.

The band's cover opens simply, with Wayne's strained vocals paired against a lone electric guitar. The guitar builds in intensity and the drums thunder in after the second verse, though all of the instruments drop out again as he sings the last verse against the counterpoint of Michael's bass. The song provides a striking ending for the album, and it is a heartfelt and tender performance, though some fans in the jaded indie-rock underground assumed that the Flaming Lips were being sarcastic when singing about trees of green, skies of blue, babies crying, and fairies saying "I love you."

"They thought we were really saying, 'It's an evil, shitty world,' and in some ways, I think that's why Jonathan liked it," Wayne said. "But I just took it as this great song. I found myself thinking, 'This really is a simple, perfect sentiment,' and the way that the melodies and the chords all work to propel the singing, it really is perfect. I don't know why we stumbled on it as something you would associate with the Flaming Lips, but I guess by doing it, it became that. We were struggling with it—I still don't know what the chords are—but when Dave Fridmann was recording us, he said, 'You know, you aren't doing that right, there are some big holes in the ship, but that's what makes it unique and beautiful.' Other guys wouldn't have done that, they'd have tried to make us fix it, but that's one of Dave's strengths."

When the sessions ended in September 1989, everyone who worked on *In a Priest Driven Ambulance* believed that they'd created something special, and the community of do-it-yourself fanzines, alternative newspapers, and college radio stations later agreed. "Far be it from me to say that we thought it was a masterpiece," Michael said, "but it did seem like there was a cohesiveness to the whole record from start to finish. There was no 'Oh, these songs are actually pointing to the next record.' There was something about all of it: the way it looks, the song titles, the time, how it was done, and the way the band looks on the cover."

In an effort to encourage radio play, the band jokingly listed the running time of every song as three minutes, twenty-six seconds, purportedly the ideal length of a hit single. That possibility no longer seemed absurd—some of the other bands on Michele V.'s Bulging Eye roster were garnering attention outside the indie-rock world, especially Nirvana, whose debut album, *Bleach*, had been in heavy rotation in Old Blue, the Flaming Lips' van, all summer—but the enduring weirdness of the Flaming Lips' sound and problems with their record company would ensure that they'd remain underground favorites for some time.

In the late eighties, the major record companies saw the growing college-rock audience and sensed that some underground bands were poised to enter the mainstream. The conglomerates forged pacts with some of the more respected indie labels, which sometimes grew too fast as they were subsumed by the larger corporations and lost touch with the practices that had made them successful. Capitol/EMI had bought co-ownership of Enigma Records, and its staff swelled from 40 in 1986 to 129 three years later. By 1990, when the Enigma labels had failed to produce the hits the parent company expected, layoffs and budget cuts ensued, and Capitol began to divest.

"We got in business with a major and found there was a cultural problem," Enigma co-founder Bill Hein said. "It's not unusual for an independent label's entire overhead to be less than a top executive's salary at a major, and it creates a very odd relationship. So we split up the joint venture." When the companies separated, Capitol kept best-selling acts such as Stryper, Poison, and the Smithereens. (Capitol briefly considered signing the Flaming Lips, but it ultimately passed.) Enigma/Restless took the rest of its acts, but it now had fewer staffers, weaker distribution, and less money for promotion than ever. Many of the resources it did have it allocated to an ill-conceived self-titled comeback album by David Cassidy, the aging teen heartthrob and former star of *The Partridge Family.*

As these problems delayed the release of *In a Priest Driven Ambulance,* the Flaming Lips returned to the studio in Fredonia in January 1990 and recorded a four-song EP as a one-off release for another indie label, Atavistic. Packaged in an impressive sleeve adorned with a silver holograph and pressed on chocolate-brown vinyl, it led with "Unconsciously Screamin'" and was completed by three new songs, including the aggressive noise-rocker "Lucifer Rising," the plaintive psychedelic ballad "Ma, I Didn't Notice," and the catchy toss-off "Let Me Be It." Unfortunately, Atavistic had no promotion and poor distribution, and the EP was hard to find in record stores.

The Flaming Lips' best album to date didn't fare much better. Restless finally issued *In a Priest Driven Ambulance* in September 1990, after a year's delay. "We made the record, and then Restless collapsed, so it came out, but it was obscured at the same time," Wayne said. "On one level, we didn't really care: We had made it for ourselves. We didn't make it thinking we would be able to get signed to a major label, although that was starting to happen to indie-rock bands at the time, but we did have these leaps and bounds, and we thought, 'Fuck, we really did this thing that we were trying to do!' And then reality set back in."

CHAPTER 5

ⲰꞶITIN' ꟻOⲢ TꞶⲈ ꟻⲢOGS TO ꟻⲀLL DOⲰN ON ⲘⲈ

HIT TO DEATH IN THE FUTURE HEAD (1992)

TꞶⲈ ꟻIⲢST time Warner Bros. Records called, the Flaming Lips hung up. During the yearlong wait for Restless to release their fourth album, the musicians sometimes amused themselves by calling Jane's Addiction's label in Burbank and announcing, "This is Perry Farrell, and I wanna talk to the person who signed us *right now!*" They never got past the switchboard.

After his parents finally succeeded in selling their house, Michael Ivins shared an apartment with Jonathan Donahue and Wayne Coyne in a duplex on NW Twelfth Street, the building pictured in the pink-tinted photo on the inner sleeve of *In a Priest Driven Ambulance*. Their friend and fellow music obsessive Scott Booker lived in the adjoining unit with his first wife, Paula. When a woman from Warner Bros. called in late 1990, Jonathan assumed they were about to be chastised for the prank calls, and he hung up without saying a word.

"Then the phone immediately rang again, and they made me answer it this time," Booker said. The manager of Oklahoma City's coolest record store, Rainbow Records, Booker was always willing to help the band out. This time the caller was adamant: "Don't hang up, I'm serious: I work for Roberta Petersen, and she's an A&R person here. She'd like to see your band. She can be there Wednesday."

Petersen had first heard the Flaming Lips through her intern David Katznelson, a DJ at the University of San Francisco radio station, KUSF-FM, who had been a fan of the band since age fourteen. He had played *In a Priest Driven Ambulance* for his boss, and Petersen loved it. "When I heard the Lips, I thought, 'I *have* to see this band,'" she said. "I will never understand why

'Shine On Sweet Jesus' wasn't a huge hit. I'm still thrown for a loop when I hear that."

In the music-industry capitals of New York, Los Angeles, and Nashville, bands courting major-label deals often arrange private showcases at fancy rehearsal studios to audition for A&R reps or talent scouts. "Now in hindsight, what Roberta meant was 'You play and I'll come watch,'" Booker said. "This happens in L.A. all the time, but in our heads, it was like, 'We've got to get a show!'" He booked a last-minute gig for his friends at a club in Norman called Rome. "We told everyone we knew that they had to come, and the place was packed."

The opening act had finished and the Flaming Lips were delaying their set, anxiously waiting for Petersen, when Booker got a call from her hotel. "It was a Wednesday night, and in the Buckle of the Bible Belt, Wednesday night is a church night. There are only one or two cabs in Norman anyway, and they were busy taking all the old ladies to church." Booker sped off to pick her up in his Chevy Chevette.

"His car had something wrong with it, and he kept apologizing the whole way," Petersen recalled. "He was the sweetest guy." Booker earned additional points for a placard in the Chevy's rear window. "It was a BoDeans logo; I liked their first record, and I had no idea she'd signed the BoDeans," he said. After stalling for as long as possible, the Flaming Lips hit the stage just as Petersen and Booker arrived at the club.

Longtime fans in Oklahoma remember the gig as one of the most frenetic the band ever played. After a taped snippet of Robert De Niro in *Taxi Driver*—"Someday a real rain will come and wash all the scum off the streets"—the group launched into the chaotic noise assault of "Lucifer Rising," then delivered the tuneful but punishingly loud one-two punch of "Unconsciously Screamin'" and "Shine On Sweet Jesus." The middle of the eight-song set featured two covers illustrating the group's essential dichotomy: the Dead Boys' punk-rock classic "Sonic Reducer" and the Bee Gees' psychedelic nugget "Every Christian Lion Hearted Man Will Show You."

The Flaming Lips had borrowed one of the Butthole Surfers' most striking stage effects, which involved filling an upside-down cymbal with alcohol. The band's friend George Salisbury lit "the Flames of Destiny" and struck the cymbal, sending burning alcohol shooting everywhere and setting himself on fire. A panicked club staffer doused him with an extinguisher, prompting Wayne to crack, "I'd rather burn to death than be sprayed with that shit."

A short, blond powerhouse decked out in a cross between Hollywood chic and hippie fringe, Petersen had elbowed her way to the front of the stage.

She was older than the Flaming Lips expected, and they weren't yet aware that she was considered royalty at Warner Bros. Her brother is renowned producer Ted Templeman, and she'd been best friends with company president Lenny Waronker since the late sixties, when he produced Harpers Bizarre, a band that included both her brother and her husband, John Petersen. Known for her eclectic tastes, she adored artists who were true eccentrics, and she had played a role in the careers of acts as diverse as Jane's Addiction, Devo, Faith No More, and k.d. lang.

The Flaming Lips held Petersen spellbound. "It was the most incredible show. I was mesmerized, I really, truly was, and then they did this thing where they set something on fire. That didn't work for me—I thought the place was going to burn down—but I also thought, 'This is a band I've *got* to have. If there's a fire, I'm gonna die here, but that's okay: I just wanna die with this band.'"

"IF THERE'S A FIRE, I'M GONNA DIE HERE, BUT THAT'S OKAY: I JUST WANNA DIE WITH THIS BAND." THE BAND'S FRIEND GEORGE SALISBURY IGNITES "THE FLAMES OF DESTINY," 1990.

As the group broke down its gear and loaded trusty Old Blue, Petersen told Booker she'd like to take everyone to dinner, anywhere they wanted to go. To her amusement they chose Denny's, and the four musicians, their girlfriends, Booker, and the Warners A&R rep huddled around a large table under the harsh fluorescent lights. The band tried its best to stay cool, even after Petersen dropped a bombshell. "She just came right out and said, 'I want to sign you to Warner Bros.,'" Booker recalled. "Everyone was just sitting around like, 'Yeah, cool, whatever.' I don't think it even really sank in."

By 1990 numerous indie-rock fans, former college radio DJs, fanzine editors, and underground promoters had infiltrated the major labels' lower ranks, and they had begun to influence the A&R departments. Warner Bros. and its affiliated labels, Reprise and Sire, already had raided the indies to sign the Replacements, Hüsker Dü, and Jane's Addiction, and the company recently had started domestic distribution of England's adventurous Creation Records, which had launched the Jesus and Mary Chain and psychedelic "shoegazer" bands such as My Bloody Valentine.

Warner Bros. wasn't the only company sensing a trend. In early 1991, Nirvana left Sub Pop for Geffen Records, in part because Kurt Cobain was impressed that it had signed Sonic Youth. Around the same time, Capitol signed the Butthole Surfers. Geffen released Nirvana's second album, *Nevermind,* in September, and it sold an astounding three million copies before the end of what came to be called "the year punk broke."

Michele Vlasimsky and Bulging Eye booked and promoted Nirvana, and the Seattle trio opened for the Flaming Lips several times. The bands came to share a mutual admiration, though Wayne hadn't been impressed at first, and he had told Michele V. that she shouldn't bother with the group. "The first time we saw Nirvana, they sucked," Wayne said. "Cobain was in his Lynyrd Skynyrd hair and he had a beard and they were total drunks. I called her and said, 'It just seems like they want to be rock stars.'"

The two bandleaders never talked much. "The times we were around him, his stomach hurt, and he was always quiet in the corner," Wayne said, though Cobain did befriend Flaming Lips drummer Nathan Roberts. According to Nathan, after a show in Ann Arbor, Michigan, in early 1990, Cobain brought him along to pay a visit to self-destructive punk rocker GG Allin, then confined to a state prison for indecent exposure and assault and battery. "After we told him who we were and that we were big fans, he proceeded to curse and spit at us and kept yelling that we were 'just a couple of Kansas City faggots who want their dicks sucked,'" Nathan told the Flaming Lips Trading Post Web site.

Wayne called Michele V. again the second time the Flaming Lips and Nirvana shared a bill: "Whatever I said before, forget that. They've changed now, and they rock!" Wayne and Michael loved Nirvana's 1989 debut, *Bleach*, and they had held it up as an example for Dave Fridmann of some of the sounds they wanted to capture on *In a Priest Driven Ambulance*. But like most fans, they never expected their fellow indie rockers to become multiplatinum superstars.

With the success of *Nevermind*, the alternative-rock era began in earnest, prompting a full-fledged feeding frenzy by corporations suddenly eager to sign the weirdest acts in the underground. Roberta Petersen's interest in the Flaming Lips preceded the alternative explosion by almost a year, and it stemmed from her appreciation of Wayne as a fellow original. She also loved his smile. "He was this complicated, incredible guy, like Captain Beefheart or something. You knew that he had a lot in him, and it was going to come out. I loved the whole band—I'm really a band person—but he was brilliant, a total eccentric, and I'm the same way."

"Roberta was an angel from the West Coast who showed up and literally saved three men's lives," Jonathan claimed. Despite the guitarist's flair for melodrama, Wayne said, Dingus wasn't really exaggerating: After spending all of their last advance from Restless recording *In a Priest Driven Ambulance*, the musicians subsisted on frozen burritos from 7-Eleven that they charged on Michael's parents' credit card. In order to pay the rent for their shared duplex, they regularly sold plasma at a local blood bank. That ended when the nurses began to suspect they were drug addicts, though the track marks actually stemmed from the previous weeks' donations.

"We really were on the edge of being able to maintain being in a band," Wayne said. "We weren't twenty years old anymore, but were still saying, 'We are going to be in a band and make this work.' Anyone with any sense would have looked at us and said, 'Isn't this a sure sign that it's *not* working? Look at how you are living!' But we were looking around and seeing a lot of people doing music that was similar enough to what we were doing—heavy rock, but freaked-out heavy rock—and we thought, 'Maybe we've got another couple of years here.'"

Wherever the Flaming Lips were going, it would be without their first manager. At Christmas 1989, Michele V. had returned to Oklahoma from San Francisco and severed all of her personal and professional ties with Wayne and the Flaming Lips, and they never spoke again. Michele continued to run

Bulging Eye for another year, and many in the music business believe she was positioned at the right time with the right roster to build the next great talent agency, a company to rival giants such as William Morris or Triad. Instead, she gave notice to her staff and her remaining bands and quit.

"It just came to a point where we were overwhelmed," said Scott Haulter, who worked as an agent at Bulging Eye for two years. "I don't want to say that Michele was unorganized; it was just that she was flying by the seat of her pants. We were trying to do much more than we had the resources for. She was idealistic and passionate, and we all loved the music, but suddenly *Nevermind* was coming out and everyone had the idea that there was a bigger and better way to do this. That is why I always respected the Lips: They took the long road to get to the point where they are. They never gave up, and they never compromised their integrity." (Today, Michele V. still works as a publicist for some bands, but she focuses most of her energy on Space Baby, a company she launched to design and market hip clothing for infants and toddlers.)

Now the Flaming Lips needed a new manager. When Michele had left Oklahoma in late 1988, she had tapped Scott Booker to oversee local shows by Bulging Eye bands, much as David Fallis had pegged her to succeed him in promoting hardcore punk shows three years earlier. "Why she picked me, I still don't know, because I had never promoted a show before," Booker said. "But people knew me because I worked at a cool record store, and they knew I never cheated anyone when they brought used records in to sell."

Gregarious in a charming, low-key way, Booker had grown up as a self-professed nerd in a conservative Baptist household in Midwest City, ten miles southeast of Oklahoma City and the home of Tinker Air Force Base, where his father worked as a civilian mechanic. Booker never took a drink of alcohol until he was twenty-six, but he did have one vice: He started working in record stores at age fifteen, and he spent every cent he earned buying albums and going to concerts. He abandoned his plan to become a history teacher after graduating from the University of Central Oklahoma with a degree in education, and started thinking about a career with the devil's music.

Booker had become a Flaming Lips fan in the fall of 1985. After he and a group of friends saw Sting perform at the Lloyd Noble Center in Norman during the jazzy rocker's first solo tour, they emerged to find that the Flaming Lips had put fliers on every car in the parking lot advertising their own show at Subterranea later that night. Booker persuaded his pals to check them out. "There were maybe ten or twelve people there, not counting my friends, but right when we walked in, the Lips were doing their version of Sting's 'If You Love Somebody, Set Them Free,' which was just pure, unadulterated noise." His friends got their money back and left. Michele V. asked Booker if he wanted a refund, too, but he stayed. "I was mesmerized. I thought, 'Oh my God, this is the coolest thing I have ever seen in my life.'"

The first time Booker met Wayne, the musician walked into Rainbow Records wearing his motorcycle helmet and never raised the tinted visor. "I thought he was going to rob me," Booker said. Michael also frequented the store, and Booker befriended the quiet bassist by talking music and comic books. "I never knew if I was actually having a conversation with him—Michael was so quiet in those days, it would always be like a yes-no-maybe kind of conversation—but he would buy stuff and I would totally take care of him. Used records we'd paid a quarter for, he got for fifty cents, even though they were marked five dollars. I loved the Flaming Lips, and he was in the

"YOU SHOULD BE THEIR MANAGER." SCOTT BOOKER,
SEVERAL YEARS AFTER HE REALIZED HE'D ASSUMED THE
JOB BY DEFAULT, WITH WAYNE AT STUDIO SEVEN, 1993.

Flaming Lips, and he talked to me, sort of. Years later I asked Michael how we ended up being friends, and he said, 'Because you talked to me.' It was as simple as that."

Eager to learn other aspects of the music business, Booker jumped at the chance to promote the Bulging Eye gigs. His first show found the Flaming Lips opening for Firehose, the band Mike Watt formed after his partner in the Minutemen, D. Boon, was killed when he was thrown from their van while touring.

Booker paid Watt sixteen hundred dollars and gave the Flaming Lips the rest of the take at the door. Wayne raised a quizzical eyebrow when Booker confessed that he'd kept twenty dollars for himself to buy a late-night burger at Denny's. "Oh, great, he thinks I cheated him," Booker thought, but Wayne just shook his head, smiled, and walked away.

A few months later, Booker oversaw his fourth and biggest show as a promoter, a gig by Nirvana. He pulled out the stops with fliers, posters, and newspaper ads. Hours before the club opened, a line stretched around the block, but Booker panicked as showtime drew closer with no sign of the headlining act. "I finally got Michele V. on the phone, and she was crying, " Booker said. Whether Michele admitted that she had forgotten to tell Nirvana about the gig (Booker's memory) or told him that bassist Krist Novoselic had called to explain that Kurt Cobain was distraught about breaking up with a girlfriend and refused to drive to Oklahoma (Michele's version), the news that Nirvana wasn't coming crushed Booker. "I was just standing there by the pay phone, sinking down against the wall, and thinking, 'Oh my God, I'm fucked.' I had to rent the room, rent the PA, and pay the opening band."

The club owner agreed to cut a deal, letting Booker keep the take from a marked-down admission at the door for the opening acts so he could recoup his expenses. Then the venue got a call from someone claiming to be Nirvana's road manager saying that the group was on its way after all, and the club let the crowd in at the original, higher price. "It turned out it was a hoax—it was just someone kidding around—but afterwards, the club owner was like, 'Now you're fucked,'" Booker said. The venue had to refund the full admission to everyone who'd entered, and Booker had to pay for all of the expenses himself. "I had five hundred bucks in my savings account, and it was all the money I had in the world," but he honored his commitments and paid for the PA and room rental.

Later that night, Wayne showed up at the prankster's apartment brandishing a baseball bat and threatening physical retribution for the loss his friend had suffered. Wayne's loyalty moved Booker, and in turn the Flaming

Lips were impressed that Booker had kept his word and behaved ethically in the midst of a lousy situation.

Los Angeles music business attorney Bill Berrol had represented the Flaming Lips since they signed with Restless in 1986. Now, in early 1991, he negotiated their new contract with Warner Bros., accepting a seven-album deal with a 13 percent royalty rate, standard at the time for an indie band making the leap to the majors. When it came time to sign the paperwork, Wayne asked Booker to accompany the band to Burbank. "Just being able to go out to Warner Bros. when they got signed—what an amazing thing for a

"I WAS USED TO CRUDDY ENGLISH GUYS, BUT THESE WERE CRUDDY GUYS FROM *Oklahoma*." SIGNING THE CONTRACT WITH WARNER BROS., 1991; STANDING FROM LEFT: SCOTT BOOKER; ROBERTA PETERSEN; LENNY WARONKER; THE BAND'S ATTORNEY, BILL BERROL; AND MO OSTIN.

guy who would look at the back of records and see names like Mo Ostin and Lenny Waronker, to get to meet these people," Booker said.

Ostin, CEO of the Warner Music Group, and Waronker, president of Warner Bros. Records, were legendary, the "record men" responsible for the company's reputation as the most artist-friendly of the major labels. Waronker had signed Randy Newman, Rod Stewart, and Curtis Mayfield, among many others, while Ostin had run Reprise Records for Frank Sinatra, signed the Kinks, Jimi Hendrix, and Neil Young, and was then the top executive at the world's largest record company.

Following the routine for every band that signed to the label, the Flaming Lips toured each department to meet the marketing, publicity, radio, and promotions people prior to signing the contract. Nervous but trying to look cool, the musicians let Booker do most of the talking. The night before the visit, Nathan had overindulged from the hotel room's minibar, while Michael had dyed all of his clothes black in the sink. Now, Nathan sacked out on the sofa in Petersen's office, and Michael silently extended a hand stained a deep shade of ebony to everyone that he met. Marketing executive Jo Lenardi would become one of the band's biggest allies at the label, but she recoiled the first time she met the group. "They were cruddy," she said. "I was used to cruddy English guys, but these were cruddy guys from *Oklahoma*."

Finally the group arrived in Waronker's office. The president gave a speech about how the drummer is the heart of every great band; nursing his hangover, Nathan hoped he wouldn't have to vomit. The musicians and the Warners execs signed the contracts, and as everyone posed for the obligatory photo for the music trades, Ostin turned to Booker. "Well, who are *you*?" the Warners chairman asked. "Um . . . I'm their friend Scott," Booker mumbled. Ostin rolled his eyes behind his trademark oversized glasses. "Oh, great."

After the meeting, Petersen took Booker aside. "You should be their manager," she said. "You can do this, and they need you." Concerned about his lack of experience, Booker solicited several more established managers on the band's behalf, including Nirvana's John Silva, but all of them passed. "It was probably a year later when someone asked, 'Are you the Flaming Lips' manager?' and I finally just said, 'Yeah, I guess I am.'" (In 1993, the band drew up a contract formalizing the arrangement, but it lapsed a few years later, and it has never been replaced; Booker earns a commission based on any work he does for the group, an agreement the Flaming Lips honor based on a handshake.)

After the trip to Burbank, the band returned to Oklahoma and geared up to make its first major-label album. Warners sought a "name" producer—

"Roberta probably wanted Brian Eno or someone, which would have actually been kind of cool," Booker said—but the musicians were eager to work with Fridmann again. The band made demos for the new disc with Fridmann at Alien Studio, an eight-track setup in Norman run by Robbie Egle (whose brother, Billy, played in a struggling group called Janis Eighteen), but Petersen disliked the recordings and expressed concern about Fridmann's abilities.

"We all thought the demos sounded like shit, and there was some serious discussion as to whether or not I'd be able to continue," Fridmann said. "But Wayne knew he could tell me what to do, and I'd do my very best. He didn't want to have to be sitting in there with Dave Jerden or whoever was the hot producer of the moment, taking shit from him." Wayne argued Fridmann's merits, and Petersen relented. Warner Bros. didn't have much to lose by letting the Flaming Lips try it their way: The young producer cost only a fraction of what a bigger name would have charged. "I tried to get points," Fridmann said, referring to the standard practice of producers earning a percentage of the profits from every album sold, "but they were not going for that."

"It wasn't a big deal, like something we had to fight for," Wayne said. "We just said, 'The record that you liked was done by Dave Fridmann, and if you like us, we're really just beginning to get started with Dave Fridmann.' We wanted to do more of what we had just done with *Priest Driven Ambulance*."

Although there are great moments on *Hit to Death in the Future Head*—a meaningless title chosen to make a bad pun with the cover photo of a toilet, which Wayne intended as a tribute to the gritty work of Oklahoma photographer Larry Clark—the album is not the artistic equal of *In a Priest Driven Ambulance*, lacking the conceptual unity and the thrill of discovery that marked the Flaming Lips' first experience with unlimited recording time.

Once again Fridmann gave the band free rein to try anything, from recruiting a mini-symphony of orchestral musicians, to recording a piano through a length of vacuum-cleaner hose, to swinging a microphone in a giant arc over the session in an attempt to capture a sort of low-tech surround sound, a precursor of the experiments that would culminate in *Zaireeka*. But at a time when the rock world was embracing the straightforward energy of the music the press dubbed grunge, the album bogged down with a few too many slower psychedelic songs and a dense and complicated sound.

The band's fifth album starts out strong with two propulsive rockers rife with explosive shards of noise guitar. Despite the obviously Dylanesque title, the lyrics of "Talkin' 'Bout the Smiling Deathporn Immortality Blues (Everyone Wants to Live Forever)" are built on a simple one-liner: "Everyone wants to live forever / But no one ever gets it together." Its strengths are the insistent rhythm, the odd swirl of noisy tape loops in the background, and the bizarre "doo-wop-wop" backing vocals, which once again find Michael singing through the Satanic megaphone effect introduced on "Ode to C.C. (Part I)." Wayne intended it as an homage to the Drifters. "I was trying for something like 'This Magic Moment,'" he said.

Built on rock's time-honored lyrical gambit of equating sex and violence, a kiss with a punch in the face, "Hit Me Like You Did the First Time" is another rollicking tune driven by Jonathan's slide guitar and Michael's tuneful bass, but the pace slows considerably for "The Sun," a plodding number written by Jonathan and decorated with staggered backing harmonies, French horn, sawing cello, and a concluding orchestral flourish, and "Felt Good to Burn," a hazy, meandering drone that evokes a George Harrison psychedelic toss-off such as "Blue Jay Way." Wayne and Jonathan shared the vocals and alternated lyrics, veering between cosmic ("Felt like a movie star when you hold my slippery brain") and carnal ("We just sucked and fucked and got high / And all we'd steal, we lit up on the Ferris wheel").

Written and sung by Jonathan, "Gingerale Afternoon (The Astrology of a Saturday)" is a cheerfully effervescent pop song that has more in common with his later efforts in Mercury Rev than it does with the Flaming Lips. It leads into another of the album's standouts, the supremely strange "Halloween on the Barbary Coast." A psychedelic epic built on a monolithic guitar riff, a martial drumbeat, a jangling tambourine, and what Wayne called his "drunk-sounding" vocals, it tells the story of a culture clash while on tour in Las Vegas: "Well, the retards laughed when the evening came / The Librium makes them all the same . . . It's Halloween on the coast again."

"After being escorted out of Caesar's Palace because we stunk, literally, we were walking to the Barbary Coast Hotel and Casino when we encountered a picket line of striking Barbary Coast employees," Nathan told the Flaming Lips Trading Post Web site. "One guy had a megaphone, and as we approached, he started cursing at us about how it's un-American to cross a picket line. As we passed, he started screaming, 'Look, everybody: It's Halloween at the Barbary Coast!'"

"We always looked like pirates in those days, and being a band crossing the country in a van was like being on a pirate ship," Wayne said. Though he was renowned at the time for his mass of tangled dreadlocks and the infrequency of his showers, and he had credited himself as "Stinky" in the liner notes for *In a Priest Driven Ambulance,* he maintained that he never had a problem with body odor. "I don't smell that bad; I don't sweat that much, although we always made these jokes about it."

A generic garage-rocker that could have fit on one of the Restless albums, "The Magician Vs. the Headache" is distinguished only by the way Michael and Nathan turn the rhythm inside out, the reappearance of the megaphone backing vocals, and the inscrutable nature of the minimal lyrics ("Sometimes I come home and there's a monkey puttin' down/He's makin' love to the hole in my head"), which seem to owe a debt to the dadaist couplets of the Pixies. The song ends with a loop of delay-and-reverb-drenched guitar noise, which reappears at much greater length at the end of the album.

"If you ask me, 'You Have to Be Joking (Autopsy of the Devil's Brain)' is the best thing on the record," Wayne said of the next track, which includes a sample of the orchestral score from the Terry Gilliam film *Brazil*. The band often kept movies running on the VCR during recording sessions, and a snippet of the soundtrack by Michael Kamen, who had orchestrated *The Wall* for Pink Floyd, lined up at exactly the right moment in the Flaming Lips' spare and frightening story-song. "The sample just worked so perfectly with the sentiment of the song. At the time, Roberta told us a story about some Middle Eastern guys killing babies on film, and she said she had seen some of these films. It's so brutal, putting an idea like that out there in the world, and lines like 'You have to be kiddin' me/They wouldn't do those unspeakable things' are my reaction."

Shifting moods, the uplifting sing-along "Frogs" revolves around an absurdly catchy chorus that finds Wayne declaring, "I'm lookin' at the sky/I'm waitin' on the rain/I'm waitin' for the frogs to fall down on me." Eight years before Paul Thomas Anderson's impressionistic film *Magnolia,* the lyrics were inspired by an example of the sort of scientific trivia that had always fascinated Wayne: Sometimes dismissed as biblical folklore or urban legend, storms that rain down fish or amphibians can indeed be caused by the rare meteorological phenomenon of waterspouts, which pick up creatures from a body of water and carry them for miles before depositing them back on earth.

The album ends with another slow and tuneless psychedelic drone, "Hold Your Head," featuring acoustic guitar, timpani, and free-associative lyrics, before listeners are tormented with a twenty-nine-minute (but seemingly unending) loop of the grating guitar noise first heard at the end of "The Magician Vs. the Headache." A perverse attempt by the band to fill out the running time of the CD, as well as a nod to the hidden track "Endless Nameless" on Nirvana's *Nevermind,* the Flaming Lips thought it was a great joke, though most listeners just found it annoying. "I still get people who tell me that when it's on a jukebox somewhere, they walk in and put that on just to hear people going, 'What the fuck is *this?*'" Wayne boasted.

Recorded in several bursts of activity, most of the album's harder-rocking songs came together at the student studio in Fredonia, while the slower material stemmed from sessions at Sweetfish Studios in Argyle, New York, a six-hour drive east on the outskirts of Saratoga Springs. Frustrated with the tedious process of getting good drum sounds, the band avoided conventional rhythm tracks at Sweetfish, substituting a spare kick and snare drum, timpani, or a tambourine. The experiment wasn't entirely successful, but the musicians enjoyed these sessions—until work abruptly ended one day when police burst into the studio with guns drawn.

A fellow graduate of the SUNY Fredonia's Sound Recording Technology program, Keith Cleversley had lived across the hall from Fridmann in the dorms, and the two had become friends and rivals. Cleversley had helped on some of the sessions for *In a Priest Driven Ambulance,* and he worked as the assistant engineer on the follow-up. The Flaming Lips only learned that Cleversley had been a suspect in a drug investigation when police led him out of Sweetfish in handcuffs. "We all just quietly dispersed, because it seemed like, 'Leave now or go to jail with him,'" Wayne said.

"They literally thought I was the kingpin drug lord of New York and Pennsylvania," Cleversley said. When the informant who fingered him disappeared before the trial, prosecutors dropped the charges against Cleversley, but the drama provided a tense conclusion for sessions that already had been fraught with stress. "We were all feeling the pressure to do something," Fridmann said. "We knew that we had to perform and to push to make it accessible to Warner Bros., even though that sounds dumb now, and we probably shot ourselves in the foot repeatedly in our attempt to make it better. We knew exactly what 'better' was: We sat there with a Jane's Addiction record and said, 'We've got to make it sound like this,' but that was done in a million-dollar studio. There's a reason that all that good gear sounds so good."

Drum and guitar sounds that seemed to have come together instantly for *In a Priest Driven Ambulance* eluded the band or took a week to recapture for *Hit to Death in the Future Head.* "I don't know what happened, but it seemed as if everyone had suffered amnesia," Michael said. "We couldn't figure out how to use what we had already learned as a springboard, and it was like we had to start over again." Added Wayne, "We didn't know this at the time, but we were already past that magical time when we made *Priest Driven* and made all these strides. We were thinking, 'We're going to go back up to New York and it's going to be great,' but you can't go back. You have to keep moving along."

The group's anxieties proved unfounded when Petersen embraced the finished album—she didn't even question the wisdom of releasing a CD that ended with twenty-nine minutes of unlistenable noise. But the band soon encountered another problem.

In 1989, comic rapper Biz Markie had scored a platinum-selling hit with *The Biz Never Sleeps* for the Warner Bros.–distributed Cold Chillin' label. The company expected big things from the follow-up, *I Need a Haircut*, released in August 1991, but the album became entangled in a lawsuit filed by faded English pop star Gilbert O'Sullivan. In crafting the track "On and On," Markie, a music geek who boasted of owning ninety thousand vinyl recordings, had sampled a short and dissonant piano intro from O'Sullivan's saccharine 1972 ballad "Alone Again (Naturally)." Few besides the song's author could even identify the sample, but U.S. District Court Judge Kevin Thomas Duffy, a man so clueless about popular music that he had to ask for a definition of "R&B," sided with O'Sullivan, issuing a permanent injunction against selling the album, and referring the case to the U.S. attorney for criminal prosecution in an infamous opinion that began with a quote from Exodus 20:15: "Thou shalt not steal."

The case set a precedent forcing artists to seek permission and pay for every sample they used, no matter how short, insignificant, or unrecognizable. In the wake of this costly fiasco, Warner Bros. hired a full-time staffer to scour every release in search of unauthorized samples, and the snippet of orchestration from *Brazil* on "You Have to Be Joking" set off an alarm. The label hired an attorney specializing in clearing samples, but the Flaming Lips proved to be a difficult case. They had taken the music from the soundtrack of a videotape, so the lawyer had to deal with the film studio.

Universal/MCA and director Terry Gilliam had engaged in an even more bitter legal battle than Biz Markie and O'Sullivan. Universal CEO Sid Sheinberg famously disliked Gilliam's cut of the film, a parable about losing your soul under a harsh bureaucratic system, and the studio chief edited his own version, removing the moody score by Kamen and replacing it with generic rock music "to appeal to teens." Gilliam feuded with the studio for more than a year. Though the film as finally released was basically Gilliam's version, eventually five different cuts of *Brazil* circulated, and MCA never released an album of Kamen's score until eight years later.

While the sampling issue was sorted out, Warner Bros. released a three-track EP, *Yeah, I Know It's a Drag . . . Wastin' Pigs Is Still Radical,* on Halloween

1991, featuring a striking cover photo shot by Jennifer Flygare of Wayne's new girlfriend, Michelle Martin, licking the eye of the band's pal George Salisbury. Eight months later, the label would become embroiled in another controversy when the song "Cop Killer" by Ice-T and Body Count drew the ire of the FBI and police benevolent organizations, but at the time, no one questioned the anticop title of the Flaming Lips' EP, which came from a line in *River's Edge,* one of Michael's favorite movies. (The bassist sometimes dressed as Crispin Glover's character when screening the film for friends.) The disc led with "Talkin' 'Bout the Smiling Deathporn Immortality Blues (Everyone Wants to Live Forever)," the album's first single, and was completed by a pair of songs by Echo and the Bunnymen, "All That Jazz" and "Happy Death Men," and the demo for a beautiful ballad called "Jets (Cupid's Kiss Vs. the Psyche of Death)."

The label had planned to release *Hit to Death in the Future Head* a few weeks later, in February 1992, but it couldn't clear the troublesome sample until the summer, when it finally gave up on the movie studio and went directly to Kamen, who readily approved. "In the end, it didn't cost us hardly anything—a couple of thousand bucks—but every week that it took to get it cleared, they pushed the record back two weeks," Booker said. "It grew exponentially—two weeks became four weeks became six weeks—until the next thing we knew, it was seven months later, and in that time, Jonathan and Nathan had quit the band."

In between recording and touring with the Flaming Lips, Jonathan had continued to record with his other band, Mercury Rev, which also featured Fridmann on bass. The group released its first album, *Yerself Is Steam,* on England's Rough Trade Records in early 1991. Some of the songs on the album dated from sessions that coincided with recording *In a Priest Driven Ambulance—* Nathan had played drums on Mercury Rev's "Frittering," and members of that band had contributed to the Flaming Lips' recordings—while their first single, "Car Wash Hair," was completed circa *Hit to Death in the Future Head.*

Alternately orchestral and lulling, experimental and avant-garde, *Yerself Is Steam* brings to mind Pink Floyd mixed with Pere Ubu—David Baker, who shared vocals with Jonathan, evoked Pere Ubu singer David Thomas with both his odd voice and his sizable girth—as well as displaying the significant influence of the Flaming Lips. While the album was difficult to find in the United States after Rough Trade's American branch declared bankruptcy shortly after its release, British critics showered it with praise, and "Car Wash Hair" became a modest hit in the United Kingdom. In retrospect, the touching ballad can be heard as Jonathan's comment on his time touring with Wayne and Michael: "Catchin' a ride from a band/I sat in the back of the van/They tried to make me understand."

The British raves for *Yerself Is Steam* attracted American major labels eager to enter the alternative rock sweepstakes. "In the time of *Oh My Gawd!!!*, no one cared about success, because no one thought indie rock was going anywhere," Jonathan said. "You were just happy that you had a nice, warm living-room floor to sleep on and the chance to play, and then you'd go back to your job and tell everybody you had been somewhere. Later, by the pink album [*In a Priest Driven Ambulance*], it began to dawn on people, 'Hey, some people are making money at this; some people don't *have* to go back to their jobs.' That's when the music business started fucking with people's minds."

Mercury Rev became the subject of a bidding war. Technically, Warner Bros. owned the rights to anything Jonathan recorded, since he had signed to the label as a member of the Flaming Lips. The company wanted Mercury Rev, too, but Jonathan didn't like that idea. "I felt that it would be distracting to the Flaming Lips and the public perception of the Flaming Lips, as if it was just one giant band and the cell divided. The Flaming Lips had been going for seven years at that point; they were an established college/indie band. I was making a record that I felt was going out to friends on an eight-track cassette." Instead, Mercury Rev accepted an offer from Columbia Records, which reissued *Yerself Is Steam* after some legal wrangling with Warner Bros. to free Dingus from his contract.

"I didn't leave the Flaming Lips because I was unhappy," Jonathan said. "I loved being with and working with Wayne. I spoke to Wayne and Scott the same day and told them I had made a decision. Wayne said, 'Well, you've gotta do what you've gotta do.' I was a young man with a great head of steam and a big imagination and a willingness to try everything and anything, but I wasn't the guy singing the songs. That was Wayne. I don't know what my leaving meant to him; I've never asked him, and I'm not sure I want to know. We had a symbiotic relationship where we seemed to understand what each other was trying to manifest, but the emotional heart between us was never written. It was always unsaid, the same with him and Michael."

While recording *Hit to Death in the Future Head*, Nathan also decided to leave the band, and he told Jonathan first. "Dingus kind of looked out for me, me being quite naïve at the time," Nathan told the Flaming Lips Trading Post Web site. "He made sure I didn't indulge too much (women, drink, etc.) . . .

When I left the band, I had no idea that he was planning to do the same." Nathan chafed under what he called Wayne's "control freak" leadership, and he disliked the Buzzard's confrontational style. "The thing with him and me is that I was raised with a lot of pride, which is a weakness, and I'm not a good debater, so Wayne loved to get on me and ride me, and ride me, and ride me," Nathan told me. "If you knew my brother, who is a right-wing, crazy Nazarene, I love him, but most of the time I want to smash his face in, and I feel the same way about Wayne. I love him, but geez, gimme the chance, and I'd pound him."

The drummer also disliked the direction the band had taken on *In a Priest Driven Ambulance* and *Hit to Death in the Future Head.* "All I knew is that I wanted to sell a lot of records, and it didn't sound like something that would sell a lot of records. I was like, 'I'm not making any money, I have to put up with Wayne's crap all day, and they are turning into an art rock band, which is fine and I love art rock, but I don't want to play it.' I'm a rock drummer; that is why I play. I like to get stressed out and rock, and I was kind of turning into a philharmonic player. I didn't want to play philharmonic music; that's why I quit the orchestra."

Nathan described an emotional scene when he announced his decision to Wayne and Michelle Martin, who'd been a friend since high school. "Michelle was sobbing and Wayne was threatening to beat my head in with a tire iron. He was flipping out, but even after all that, when they were leaving, he stopped and came back and said, 'Look, think about this for a few days and let me know.' I had been thinking about it for a long time, and my mind was made up. I think he felt I was being disloyal, but I just wasn't happy anymore."

Two years after the leg of their trip that began in Charlotte, North Carolina, when Richard English quit and left them to perform as a duo, Wayne and Michael were back where they'd started. "All of the sudden the dust cleared and Wayne looked at me, I looked at Wayne, and we were both like, 'What the hell?'" Michael said. Wayne insisted that he didn't worry about either resignation, and he didn't try to persuade Nathan or Jonathan to stay. "Nathan quitting was really no big deal. I could figure that out: We'd get another drummer, and we were thinking of getting another drummer before he thought about quitting because he was just so drunk, lazy, and unmotivated." Jonathan was a bigger loss, but Wayne had begun to tire of the guitarist's style of self-mythologizing, which differed from his own. "Jonathan and I are a lot alike in that pursuit of something, but Jonathan isn't trying to be authentic. He is trying to present people with a mystery, so you never know what he is talking about, and I am the opposite. He wanted to appear like a drug addict, some Lou Reed/Bob Dylan character, all these stupid rock 'n' roll clichés, but I was like, 'That may work with the journalists in England, but I *know* you.'"

The news that half the band had defected before the release of its first album distressed its label—"If I was at Warner Bros., I would have dropped them," Booker said—but Wayne assured everyone that he would put together an even better group, and Petersen's faith in the Flaming Lips' front man didn't waver. "I always think that all bands should stick together from the beginning," she said. "Don't kick anyone out, ever; try to keep it together. I've been through it with tons of bands, and it always bothers me, but when Wayne has his mind made up, that is it, and he is a smart, smart man."

Within weeks the band had recruited a new drummer, Steven Drozd, a devoted twenty-two-year-old fan who'd been playing with Janis Eighteen. A few months later, twenty-one-year-old Ronald Jones filled the role of lead guitarist. Warner Bros. finally released *Hit to Death in the Future Head* in August 1992. The old lineup with Jonathan and Nathan had made an inspired video for "Everyone Wants to Live Forever," a performance clip that climaxed with the group dumping buckets of fake blood into a fan and its friend Jon Mooneyham sliding through the mess. The new band with Steven and Ronald appeared in another clip for "Frogs," and both videos got a handful of airings on MTV's late-night alternative rock show, *120 Minutes,* but the exposure had little impact.

With sales of fewer than forty thousand more than a decade after its release, the album remains the Flaming Lips' least successful effort for Warner Bros., and it barely sold better than the group's Restless recordings. The reconfigured band did two tours to support the disc—one of the highlights of these jaunts came when the group paid a visit to Beat novelist William S. Burroughs at his home in Lawrence, Kansas, and spent an afternoon firing shotguns with him and his assistant, James Grauerholz—but by the end of 1992, the Flaming Lips were eager to leave *Hit to Death in the Future Head* in the past. They were already looking ahead to the next album and aiming for the stars— or the satellites, as the case may be.

CHAPTER 6

TURN IT ON AND ALL THE WAY UP

TRANSMISSIONS FROM THE
SATELLITE HEART (1993)

THE FADING summer sun cast a gentle orange glow, but the temperature still hovered in the nineties as the Flaming Lips hit the stage at the World Music Theatre south of Chicago for Lollapalooza 1994. As the first notes rang out, roadie Cory Franklin powered up a row of six machines and a couple of giant fans mounted on the lighting scaffold, and the audience cheered as the air filled with thousands of glistening bubbles.

Former Jane's Addiction singer Perry Farrell had launched the traveling day-long alternative rock festival in 1991, but Lollapalooza's popularity peaked during its fourth year, when it drew sixty thousand fans over two nights in Chicago alone. Nirvana had pulled out of the headlining slot in March following Kurt Cobain's attempted overdose in Rome—a month later, he succeeded in taking his own life with a shotgun at home in Seattle—and the top slots on the main stage for the forty-three-date summer tour went to the Smashing Pumpkins and the Beastie Boys.

The Flaming Lips' sixth album, *Transmissions from the Satellite Heart,* had yet to make much of an impact on MTV or modern rock radio, which had exploded in the wake of *Nevermind* to become the most successful music format on the dial, but the second single, "She Don't Use Jelly," had become a local hit in Chicago, and John Rubeli, an agent with Lollapalooza's co-owners, Triad Artists, tapped the band to headline the second stage. "I was a fan, and I met them in 1989 when I booked them at Marquette University and Steel Pole Bathtub and Nirvana opened," Rubeli said. "I used to yell at all of the Warners people to watch the crowd reaction during 'Jelly'; it was epic and beautiful. I just knew that they were going to have a hit with that. Lollapalooza that summer really cemented the Lips' position in the alt-rock hierarchy, and you'd see Nick Cave, the Breeders, L7, the Pumpkins, and the Beasties all flocking to see them."

The second stage generally drew a smaller and less intense crowd, but in Chicago, the majority of concertgoers opted to skip George Clinton's P-Funk

Allstars on the main stage in favor of the Flaming Lips, who played on a temporary platform set up in an asphalt lot that was filled with bobbing heads as far as the eye could see. Amped-up teenage boys formed mosh pits in the center of the throng, slamming into one another with limbs flailing, while dozens of young girls body-surfed on the crowd's upraised arms. Occasionally, a fan climbed onstage and darted in between the band members before diving back into the churning mass of humanity.

Acknowledging Generation X's love of irony and its penchant for campy nostalgia, the Flaming Lips opened with a giddy cover of "Space Age Love Song," the 1983 hit by the oddly coiffed New Wave band A Flock of Seagulls, a favorite of new guitarist Ronald Jones. Reflecting the strong glam-rock influence on its sixth album, the band closed its set with "Under Pressure," David Bowie's 1981 collaboration with Queen, but the group's new originals garnered the biggest response. Inspired by his girlfriend Michelle Martin's twenty-second birthday and exploring one of Wayne Coyne's favorite themes—maintaining your individuality in the face of becoming another cog in society's wheel—the pounding drums, throbbing bass, and wailing noise guitar of "When Yer Twenty-Two" mirrored the nervous energy of the crowd. "Stuck in the perpetual motion, dying against the machine," Wayne howled. "The sound is so huge when you're twenty-two."

Offering ample evidence of why it would become a hit, "She Don't Use Jelly" prompted fans to sing along with every absurdist couplet about Vaseline, tangerines, and toast, while the unapologetically hokey "Chewin' the Apple of Yer Eye" offered a postmodern take on Neil Young's "Sugar Mountain," providing a brief acoustic respite from the full-on rock assault. This tune also seemed to comment on the liberating experience that thousands of young nonconformists were having at Lollapalooza as they spent a day among like-minded misfits sporting nose rings, tattoos, purple Mohawks, and sarcastic sneers. "It's like at the circus when you get lost in the crowd," Wayne sang. "You're happy but nervous, a definite sign that you lost it."

The Flaming Lips had made a giant leap forward from *Hit to Death in the Future Head,* and "Moth in the Incubator" best illustrated its new approach. An alternative version of the "pocket symphony" Brian Wilson envisioned when crafting "Good Vibrations" for the Beach Boys, the song started simply, with a sparse guitar part and Wayne crooning about transformation: "Something in you, it jitters like a moth/And I see that your arms are out to God." Running his Fender Jaguar through a massive array of effects pedals, many of them homemade, Ronald slowly added layers of strange noises and otherworldly squeals to usher in the next phase of the tune, a grinding riff that evoked the sexual bravado of seventies glam-rockers T. Rex. "Your incubator is so tight," Wayne sang, his excitement building as he went on to proclaim that he'd been "born before" and was getting used to it.

With that, the song became something else entirely for its last third, an insanely catchy instrumental built on a massive, repetitive guitar riff. Ronald piled on buzzing harmonics, bringing to mind a swarm of locusts amplified to the threshold of pain, as Steven Drozd pummeled his twenty-six-inch bass drum and oversized snare. Mixing the classic-rock stomp of Led Zeppelin's John Bonham and Black Sabbath's Bill Ward with an unrestrained punk fury, Steven pushed the tempo faster and faster until the band finally lost control, the melody gave way to sheer dissonance, and the song ended in a frenzied explosion of clattering cymbals and screeching feedback.

The lineup with Jonathan Donahue and Nathan Roberts had been an undeniably weird and powerful rock band. The new Flaming Lips were just as intense and strange, but much more musical and melodic. Clad in the all-black "cyberjunkie" look that followed his tuxedo-and-bow-tie "James Bond phase," with a new close-cropped cut replacing the Afro that inspired "the Church of Michael Ivins's Hair," the stoic bassist remained the reliable anchor amid the chaos, while Wayne displayed an increasing self-confidence as singer and a growing desire to entertain in his role as front man, telling rambling stories about the events that inspired his songs, hammering his trashy Harmony Rocket guitar, and screaming until the veins on the side of his neck popped out. But much of the excitement came from the band's new members, the manic drummer and the lanky guitar wizard, both a decade younger than the duo that formed the group, and each a musical force unlike any other on the alternative rock scene.

Steven Drozd grew up on the outskirts of Houston, Texas, in a tight-knit community of German and Czechoslovakian immigrants, surrounded by polka music and its Mexican cousin, conjunto. Like Wayne, he came from a large family, with an older sister, two older brothers, and one younger brother. It wasn't the only similarity in their upbringings. Steven's formal education also ended with high school, and not only did his older brothers introduce him to the music of bands such as Led Zeppelin, Black Sabbath, and Pink Floyd, but they also had trouble with drugs and the law.

Renowned as the saxophonist in one of the state's best polka groups, the Gil Baca Band, Steven's father, Vernon, played rock 'n' roll in the mid-fifties

"THE SOUND IS SO HUGE WHEN YOU'RE TWENTY-TWO."
LOLLAPALOOZA, CHICAGO, 1994; CLOCKWISE FROM TOP LEFT:
WAYNE (NOTE THE "I ♥ MICHELLE" BUTTON), MICHAEL,
STEVEN DROZD, AND RONALD JONES.

with Huey Long and the Wild Ones and spent seven years as a sideman with country legend Johnny Bush, the author of "Whiskey River." Between gigs, Vernon drove a truck delivering beer. Steven was the only one of his children who followed in his footsteps as a professional musician. "I come home one day from the beer route and I said, 'What is that little fart doing in the garage with that box of Schlitz? He's beating it, beating it, beating it!'" Vernon said. "So I bought him a small set of toy drums, and he busted them to pieces in no time. Then I worked my tail off and saved up about a thousand dollars and bought him a real drum set, used. After that there was no stopping him: He'd be practicing at eleven o'clock at night, just driving me nuts. He was obsessed with music."

Steven was ten years old when his parents divorced. Vernon soon remarried, and the young drummer moved with his father, two of his siblings, his new stepmother, and her five children to Lawton, a poor, crime-ridden town an hour southwest of Oklahoma City. "It was chaos, but it was all I knew," Steven said of his crowded home life. At the time, Vernon played in a band called Rawhide, covering Top 40 country hits. One night the group's drummer didn't show up, so Steven's stepmother took him to the club to sit in. The preteen began playing with his father's band every weekend thereafter.

When he was thirteen, Steven taught himself to play piano. Despite his lack of formal training, he could soon figure out any song he heard—"Steven can hear a train whistle and tell you what key it's in," Wayne said—and he honed his chops playing for his older brother, Tony, better known as Bubba, who had been paralyzed in a car accident. "We spent a lot of time together while I was in high school just because he lived with us and he couldn't go anywhere," Steven said. "He's one of the reasons I became the piano player I did, because I would come home from school every day and he would say, 'All right, come on in here and play the piano.' He'd make me play a Stones tune or some Journey song, and he would just sit there and watch me play piano for hours."

After high school, Steven lingered in Lawton, dreaming of becoming a session musician in Los Angeles, until he got an offer to join a band called the Van Goghs back in Houston. "This was 1988, and living in Lawton, I really didn't know anything about indie rock. I had never heard Sonic Youth or Dinosaur Jr., and when I did, it blew my head off." Drummers were always in demand, and he soon moved on to an outfit called Monster Zero, trading Houston for the city that has always been the center of the Texas music scene. "Now I was in Austin and I was twenty-one, so I lived up to every cliché you can imagine: drugs, drinking, sex, you name it." He dyed his hair blue-black

"HE WAS OBSESSED WITH MUSIC."
STEVEN AS A TEENAGER IN THE MID-EIGHTIES.

with Clairol Nice 'n Easy, wore a nose ring, worked a dead-end telemarketing job by day, and hit the clubs every night.

In the summer of 1990, Steven landed his best gig yet with Janis Eighteen, which had relocated to Austin from Oklahoma a few months after the Flaming Lips used bandleader Billy Egle's brother's studio to record the demos for *Hit to Death in the Future Head*. "They were this second-rate Nirvana/Pixies/Jesus Lizard wannabe band," Steven said of his new group, "but they had already done a couple of tours, and then we rehearsed for a week and took off for the Midwest: Minneapolis, Madison, Milwaukee, Lawrence, Iowa City, Chicago. We didn't make a dime at any of these places, and no one came to see us, but it was great. We were in a band together and we were living the rock 'n' roll dream."

Steven's new bandmates turned him on to the Flaming Lips. "I had heard *Oh My Gawd!!!* and I thought it was pretty cool, but I just forgot about them. Then when I joined Janis Eighteen, they played *Priest Driven Ambulance* for me, and it knocked me out. I couldn't believe what I was hearing. My ideal for kick-ass rock 'n' roll or psychedelia was pretty heavy, but deep down, I also loved seventies Carpenters and stuff like that. Part of the appeal of *Priest* was all the really heavy stuff, like 'Mountain Side' and 'God Walks Among Us Now,' but in December of '90, the Flaming Lips came to the Cannibal Club in

Austin, and they covered 'Every Christian Lion Hearted Man' by the Bee Gees, and that was it. They became my favorite band."

By the spring of 1991, Janis Eighteen was falling apart, but Steven followed the group back to Norman. "Nothing was happening in Austin, and they decided to go home and lick their wounds." He was working at a restaurant and rooming with two members of a band called Glue when Wayne dropped by to hang out. "My roommate Robbie had an eight-track, and Wayne and Michael were making demos; Jonathan and Nathan had quit the band, and it was just the two of them. I don't think I let on that he was my favorite musician of the last couple of years. The second time I met him, I was sitting there with an acoustic guitar, and I had just learned how to play 'Hello It's Me' by Todd Rundgren. He had just heard it on the radio, so he was like, 'Wow!'"

By their third meeting, Wayne had seen a videotape of Steven drumming with Janis Eighteen. The Flaming Lips' bandleader extended a casual invitation—"Come to Oklahoma City and set up with us and play through some songs"—but Wayne already knew he'd found his new drummer. "We knew he could play like a motherfucker, but just as important, he truly is an excellent person: smart and funny and charming. Every time someone left, Michael and I would reassess our standards of tolerance: We were like, 'Look, we know how to be in a band, we can show you that, but we can't show you how to act like a human.' Steven was a fucking awesome drummer and a really cool guy."

For several weeks, Steven practiced with Wayne, Michael, and their longtime friend Jon Mooneyham, who had played guitar in several noise bands, regularly introduced the Flaming Lips to esoteric music they'd never heard, and helped design some of their album covers. "After Jonathan said he was quitting, I told Wayne, 'You need to get Ron Jones,'" Mooneyham recalled. "Actually, I was thinking about *you*," Wayne said. Mooneyham insisted he wasn't a great guitarist, but Wayne said he didn't want a virtuoso, he wanted someone with good ideas. Mooneyham agreed to give it a go.

The lineup with Mooneyham on second guitar also featured cellist Mary Beth Leigh, later of the Starlight Mints, but it lasted for only one show in December 1991. "The next day, Wayne called me and said, 'Well, I think we're going to get rid of Jon Mooneyham,'" Steven recalled. "I was like, 'Why? Because he can't play and his gear never works?' Wayne said, 'No, we just can't deal with his personality anymore; he's driving me and Michael crazy.'" Mooneyham harbored no bad feelings, and the band turned to the guitarist he had recommended in the first place.

A dedicated fan, Ronald Jones had often come straight from his job bagging groceries to sit in the corner and watch the Flaming Lips rehearse with their new drummer and Mooneyham. "Every once in a while, he'd make a suggestion: 'If you play that guitar chord like this, it will sound more like what's on the record,' stuff that only a total muso would know, and I always thought that was pretty impressive," Steven said.

Born in Hawaii to an outgoing African-American father and a quiet Filipino mother, Ronald wound up in Oklahoma when his dad, an amateur musician, took a job at Tinker Air Force Base. While attending Del City High School, the Flaming Lips' future guitarist crossed paths with the band's future manager—Scott Booker did his student teaching there prior to abandoning his goal of becoming a history teacher—but it was a few years later before they started talking, when Ronald would rummage through the bins of dollar cassettes at Rainbow Records, and Booker would sell him albums by ABC or A Flock of Seagulls for a dime apiece.

As a teenager, Ronald had pursued his twin passions for racing BMX dirt bikes and playing guitar. He sat in his bedroom for hours playing along with albums by his beloved New Wave bands and progressive rock groups such as Genesis, and he developed a unique sound by employing ingenious effects such as holding a small Realistic telephone amplifier next to his pickups to create a roar like a million electric razors. Prior to joining the Flaming Lips, he played in a band called Snail—"They were really over-the-top New Wave, part Roxy Music glam rock and part Chrome and Helios Creed guitar weirdness," Steven said—which stood out on the Oklahoma music scene as much for its flamboyantly gay African-American front man as it did for its distinctive sound.

One day when Wayne and Booker were hanging outside the duplex on NW Twelfth Street, Ronald came over to visit another of their neighbors, the Flaming Lips' former roadie Ted Drake. Ronald sat on the porch and performed "There You Are" on acoustic guitar, then sheepishly asked Wayne if he had played the tune correctly. The song's author looked at him in astonishment. "Well, yeah, you're playing it right, but you're playing both guitar parts at once!"

"It was like a light bulb went off or a sledgehammer hit me in the head, and I said, 'Wow, this guy is good! He should be the Flaming Lips' new guitarist,'" Booker said, but Wayne and Michael were committed to giving Mooneyham a shot. Booker encouraged Ronald to attend their rehearsals and report back. "He was like my spy," Booker said, laughing. "I'd ask him, 'Dude, how is it?' It would be hard for him to answer: He'd stare at the ground, shuffle his feet, shake his head, and finally say, 'Um, well . . . It's not so good.' He knew he could do better."

When the Flaming Lips played with Ronald for the first time, Steven nursed a psychedelic hangover from the hit of acid he'd dropped the night before. "I felt pretty crummy as Jones set up all this crazy gear, but we played for about two and a half hours straight. Ronald and I knew every song in Wayne and Michael's catalog, and we were these rabid fans: 'Come on, let's play another one off of *Hear It Is!*' I swear there was a moment somewhere in the middle of it where I felt like I was levitating, it was so intense. I didn't know I could get any higher than I already was."

Steven quickly bonded with the Flaming Lips' veterans. He and Wayne shared similar backgrounds, and the drummer's easygoing personality prompted the usually silent Michael to open up. "I'm not one who can sit in silence comfortably," Steven said, so Michael made him nervous at first, until one night when the two drove from Norman to Oklahoma City. "I think I realized that Michael had accepted me as a new friend when he got in the car, lit up a Marlboro, and was like, 'Are you interested in World War II? I was reading this book about how the Nazis had perfected audio sources as weapons of destruction,' then he talked about that for the next thirty minutes."

Ronald proved to be harder to get to know. Tall, awkward, and soft-spoken, the guitarist surpassed even Michael in his shyness; by comparison, the introverted bassist seemed as loquacious as Wayne. For months after joining the band, Ronald covered his face with his hands during photo sessions, and in group interviews, he almost never said a word. He expressed himself primarily through his playing, and in that regard he amazed his bandmates. "As soon as we heard Ronald play, all the things that we thought we could never do were suddenly within our grasp," Wayne said. "Me and Michael, we understood how to make noise, but there were some elements of the songs we were starting to make—the musicality of them—that was beyond us. Ronald understood harmonies and textures. Jonathan and Fridmann understood that stuff, too, but they couldn't play on his level. Jonathan was a good guitar player, but if I'm a two on a scale of one to ten, Jonathan is a five, and Ronald is a twenty. We'd never played with anybody that good."

The day after the new quartet's first rehearsal, Wayne called Booker and announced, "We're ready to roll; get us some shows!" The band solidified as a live act in 1992 as it supported *Hit to Death in the Future Head* on tour, opening for the English band Lush, whose leader, Miki Berenyi, Steven dated, and then for Throwing Muses. The latter jaunt included a high-profile showcase

"THOSE GUYS ARE BOTH SUCH AMAZING MUSICIANS,
I FEEL SORRY THAT THEY'RE STUCK WITH A
SINGER LIKE ME." STEVEN AND RONALD, 1994.

in October during the College Music Journal Conference in New York, and afterward, the band talked with its marketing rep.

"I remember Jo Lenardi from Warners came to us and said, 'Guys, I realize that *Hit to Death* just came out a month and a half ago, but when you get done with this tour, I want you to go home and start working on a new record,'" Steven said. "I think they felt they dropped the ball on the record coming out at the right time because of all the Michael Kamen stuff, so they said, 'You guys have been heightening your profile by touring, you sound great, let's just forget all that and move on.' So we went home and started working on *Transmissions*."

After recording two albums in western New York, the Flaming Lips decided to work on the next one at home in Oklahoma City—without the producer who'd become their ideal partner. Wayne maintained that Dave Fridmann was busy at the time with Mercury Rev, but Fridmann had a different recollection. "Once Jonathan left the band, I was excommunicated; instantly, it was over. It was 'You're from Mercury Rev and you're staying with Jonathan.' Nobody believed me that I didn't know he was quitting, though them knowing Jonathan, they should have known better. Within a month or two, they came to accept what I was saying and it was no longer a big deal, but with Warner Bros., it still mattered. They had signed Jonathan to a contract, and they thought he should contribute to the Flaming Lips, so they sued Columbia and made Columbia buy Jon, and I was not allowed to work with the Lips from the Warner Bros. side, period."

Instead, the Flaming Lips turned to Fridmann's old assistant and Fredonia rival, Keith Cleversley, who had been running live sound for Spiritualized, the new band formed by Jason Pierce of Spacemen 3. The English group and the Flaming Lips were both playing in San Francisco, and when Cleversley stopped backstage to say hello, Wayne asked him to produce the Lips' next album. "You mean you want me to produce it with Dave?" Cleversley asked. Wayne said no, he'd be doing it on his own. "My mouth dropped open," Cleversley said. "Jason had just asked me to produce his record, and both bands were going to start in January. I had always dreamed of recording both these bands, but there was no way I could do both, so I decided to go with the Flaming Lips because I missed the States and I adored the band as people. Wayne was like a god to me. When I first heard their music, I was in awe, and I had this vision of a guy standing on a mountaintop, playing guitar, pumping out music that moved me."

The band spent the first few months of 1993 in Studio Seven, which usually hosted bluesy bar bands and gospel groups. The studio was located in a dicey neighborhood a mile from downtown Oklahoma City, and one night during the sessions, the musicians were experimenting by recording vocals in a car parked out front when a house across the street exploded. They watched it burn to the ground before the fire department arrived, and the debris still sat untouched years later. "The studio was a mess, and I spent a large amount of time just rewiring it," Cleversley said. "The only good thing about it was this old storm room that was perfect for drums: a loud, obnoxious, bouncy concrete room."

In contrast to its last two albums, the group didn't have a big backlog of songs that had already been demoed, and the sessions started slowly. "We were just recording Steven and Ronald the way we recorded everybody who came before, and it sucked," Wayne said. The band taped a cover of "Ballrooms of Mars" by T. Rex; a new version of "Five Stop Mother Superior Rain" that was "vastly inferior to the *Priest* recording," according to Steven; and "Teenagers in the Himalayas," an original by Wayne. "The only part of that song which made it worthwhile was this guitar part that Ronald played that sounded like the weird keyboard part of 'Benny and the Jets' by Elton John," Steven said. "The rest of the song was a piece of trash." Added Wayne, "We literally erased the tape, it was so bad."

In his earlier groups, Steven had never contributed to the songwriting,

"WHEN I FIRST HEARD THEIR MUSIC . . . I HAD THIS
VISION OF A GUY STANDING ON A MOUNTAINTOP, PLAYING
GUITAR, PUMPING OUT MUSIC THAT MOVED ME." RECORDING
Transmissions from the Satellite Heart, 1993: FROM LEFT,
MICHAEL, WAYNE, BOOKER, DAVID KATZNELSON, ROBERTA PETERSEN,
STEVEN, KEITH CLEVERSLEY, AND RONALD, HIDING AS USUAL.

but now he played his bandmates a four-track demo that he'd made over the holidays. "It had the drums, the chords, the melody, everything in place," he said, and the group decided to try a version of the tune for the album. "We recorded the drums and distorted the hell out of them and added a few other parts. Wayne already had the lyrics, it all just fell together, and we said, 'Okay, now we're off to the races.'"

"Slow Nerve Action" broke the creative logjam and provided a model for a new way of working in the studio. "That song really set into motion the way that we record now," Wayne said. "Steven plays everything, I sing, and if anybody else has anything to contribute, get in line!" From that point on, the majority of the songs came together as the tape rolled, either starting with a musical idea from Steven, or with Steven and Wayne honing an idea that Wayne had developed on his own. Wayne added lyrics and vocal melodies, while Ronald became "the decorator guy," as Steven said, a role similar to Brian Eno's in Roxy Music, obsessing with strange sounds, adding layered harmony riffs, "and really taking the songs to the next dimension."

Where Fridmann had epitomized a laid-back, patient, and encouraging approach to producing, Cleversley represented the opposite extreme, and his style grated on the musicians. "I think his whole raison d'être is power: He wants to hold the power over bands, in contrast to Fridmann, who should be a United Nations ambassador," Steven said. "Cleversley's got the biggest ego out of any band guy I've ever met. I think he wanted to create a name for himself, get as many bands on his résumé as possible, be a really famous producer, do drugs, and fuck women. He gave Wayne an amount of respect that the rest of us didn't get, and he'd do these power plays with Ronald and Michael."

"I was completely unprepared maturity-wise to be producing a band for a major label," Cleversley granted. "I was fresh out of school, twenty-three years old, and here I was producing a band I really loved. My skull was on a platter, because I thought my whole life depended on this record. Plus, I was so in awe of Wayne, I was blinded beyond that narrow vision." Cleversley pushed, goaded, and cajoled Michael and Ronald, but he maintained that it was what Wayne wanted. "Wayne's two big phrases during those sessions were 'It's not about money, it's about fear,' and 'If someone else can play the part, let them play the part.' Michael would come in, but Drozd could play every instrument better than everybody else. Wayne wasn't threatened by this, but Michael was extremely threatened. Wayne would say, 'Keith, he can't spend eight hours doing a bass track when Steven can do it in five minutes.' Michael and Wayne got into a fight about it, and Michael ended up crying."

At one point, Cleversley said, he taped Wayne yelling at his bandmates and played it back to him. "In my pea brain, I thought, 'If he could hear the way he treats other people sometimes, maybe it would be eye-opening. Maybe he isn't aware how angry he gets.' He'd be yelling, 'What are you doing? It sounded like art, and now it sounds like fucking whales!' Everything was a debate: 'If you don't like tomatoes, how can you say you like ketchup?' So I recorded this, took him aside one day when we came in early, played it for him, and he freaked out. He went to my apartment, and every tape, DAT, anything I had, he took it all."

"That's not true," Wayne countered. "Keith did record us talking in the studio, but I believe it was always to see what we were saying about *him*. He was very manipulative in that way. I *would* yell at the band—'Look, we don't have to be polite to each other; we have to get this shit done!'—and I regret some of that, but I think I'd earned the luxury of being able to yell at these guys. At the end of the day, I felt like they wanted me in charge because I had some experience, some vision, something to offer them, and I didn't want to let them down. We were all in it together: I loved these guys, and I always felt we should work harder and push ourselves."

While Michael agreed that he resisted yielding some of his bass parts to Steven—"It was like, 'Wait a minute, if I'm not playing bass, there's nothing for me to do'"—he came to see Wayne's point about wasting time in the studio, though he resented what he viewed as Cleversley's efforts to edge him out of the band. "If you look at his history of bands he has worked with, I think every one of them had a personnel change except for the Flaming Lips, and I think he tried really hard to have one happen. I actually wish I had been meaner to him. Hate is a weird emotion; it's so powerful, and I don't really invest myself in it too much. It takes a lot for me to say I hate another human being, but since I'm venting now, yeah, I actually hated him."

Despite the intense emotions behind the scenes, *Transmissions from the Satellite Heart* stands as one of the Flaming Lips' best albums. It kicks off with "Turn It On," an optimistic anthem that introduces the new lineup by restating psychedelic guru Timothy Leary's call to "tune in, turn on, drop out." As Ronald evokes the sound of radio waves bouncing off the satellites and Steven assaults the drums with pile-driver intensity, Wayne urges a new audience to "turn it on and all the way up." The song predated *Hit to Death in the Future Head*, but it seemed especially timely in 1992 thanks to the proliferation of online communications. "Not to say that I could peer into the future and see it coming, but there was some vague notion of whatever the Internet was pointing towards," Wayne said, "where you're sitting in your own house and you're connected to everything around the world, all your friends and all the things you really like, in your own little space and time."

Built on one of Steven's riffs and more typical of a growing whimsy and surreal playfulness in Wayne's lyrics, "Pilot Can at the Queer of God" patterned its title after that of Pink Floyd's 1967 debut, *The Piper at the Gates of Dawn,* in part because Steven lifted the memorable drumbeat that opens the tune from Nick Mason's playing on "Take Up Thy Stethoscope and Walk." As Wayne asks a series of questions about an unnamed woman—"Has she joined the Army?" "Has she turned queer?"—the group answers with beautiful call-and-response harmonies, and the song builds to a climactic chant of "She's got helicopters." Wayne based the tune on a coworker who left Long John Silver's to serve in the Army. "When he would come back from his duties, I felt like he was changed for the better. He went away and he was a hick, a chauvinist, but he came back and he'd surprise me with the things he would say about this woman, a lesbian pilot who flew Blackhawk helicopters and shot missiles and stuff. He was really impressed with her."

Much less linear, "Oh My Pregnant Head (Labia in the Sunlight)" strives to evoke the feeling of a bad acid trip, with a rhythm that turns itself inside-out and beautiful symphonic swells created by Ronald, the disorienting one-man orchestra. Free-associative couplets such as "Somewhere the star burns the universe / Gold eagle paints in my fingers" read like Beat poetry and find Wayne reveling in the sound of the words without unduly worrying about their meaning. "When you have a title like that, and the sound of the music, you really don't need a song," he said.

Equally surreal but more structured and tuneful, "She Don't Use Jelly" came in a burst of inspiration as Wayne toyed with his acoustic guitar. "I just sat there and strummed those chords and sang a verse with that melody in exactly the amount of time it took to play it. We were at the beginning stages of *Transmissions,* and it was so rich with all this new stuff that we were able to do with my simple songwriting and Ronald and Steven's crazy playing that I could see a good arrangement happening, even though it's really not that different from a million other songs I'd written." The tune was distinguished by the addition of Steven's martial drumbeat and the signature hook that he played on pedal steel guitar, but no one thought it was a more likely hit than any other track. "It was just, 'That's a weird, silly song, but it isn't hard to listen to,'" Michael said.

When radio and MTV began playing "She Don't Use Jelly" a year and a half after the album's release, some reviewers contended that the whimsical characters portrayed in the verses—the girl who thinks of ghosts and puts Vaseline on her toast; the guy who goes to shows and uses magazines to blow his nose; and the girl who reminds Wayne of Cher because she's always changing the color of her hair—were symbolic of the unholy trinity of sex, drugs, and rock 'n' roll. "I guess the guy who blows his nose was supposed to be about blow, the girl who dyes her hair orange is supposed to be some sort of take on the alternative movement, and the Vaseline that the girl puts on toast is really meant as some sexual thing. But I never heard about that sort of thing in Oklahoma," Wayne said, laughing. "It's really not; it's really all pretty normal until the slight twist on things in the last line. One couplet in each of those verses and the whole thing goes to hell."

A relatively stripped-down number built around acoustic guitar, "Chewin' the Apple of Yer Eye" was one of the first songs Steven ever wrote; it's also the last Flaming Lips tune to feature his lyrics. "I wrote the first verse, then Wayne wrote the second verse. His words were much better than anything I could come up with; it was like, 'When you have a lyric-writer guy like Wayne, why bother?' Honestly, I was just so happy being in this position where I was actually contributing musical ideas that were being used. It was a mind blower, and I couldn't believe I didn't have to worry about that old joke: 'What's the last thing the drummer said before they fired him?' 'Hey, guys, I've got a new song!'"

"Steven had the very beginning of that song: 'Hey, what were ya thinkin'/When they were startin' the show,'" Wayne said. "He was talking about a story that happened to him at a movie theater where his friends were smoking pot and got busted. We tried to make it into a more epic, symbolic thing, where he's watching the movie and the world is ending outside. We didn't even try to put drums on it. For a while, we ran into that scenario where either it was going to rock and destroy you, or there'd be no drums on it at all. That worked really well on that album, to have these extremes: You could be Led Zeppelin *and* you could be Simon and Garfunkel."

Listed on the back cover as "* * * * * * *" but better known as "Plastic Jesus," the album's other change-of-pace acoustic song is a cover of the tune Paul Newman delivers to his fellow prisoners on the chain gang after his mother dies in the 1967 film *Cool Hand Luke*. "If you go back to the type of song that we did on *Oh My Gawd!!!*—'This man came up to me just the other day/He asked me if I'd been born again' ["Ode to C.C. (Part II)"]—I knew even early on that people took to me as this kind of Oklahoma songwriter guy put into a space capsule," Wayne said. "I knew there was something in there, so I was always looking for another way to say, 'Yeah, I believe in that, too—not that I think it's true, but I believe that if that thing could exist, it could exist in me.'"

Cool Hand Luke ranked as one of Wayne's favorite movies because he related to what he called "the existential hero" of the title. "The movie is about a group of men trying to discover their own possibilities, and Paul Newman becomes the focus of that. I think I saw a parallel there, growing up with my brothers and all their friends and wanting to have experiences that were authentic, and somewhere in there is that rebellion against everyday acceptance and the way things are supposed to be, and the imagery of this isolated guy who has nothing but his own mind to rely on, though he's really doing it with a group of people"—a story not unlike the Flaming Lips' tale.

The rest of *Transmissions from the Satellite Heart* contrasts dramatically with the two stark acoustic songs, and it often seems as if the band had saturated every magnetic molecule of the two-inch master tape with sound. Inspired by the urban legend about someone finding the extraordinary strength to rescue a trapped child by single-handedly lifting a car, "Superhumans" builds the dynamics slowly through each verse until Steven's mounting drums, Ronald's swirling guitar, and the unexpected tubular bells explode as Wayne proclaims, "I'm sure there's planets wrapped up with you." Despite its weird sawing guitar and layers of unsettling noises, "Be My Head" is an insanely catchy sing-along that could be the theme song for the Scarecrow in another of Wayne's favorite movies, *The Wizard of Oz* ("You can be my head/Oh, I really need one"), and if "When Yer Twenty Two" is a love letter to Michelle Martin, "Moth in the Incubator" can be heard as a mash note from Wayne to his new bandmates.

"By the time we hit that song, the shit was really going, and we knew we could jump from one mood, into another mood, and then into a whole new mood at the end, no problem," Wayne said. Throughout the recording, Ronald obsessed over details, spending days crafting a part that appeared in a song for twenty seconds, while Steven threw his whole body into hitting the drums, duct-taping his headphones in place to prevent them from flying off. Cleversley's efforts to replicate the sound of John Bonham on Led Zeppelin's "When the Levee Breaks," the acoustics of Studio Seven's concrete tornado shelter/drum booth, and most of all Steven's intensely physical playing combined to produce a sound that other alternative rock bands have been trying to copy ever since.

Shortly after Roberta Petersen signed the Flaming Lips, David Katznelson won a full-time job at Warner Bros., and he now served as the band's

A&R rep, with Petersen supervising. The two monitored the group's progress throughout the sessions, and they visited Studio Seven several times. "To me that was always like, 'Let's be on our best behavior, the bosses are coming,'" Steven said. "I remember we played 'Chewin' the Apple of Yer Eye' for Roberta, and I could tell she was really into it. At the end, she just said, 'That was so beautiful.' Dave Katznelson and I would drink bourbon until three or four o'clock in the morning. Everybody involved was really jacked up about the record."

Warner Bros. released *Transmissions from the Satellite Heart* in June 1993, while the Flaming Lips toured with Porno for Pyros, the new band fronted by Perry Farrell. The label chose "Turn It On" as the first single, but radio ignored it, and MTV passed on the video directed by New York photographer Michael Lavine, which featured a young girl watching the band on TV. The group fared much better with reviewers. In addition to the usual fanzine support, the album won a smattering of attention from more mainstream outlets, and Greg Kot, the rock critic at the *Chicago Tribune,* convinced *Rolling Stone* to publish a three-and-a-half-star review in late October, four months after the album's release. "At one time, it might have been easy to dismiss the Oklahoma City quartet as overly enamored of whimsy ('One Million Billionth of a Millisecond on a Sunday Morning') or excess (the twenty-three-minute 'Hell's Angel's Cracker Factory') or British acid rock," Kot wrote. "With *Transmissions from the Satellite Heart,* the Flaming Lips join the ranks of rock 'n' roll's most endearing eccentrics."

In December, Kot named the disc album of the year in the *Chicago Tribune* on the same day that I singled it out for the same honor in the *Chicago Sun-Times,* but it seemed destined for the same fate as *Hit to Death in the Future Head* when "She Don't Use Jelly" followed "Turn It On" by failing to garner modern-rock radio play. By the end of the year, the Warner Bros. publicity, marketing, and radio staffs had turned their attentions to the next products in the pipeline, and "this was a dead, dead, dead record," company staffer Tom "Grover" Biery said. "Nothing was happening, and it didn't seem like anything would."

Given the disappointing sales of *Hit to Death in the Future Head,* Wayne and Michael realized they might not have the opportunity to make another major-label album if *Transmissions from the Satellite Heart* flopped. "I don't think anyone would say this out loud, but we knew it was an important record, and if something didn't happen with it . . . " Booker said in 1994, his voice trailing off. So the band set out to convert fans one gig at a time.

In the eighteen months after the album's release, the Flaming Lips performed in Chicago alone thirteen times, touring with the Butthole Surfers, Stone Temple Pilots, Tool, the Grifters, Codeine, Archers of Loaf, and Red Red Meat. Always up for any task involving organization or machinery, Michael assumed the role of tour manager and methodically set the band's schedule, charted its travels, and booked its accommodations on his Apple 180 laptop. As always, the band presented listeners with a musical and visual assault: It relied less on the old smoke machines during this period, but it had more bubbles than ever, and it now adorned the stage with thousands of blinking Christmas lights, powered by two electrical generators that it carried in a trailer behind Old Blue.

"Four hours a day hanging those fucking lights and pulling them down at the end of the night, that was my gig," roadie Dick Smart said, "and still Wayne would be like, 'Should we get more lights?'"

"Staying on the road and doing good shows were the only things we had control over," Booker said. "We didn't know radio people or promotions people. Touring was the one way we had to give the record company some indication of what we were capable of." Wayne didn't expect anybody at Warner Bros. to work any harder than the band. "The record company does what it can, and it does the same for everybody," he said. "It's easy for a band to say, 'We think our album is good, you should make it a hit,' but it's a lot harder to say, 'We think it's good and we're gonna go out and tour and show you.'"

"They just kept touring and touring," said Biery, who joined Petersen, Katznelson, Lenardi, and publicist Deb Bernardini in the small but devoted circle of Warner Bros. staffers reluctant to give up on *Transmissions from the Satellite Heart*. "They wouldn't go away. Even though some of the power people at the company maybe wanted them to go away, they just wouldn't."

A native of rural Sharon, Pennsylvania, Biery was another indie-rock veteran who had worked in record stores, booked punk shows, written for fanzines, and played the albums he loved on community radio; his nickname, Grover, stemmed from his handle as a DJ. The contacts he made in radio led to a job as a Warner Bros. promotions rep in Ohio, and after three and a half years working the territory from Toledo to Columbus and Cincinnati to Youngstown, he became the Midwest radio and promotions manager in Chicago. "I got to Chicago on a Friday a few weeks after Thanksgiving, 1993, and that Sunday both you and Kot named *Transmissions* the album of the year," he told me twelve years later. "I'd been a Lips fan since the beginning, and when the first Warners record came out, I thought it was great, but there wasn't anything I could really do as the local radio guy in Ohio. There would not have been a snowball's chance in hell in Cleveland or Columbus of the Flaming Lips' record being named album of the year, and I was so blown away by that happening in Chicago that my brain went into overdrive: 'We've gotta do something!' At that point, the record had been out a long time, and truthfully, no one at Warner Bros. really cared."

Biery called Booker and hatched a plan for the Flaming Lips to play a free show at Metro in February 1994 to thank Chicago for its support. A bastion of adventurous rock radio since the New Wave era, WXRT-FM had begun playing "Turn It On," and the new modern-rock outlet, WKQX-FM, had added "She Don't Use Jelly." As a result, the album was selling two thousand copies a week in Chicago, 40 percent of its weekly total nationwide. "In order to do the show, I had to go to all these different people that ran departments in the company and scrape up a thousand dollars here and a thousand dollars there," Biery said. "I put together this whole marketing plan and sent it to everybody from Mo Ostin on down. The key was that the record was selling in Chicago, and I knew that could show the company it was capable of selling everywhere else."

The label reserviced "She Don't Use Jelly" as a single, but outside Chicago, modern-rock radio still didn't embrace the track. The Lips continued to tour relentlessly, following Lollapalooza with a grueling sixty-date jaunt opening for their best-selling Warner Bros. label mates, Candlebox, a generic grunge band that had a huge following among hard-rocking frat boys. Wayne and Booker knew that the label's radio staffers would work overtime to support the Candlebox tour and, at the same time, the Flaming Lips. The group would get a push at radio and earn twenty-five hundred dollars a night for a thirty-minute set, but the tour would have hidden costs.

"We used to joke that we left home as boys and came back as men, just like coming back from a war, which is a terrible way to describe being in a band," Steven said. "A lot of times, the audiences were either totally apathetic or aggressively uninterested. For Wayne and Michael, they had been through the ringer so much, this was just another tour to make some money to continue the band, but for me and Ronald, it ended the illusion that this band was going to change the world. It was soul-destroying in a lot of ways, and that was the first time that playing in a band seemed like work."

"We had been [touring in support of] *Transmissions* for so long, and that Candlebox tour took a lot more out of us than anybody realized," said Dick Smart, who worked on the Flaming Lips' road crew for four years. "Candlebox sucked, and everyone knew they would have their fifteen minutes and then evaporate. Here the Flaming Lips are slogging away opening for this shit band for two months, and their fans could give a shit about the Flaming Lips. It was really bad and just very, very depressing."

Nevertheless, the tour had the desired effect when, shortly before the first date, Warner Bros. summoned Booker to Burbank. Label president Lenny Waronker liked and supported the Flaming Lips, staffers said, but vice chairman Russ Thyret was the executive who could really "push the button" to promote a record. "Our product manager said, 'I think it's time for you to meet Russ,'" Booker recalled. "I was like, 'Who the hell's this guy?' People said, 'He's the wizard behind the curtain,' but here was this guy in front of me who looked just like Burl Ives. Our product manager did all the talking. Finally Russ stood up as he was getting ready to leave and he looked at me and said, 'Scott, you didn't say a word. What do you want?'" Booker asked for more radio support, more albums in the stores, and some help getting the Flaming Lips on TV.

"Listen, this reminds me of the Replacements a few years back," Thyret said, "when everyone at the label loved them and all the right opportunities were popping up, but it never clicked. We didn't follow through, and the band broke up. I don't want that to happen to this band."

"Russ said, 'If you don't feel like this is happening in a week, call me and let me know, but I'm a man of my word,' and then he left," Booker said. "It was such a weird thing. Everyone was like, 'Russ really liked you,' and I was like, 'How could you tell?' But the next week, there was a person from Warners at every single show. They had to be there, they had to write a report, and they had to bring a person from a radio station with them or they were gonna get chewed out."

Marketing executive Jo Lenardi lined up dozens of in-store appearances for the band wherever it performed. "We did everything we could with them on the road and got everyone out to see them numerous times, and Wayne charmed the socks off everyone at the record stores. He would send them postcards and special silk-screened posters and remember everybody's name. Ever since then I've tried to get bands to do the same thing, because I think it made people feel like the Flaming Lips were friends, and everyone wanted to get behind them."

Finally, the third time Warner Bros. sent the single to radio, "She Don't Use Jelly" became a national hit, maintaining a presence on *Billboard*'s Modern Rock Chart from December 1994 through March 1995, and peaking at Number Nine. Some Warners staffers initially had scoffed at the video that

Wayne and independent filmmaker Bradley Beesley made for twelve thousand dollars, featuring Wayne with hair dyed orange and Michelle Martin rolling around in a psychedelic bathtub. Now, the clip won a spot in MTV's Buzz Bin, and it got a further boost when it was mocked by cartoon boneheads Beavis and Butt-head. ("Uh-oh, I think this is college music," Butt-head cracked.) MTV also played the new video that Wayne and Beesley made for "Turn It On," which found the group performing in front of a wall of Christmas lights as Michelle, Steven's girlfriend, Becky Stokesberry, and their friend Emma Rolls frolicked in a Laundromat.

Still the Flaming Lips' biggest fan, Wayne's mother, Dolly, did her part to spur the band's success. Whenever the group played within a day's drive of Oklahoma City, she rounded up as many Coyne siblings, cousins, nephews, and nieces as possible and led a caravan to the gig in the family's Isuzu minivan, though her husband, Tom, was often too busy working to join them. Dolly also launched an ambitious campaign besieging MTV to air the group's videos—a story told by Warner Bros. marketing staffers in an ad called "The Case of the Promo Mama."

"What a character she is—very proud of her son," Lenardi said in the ad. "Somehow Wayne's family had learned the name of an executive at MTV, Lewis Largent. The family wrote out boxes of postcards and sent them in gobs to Largent, each postcard demanding that MTV play the video of the band's single, 'She Don't Use Jelly.' Every postcard was signed by a different person, but the text on them all was in the same handwriting! So this, uh, threatening pile of postcards starts to deluge Largent, and then the Flaming Lips get Largent's phone number. Endless messages! Really spooked Largent. We had to explain: 'Lewis, the band is not stalking you.'" Modest to a fault, Dolly declined to let the label run the ad.

True to Thyret's word, Warner Bros. helped the band land several prestigious TV appearances. By mid-1995, the Flaming Lips had performed on *Late Show with David Letterman, The Jon Stewart Show, MTV Spring Break,* and the teen soap opera *Beverly Hills, 90210,* where they appeared surrounded by their Christmas lights at the fictional rock club the Peach Pit. "Hey, is that the Flaming Lips?" asked Brian Austin Green as David Silver. Replied Ian "Steve Sanders" Ziering: "Well, it's not Michael Bolton!" In June, a new song called "Bad Days" garnered a spot on the soundtrack for the Warner Bros. film *Batman Forever,* during the key scene where Jim Carrey is introduced as the Riddler. The group was also slotted to record the soundtrack for Spike Jonze's film version of *Harold and the Purple Crayon,* but the director never secured the financing.

The Flaming Lips had finally broached the mainstream, but the band's veteran members took a characteristically philosophical view about their success. "To me, *Transmissions*, for whatever reason, that's the breakout album," Michael said. "We'll probably always be 'the band that does that jelly song,' but that's fine. I go back to that quote from *Pulp Fiction:* 'They're *your* clothes, motherfucker!' I don't look at *Hear It Is* and say, 'Boy, that's crap; look how far

"IS THAT THE FLAMING LIPS?"
"WELL, IT'S NOT MICHAEL BOLTON!"
RONALD AND MICHAEL TAPING *Beverly Hills, 90210*, 1994.

we've gotten.' I hate bands that do that. Maybe you are a different band now, but you did that stuff, and you can't say 'I was drunk' or 'We were young and we didn't know what we were doing.' You seemed like you liked it and knew what you were doing back then. I would never say that's not part of who we were or who we are."

After two years promoting *Transmissions from the Satellite Heart*—and sales of three hundred thousand copies, ten times more than all of their earlier albums combined—the Flaming Lips were ready to move on, and their next release would finally be a priority for their record company. "We never wanted Warner Bros. to come in and sort of take over and make us a huge band; our idea was they give us money, we make records, they distribute them, and we'll take care of the rest," Wayne said in 1994. "I think in some ways that works real good, and in some ways it doesn't work so good. We're lucky in the regard that this time, if the new album flops, it's their fault. We can't lose now. If we sell a million records, fine. If we sell fifty thousand, it just looks like they fucked up. But it doesn't make doing records any easier, because in the end, all that shit really doesn't matter."

CHAPTER **7**

I'VE HEARD ABOUT A PLACE
WHERE THEY ENLARGE YER SPACE

CLOUDS TASTE METALLIC (1995)

BY THE TIME I visited Studio Seven in mid-April 1995, the Flaming Lips had been hunkered down for six weeks recording their seventh album, *Clouds Taste Metallic*. The musicians had returned from a tour of Australia and taken over the studio, filling every corner with a mind-boggling array of guitars, percussion instruments, analog synthesizers, and other musical gear, as well as toys to occupy their downtime, dirty laundry, and empty takeout containers. The owners didn't mind, because there weren't any other customers. "This place is probably gonna go bankrupt," Wayne Coyne said. "Then we'll have to buy it so we have a place to work."

As Wayne conducted a tour, he apologized for how "neat" the studio was. Ronald Jones recently had rolled up the loose microphone cords and vacuumed the tattered rug in the main recording space, but the guitarist didn't touch the drum room. Steven Drozd's oversized, mismatched drum kit was set up in front of a giant psychedelic mural that looked as if it had been painted at a hippie day-care center. Two dozen massive, broken drumsticks littered the floor, along with innumerable cigarette butts and an impressive collection of empty beer cans, and Steven had scrawled several inspirational slogans on his giant ride cymbal with a marker: "Fucking is gnarly," "Personally, I like myself," and "Probably the coke talking, but I like you, too."

Ronald didn't touch Wayne's vocal booth, either. The smell of stale cigarette smoke permeated the closet-sized space, and there was barely enough room to step inside without walking on Wayne's road-weary acoustic guitar, a hefty anthology of Bob Dylan's lyrics, or a hardcover copy of *Santa Calls*. William Joyce's children's book tells the story of a boy named Art, "devoted to the making of inventions, the quest for adventure, and the fighting and smashing of crime," who leads a 1908 expedition from Abilene, Texas, to the North Pole in search of Toyland, "the best of the old, the best of the new, and the best that is yet to be."

"For inspiration," Wayne said as I leafed through the colorful pages.

The night before I arrived, Wayne had recorded the vocals and acoustic guitar for "Brainville," a goofy little ditty that he'd written at home. "You'll find out where this song is going as soon as we do," he said of the work in progress. It had been nearly two years since the release of *Transmissions from the Satellite Heart*. In between, timed to Lollapalooza, the band had issued an EP self-deprecatingly titled *Due to High Expectations the Flaming Lips Are Providing Needles for Your Balloons*. The disc rounded up a collection of rarities, including "Ice Drummer," a cover of a song by Alan Vega of the pioneering electronic rock duo Suicide, and "Put the Waterbug in the Policeman's Ear," a memorable story-song in the tradition of "U.F.O. Story," recounting a run-in with police that Wayne's brother Marty had while stoned on downers. The group had recorded one new album-worthy original, "Bad Days," but it had entered the studio with only a handful of demos for other new tunes.

After his work on *Transmissions from the Satellite Heart*, Keith Cleversley ran the group's live sound for several months, until the band finally fired him. "He wanted to be the fifth Flaming Lip," roadie Dick Smart said, but Cleversley wasn't as subtle in the role of offstage Brian Eno as Dave Fridmann had been. "You couldn't hear the band, and you could tell it was pissing Wayne off. Finally he just told Keith, 'Man, you are an arrogant cocksucker,' and that was it."

Any animosity that Warner Bros. held toward Mercury Rev had subsided, and now Fridmann once again occupied the producer's chair. The morning I arrived at the studio, the producer played the basic tracks for "Brainville," and Wayne cringed as he heard himself sing the opening line, "I've heard about a place where they enlarge yer space." He gestured toward Steven and Ronald, who were tinkering with guitars on the other side of the control room's glass partition. "Those guys are both such amazing musicians, I feel sorry that they're stuck with a singer like me."

The lyrics of "Brainville" can be heard as a swipe at people who think you can't be an intellectual unless you've earned a higher degree. "They say it's the one thing everyone should have / I know it must look bad," Wayne sings in the bridge, presumably referring to his lack of a diploma. "Wayne went to college vicariously through his friends," Michelle Martin said. "He always thought, 'If you are inquisitive and broke, go get a job washing dishes in a college town.'" But the songwriter maintained that the lyrics sprang from one of his surreal stories. "I imagined these guys who put fliers up all over town saying, 'Brainville University, Tuition One Dollar' and listing this back alley as the address, and then they beat up and rob anybody dumb enough to show up," Wayne said.

The basic chords sounded a lot like those of "Garden Party," the 1972 hit by Rick Nelson, but over the next twelve hours, the two-minute-seventeen-second tune morphed into an elaborate mini-symphony as the Flaming Lips added drums, bass, keyboards, tambourine, backing vocals, and a dozen gui-

"THE BEST PART ABOUT WORKING THE WAY WE DO IS THAT YOU CAN NEVER DO ANYTHING WRONG." RECORDING *Clouds Taste Metallic* AT STUDIO SEVEN WITH FRIDMANN, CENTER, AS ROBERTA PETERSEN LISTENS IN THE BACKGROUND, 1995.

tars, including one that sounded like a banjo and another that mimicked a ka-
zoo. Now, the group was preparing to record another overdub. "What have
you got for us, Jones?" Wayne asked as he entered the main recording room.
The lanky guitarist played a heavily chorused riff, and Wayne recoiled. "You
haven't gone ELP on us, have you?" he asked. Ronald shrugged defensively,
but Fridmann piped up over the studio intercom, "No, no, that's more 'The
Sound of Silence,' Wayne." Convinced that folk-rock legends Simon & Garfunkel were cooler than progressive rockers Emerson, Lake & Palmer, Wayne
nodded, and Ronald committed the part to tape. "The best part about working the way we do is that you can never do anything wrong," Wayne said.

Throughout the session, the band members continually asked, "That's
not another song, is it?" or "This hasn't been done before, has it?" They were
happy to borrow from or reference a wide array of musical heroes, as long as
these sounds appeared in new and original contexts. With the addition of
Ronald's guitar line, "Brainville" seemed complete and ready to mix, until
Fridmann pointed out that the tune could use some percussive handclaps after
the final chorus. The four musicians pressed me to join them in a circle around
the microphone, and we all clapped out a syncopated rhythm on Fridmann's
cue. Afterward, a passionate thirty-minute debate followed about how the producer should make the thirty seconds of clapping sound. Ronald favored the giant, reverb-drenched claps that Roy Thomas Baker created for Queen and the
Cars, while Wayne preferred the subtle, dry handclaps that John Cale recorded
for the debut of Iggy Pop's band the Stooges. Michael Ivins sat quietly in a corner, distracted by the pain of having had his wisdom teeth pulled the day before. Finally Steven produced a CD of David Bowie's *Hunky Dory* and played the
song "Andy Warhol." *That* was the way rock 'n' roll handclaps should sound,
the consensus held, and Fridmann tweaked the EQ accordingly.

The band seemed content as it broke for takeout from an Indian restaurant, and Wayne expounded on his vision for the Flaming Lips' music. "I
think the one thing that a lot of people who record Christmas songs have going for them is they have all this great imagery associated with Christmas that
they can put these sounds to: You hear bells, you hear the swishing of sleighs,
and you hear horses and angels and all that, and all this great imagery really
comes through. That's the sort of thing that we try to do. There are always
these visual references that you're going to turn into sounds. It isn't 'What
notes are we going to play?' or 'What instrument are we going to use?' It becomes a real specific way of trying to get a mood across. We're the sort of
band that's always making a Christmas record."

☺   ☺   ☺

The success of *Transmissions from the Satellite Heart* turned out to be a mixed blessing for the Flaming Lips. For the first time in their career, the musicians weren't scrambling for money. Booker helped Steven and Ronald open their first checking accounts, the band finally paid off the debt it had racked up on Michael's parents' credit card, and Wayne and Michelle Martin bought a house a few blocks away from his mom and dad, near where he'd grown up.

Classen-Ten-Penn is one of Oklahoma City's poorest neighborhoods—"Basically, we're in the ghetto," Wayne said—with block after block of sad, squat ranch houses, junked-up cars sitting on cinder blocks in the front yards, and babies playing in the dirt in their diapers. Wayne and Michelle's home stood out even before the addition of the gargoyles they perched on the roof. Vaguely inspired by Frank Lloyd Wright, the rambling, two-story mansion had been built by an eccentric contractor in 1936, utilizing materials salvaged from other jobs. The unique circular staircase came from an old movie theater, the tile in the kitchen from a drive-in restaurant, and the stained-glass windows from a church.

Like the Beatles in *A Hard Day's Night,* the musicians essentially lived together in the place they called "the Compound" or "Stately Wayne Manor." Michael and Scott Booker, who'd split from his first wife, shared a guest house in the back, and Fridmann, Steven, and Ronald often crashed in one of the spare bedrooms or on the living-room couches after all-night recording sessions. It was part headquarters, part clubhouse, and the group rehearsed, stored its gear, silk-screened its posters, and shot and developed its album and publicity photos in various corners of the communal crash pad.

"Wayne's mom actually spotted the place," Michelle said. "We weren't really looking to buy a house, but we drove up and the back door was open, and once we saw it, we thought, 'This is unbelievably cool.'" The U.S. Department of Housing and Urban Development had put the house up for auction, and Wayne and Michelle won it with five hundred dollars down and a bid of twenty thousand more—which, Wayne proudly noted, they'd promptly paid off. But the band didn't stay solvent for long.

The Flaming Lips had never properly paid their corporate income taxes, and their number came up when the IRS launched an audit. Michael and his girlfriend, Catherine DoBiesz, joined Booker in rummaging through mountains of old receipts, attending workshops, and studying tax manuals in order to negotiate the avalanche of paperwork. "Right around that time, there was just sort of enough money to pay the taxes," Michael said. "Afterwards I remember driving down the street with Catherine and being like, 'Well, now we've got five dollars left in our account.' That's right when it seemed like we should put our nose to the grindstone and do another record."

Since the late eighties, the Flaming Lips had established a pattern of following each of their strongest albums with a recording that consolidated the accomplishments of its predecessor, seemingly biding time until the next leap forward. Although there are great moments on all of them, 1989's *Telepathic Surgery* is overshadowed by 1987's *Oh My Gawd!!!*; 1992's *Hit to Death in the Future Head* pales in comparison with 1990's *In a Priest Driven Ambulance*, and 1995's *Clouds Taste Metallic* doesn't live up to the expectations created by *Transmissions from the Satellite Heart*, though it stands as the most unjustly overlooked gem in the band's catalog.

The album opens with its most ambitious track, "The Abandoned Hospital Ship," which starts quietly with Wayne singing over Steven's mock tack piano and the percussive sound of a rolling film projector. The tune stemmed from a relatively rare full-band jam on the majestic riff that comprises its second half, while Wayne's lyrics came from another of the short stories he car-

"WE WEREN'T REALLY LOOKING TO BUY A HOUSE, BUT . . . ONCE WE SAW IT, WE THOUGHT, 'THIS IS UNBELIEVABLY COOL.'" STATELY WAYNE MANOR, OR THE COMPOUND, 1995.

ried only in his head. "It was a sort of *Twilight Zone* episode: I was thinking of a giant hospital spaceship going to different galaxies. One patient shows up, they work frantically through the night to save him, and at the end of the episode, it's God that they saved; God was in some horrible galactic accident. In a typical Rod Serling sort of way, the patient leaves, and they're all sitting there thinking, 'Oh, nice work,' but they don't realize the extent of what they did. I was playing with a lot of film loops at the time, and the projector just sort of naturally made its way onto the tune. I think we tried turning it off, but the minute we did, the whole atmosphere disappeared."

The bizarre universe-turned-inside-out lyrics of "Psychiatric Explorations of the Fetus with Needles"—"Cats killing dogs, pigs eating rats / 'Every mouth will eat you up,' the king bug laughs"—don't quite live up to the propulsive rocker's evocative title. It and the next two tunes boast uplifting, sunny melodies that contrast with the darker songs at the end of the album, and these three tracks represent the peak of Wayne's silly/surreal lyrics. The singer poses some intriguing questions in "Placebo Headwound"—"Where does outer space end?" and "And if God hears all my questions / Well how come there's never an answer?"—but he never fully explores these themes, while "This Here Giraffe" could have been written as the theme song for a children's cartoon. It grew from a synthesizer riff devised by Michael and Steven, who disliked Wayne's lyrics. "I was just like, 'Aw, geez, not another fucking song about animals,'" Steven said. "The same thing happened with 'Christmas at the Zoo.' I had the music and the melody intact on a four-track demo, and of course I didn't give him anything to go by when he asked, 'Well, what do you want the song to be about? Do you have any ideas?' My answer is always the same: 'No, I don't have a vague idea what I would want you to sing about.' So he came back a couple days later talking about the animals at the zoo and Christmas, and I was like, 'Jesus Christ!'"

"We were building on these themes: What band can sing about animals? What band can sing about Christmas?" Wayne said. "I know we can, not because it is so sincere, but we can sing about things that other bands wouldn't care to." The novelty of these tunes wore thin quickly, however, in contrast to the album's closer, "Bad Days," which stands beside "She Don't Use Jelly" as an example of Wayne at his whimsical best. Inspired by the eleven years he spent at Long John Silver's—he had finally quit after *Transmissions from the Satellite Heart*—and including a homicidal fantasy about shooting your boss (suggesting that perhaps Wayne didn't love his job as a fry cook as much as he claims), the song reveals the deceptively simple secret to happiness: "You have to sleep late when you can/And all your bad days will end."

Replete with cheering crowds, guitars that sound like trombones, bells, or tubas, the return of the voice-of-Satan backing vocals, and a carnival barker who narrates part of the action through a megaphone, the epic "Guy Who Got a Headache and Accidentally Saves the World" pursues another of Wayne's recurring themes: "the epiphany of the everyday, normal guy seeing the extraordinary in the mundane. We were going by the seat of our pants in that song. I remember playing it for Steven and saying, 'Hey, this is like Aerosmith,' still feeling like we were a heavy rock band, but with these Syd Barrett or *Pet Sounds* elements."

This formula is best exemplified by the album's most upbeat tracks, "When You Smile" and "Kim's Watermelon Gun." The former is a gorgeous love song decorated with tinkling bells and driven by Steven's fractured but powerful drum part. "It's about how everything you thought was perfect about the world came together in that second when this person smiled," Wayne said. "I remember at the time thinking that Sade could sing it." As with all of his best love songs, Michelle Martin provided the inspiration. Through all of the touring that followed *Transmissions from the Satellite Heart*, Wayne proudly sported a button proclaiming, "I ♥ Michelle."

"There are some drunk women who are very nice to talk to," Wayne said. "You can't say they're groupies, but they come backstage and their titties are hanging out and all of that. I wear the button so everyone says, 'Who's Michelle?' and I can just blatantly say, 'She's my girlfriend.'"

"Kim's Watermelon Gun" is a rollicking and insanely catchy song that paints an impressionistic portrait of another woman, Pixies veteran and Breeders bandleader Kim Deal, whom Steven befriended during Lollapalooza. "Basically it's just a great rock riff," Wayne said. "I wish we would've gone into some revelation about the human condition, but we didn't. It's just a pretty fun three minutes."

Unlike Michael and Booker, who were both big science fiction fans, Wayne never read the genre, but he did enjoy spinning his own futuristic tales. Slow, spare, and melancholy, "They Punctured My Yolk" stemmed from another of these unwritten short stories. "It's about a couple who are falling in love as they are training for a mission into outer space, and they are going to explore the universe together, but at the very end of the song, the guy discovers that for some reason he is not going on the mission, and she gets sent off into space while he's stuck here."

The giddy but lumbering "Lightning Strikes the Postman" found its inspiration closer to home. "That was an inside joke that we would have about Ronald, and it was a song that Ronald sort of wrote," Wayne said. "He had the basic chords and melody, and we filled in the gaps with the arrangement. It was about the idea that we would be in the control room after a twelve-hour session of his playing, and we would all feel like there was at least a fundamental understanding of what he was going to add to the song next, but in between him leaving the control room and picking up his guitar, the lightning would strike the postman, and whatever he was meant to deliver to us had utterly changed. We'd ask, 'Twenty seconds ago, didn't we talk about this exact thing?,' but he'd have an utterly inexplicable response to whatever we were asking for. It was funny that the one song he was the instigator of was actually about him."

If Ronald realized he'd inspired the lyrics, he didn't express dismay, though he did have a problem with the album's penultimate track. "Evil Will Prevail" begins as a low-key acoustic tune and builds into an ominous, rumbling symphony before fading out again. The lyrics are a minimalist sketch, but the title is repeated several times in the choruses, and the song ends abruptly with Wayne's naked and desperate-sounding voice declaring, "Evil will always win." The band had demoed the song six months earlier, but recording the album version proved to be an ordeal.

"Ronald didn't like that song at all, and I don't want to say he was trying to sabotage it, but he was playing parts he knew we wouldn't like," Steven said. During Lollapalooza, Ronald had a spiritual awakening inspired by the troupe of Tibetan monks who toured with the Beastie Boys. Increasingly interested in healing crystals and Rolfing, a holistic system of soft-tissue manipulation, the guitarist believed the cynical message of "Evil Will Prevail" would create bad karma.

"I think Ron met some people that cracked open the third eye a bit for him, and he was definitely having some metaphysical experiences," said Jon Mooneyham, who was close to Ronald. "People have different ways of assembling that information or those experiences: It ends up being a search for God or whatever, and I think that was the path he ended up being on. I hate to say there was a taste of New Age to it, but he was definitely exploring that a lot more, and he would take trips out of town to be with friends and fellow travelers."

"The Tibetan monks and the crystals and all that stuff is fine, but it's not based in reality; it's too cosmic for me," Wayne said. "With 'Evil Will Prevail,' I felt like I broke through the gap of the psychedelic nonsense and said, 'Fellows, we are going to sing about some stuff here, and we may be uncomfortable, but people have given us this opportunity to say something. If I can sing songs this way, with this music backing me up and the momentum of the ideas and all that, I think these songs will get beyond the whimsical and mystical, psychedelic stuff, and maybe we can get into something real about the human condition.' I had stumbled upon this idea that love is only really love if you know how truly evil people in the world are. If you can love knowing that, then that really is love."

The song seemed especially resonant a week after I visited the Flaming Lips, when Studio Seven and Stately Wayne Manor shook with the force of an explosion less than two miles away. On April 19, 1995, at 9:03 a.m., the homemade bomb that twenty-seven-year-old right-wing extremist Timothy McVeigh had assembled in a rented Ryder truck destroyed the Alfred P. Murrah Federal Building in downtown Oklahoma City, killing 168 people, including nineteen children who had just been dropped off at the employees' day-care center. Unlike many Oklahoma City residents, the Flaming Lips had no connection to any of the victims of the blast. Wayne rode his bicycle to the site immediately afterward, not because he felt like part of the tragedy, but because he didn't. "It was such a big news event—a megamoment—and you knew that everybody that you talked to was going to be talking about it," he said. "It didn't enlighten me to how evil the world is. I already knew that anyway."

Upon its release in September 1995, modern-rock radio and MTV ignored *Clouds Taste Metallic* the way they had disregarded the Flaming Lips' earlier albums, and its sales would ultimately be closer to *Hit to Death in the Future Head*'s than *Transmissions from the Satellite Heart*'s. With the benefit of hindsight, everyone in the band's camp developed a theory about the album's failure—a relative term, given that indie-rock groups a few years earlier would have been thrilled to sell sixty thousand albums.

Wayne came to agree with Steven that aside from "Evil Will Prevail," the lyrics were simply too silly—"It didn't deliver on an emotional level"—while musically, the band had settled into a formulaic groove, albeit an extremely strange one, saturating every tune with countless weird guitar overdubs. "*Clouds Taste Metallic* is the fullest expression of the weird imagery with the lyrics and the music and just how dense we can make things," Michael said. "After we were done, we would start picking things apart, saying, 'You know, there's a melody that comes in toward the middle of the song that doesn't happen anywhere else. Why?' That can be neat in and of itself, but it doesn't have anything to do with the craftsmanship of the song or trying to use the song as an actual vehicle for communication. It was just like, 'Here's a canvas; let's fill it up with a bunch of stuff.'"

Fridmann believed the band had "alt-rocked itself to death" at a time when the movement was waning. Many of the modern-rock radio stations that proliferated in the wake of *Nevermind* were run by corporate executives who previously helmed "lite FM" or classic-rock stations. They had no idea what distinguished good alternative-rock bands from cookie-cutter grunge clones such as Bush and Candlebox, and they were susceptible to the hype of the independent promoters hired by the major labels in the modern analog to the notorious "hit men" of earlier payola scandals. This produced a wave of one-hit wonders and novelty hits unprecedented since the late sixties and early seventies. Some of these acts endured to have impressive careers— including Beck, who made his bow with "Loser"; Radiohead, which initially scored with "Creep"; and Weezer, which debuted with "Undone—The Sweater Song"—but others, such as Dada ("Dizz Knee Land"), Marcy Playground ("Sex and Candy"), the Rentals ("Friends of P"), Semisonic ("Closing Time"), and Whale ("Hobo Humpin' Slobo Babe") were forgotten the week after they dropped off the *Billboard* charts. Many people in the music industry counted the Flaming Lips as part of this dismissible group, despite their already lengthy history.

"Keep in mind that we're talking about a time when we didn't know who the Flaming Lips' fan base was, because when you're used to selling twenty-five thousand records, and then all of a sudden you have this novelty hit with 'Jelly' and this awesome, super-weirdo band sells three hundred thousand records, you have no idea who's buying them," said Grover Biery. "Clearly all those copies of *Transmissions* sold because of a novelty song. Some new fans joined up, but a lot was driven by that hit. When *Clouds* came out, it deflated the idea that we had built more of a core fan base for them, but I don't know if *Clouds* is their finest moment, either."

Some factors were out of the band's control. Starting in July 1994, Warner Bros. suffered the biggest corporate upheaval in its storied history when Doug Morris and Robert Morgado, the vilified examples of a new breed of executive that rose in the wake of corporate consolidation, assumed key positions overseeing the Warners-affiliated record labels. For them the bottom line was everything, and artist development was an unnecessary expense. By the end of the year veteran record men Mo Ostin and Lenny Waronker had announced their resignations. Roberta Petersen, the A&R rep who signed the Flaming Lips, quit shortly after Waronker left in 1995. "Once Lenny was gone, everything started falling apart," she said, "and nobody cared about the music anymore."

The Flaming Lips still had a dedicated group of supporters at the label, including Biery, Jo Lenardi, and David Katznelson, but the effort these staffers had put into creating a hit with "She Don't Use Jelly" didn't matter to the new bosses. The new general manager, Jeff Gold, "didn't hear a single" on *Clouds Taste Metallic,* and he vetoed spending any money to promote it on radio or MTV, although the group made videos for three of its songs, "Bad Days," "This Here Giraffe," and "Christmas at the Zoo."

"Jeff Gold had always been a naysayer," Katznelson said. "He didn't see the musicality or the star potential behind Wayne as a true artist who people could look up to; he just saw a bunch of weirdos. Lenny [Waronker] had loved the band, but now Lenny was gone, and Jeff Gold was one of the guys running the show."

"Bad Days" had been slated to appear on the soundtrack for the Warner Bros. film *Batman Forever,* which opened in June 1995. Katznelson hoped it would give the album a boost, but Gold called to say the song needed tweaking: "We need to do a couple of edits, and we need to bring the chorus closer to the beginning." The Flaming Lips' A&R rep didn't understand. "Jeff, can you come down here and show me?" Katznelson asked. Gold confessed that he hadn't actually listened to the song, but was sure it needed work. (A remixed or "aurally excited" version of "Bad Days" ultimately appeared in the film.)

In the end, the biggest reason *Clouds Taste Metallic* didn't perform like *Transmissions from the Satellite Heart* may have been that the Flaming Lips were burned out on touring and didn't work as hard to support it. "We did the Red Hot Chili Peppers tour in Europe, which didn't help us there or here, and we were supposed to tour with them in the States, but that got canceled because the drummer broke his wrist," Steven said. "So we came home and did a tour with the Apples in Stereo, but it didn't seem like things were going onward and upward, it seemed like everything was kind of stalling and we were just spinning our wheels. This is the time period, late '95, when, as the English say, 'Everything went pear-shaped.' There was the disillusionment and the drugs . . . I was really, really fucking on the way down by then, and I just started to not care."

In the fall of 1994, during the long and soul-sapping tour with Candlebox, Steven progressed from occasionally snorting heroin when it was offered to him to regularly shooting up. "That tour was when it started to be, 'Hey,

I'm going to do this as often and for as long as I can.' We were in New York City for a week around the Thanksgiving holiday, and that was probably the first time I went off on a major bender. I remember we got to Philadelphia and I'd run out. We played this show, and it was the first time that I ever felt like I didn't play very well and that I didn't care if the show went well or not, and that was a weird and scary feeling. Before that, every time the Flaming Lips ever played, I always gave it 100 percent, everything I had, but this time I was just waiting for the show to get over with."

Steven realized he'd become addicted to heroin when he returned from the Candlebox tour. "I either had a major nervous breakdown or some attack of manic depression hit me that I had never experienced before. For a couple of weeks, I was convinced I had a stroke. I remember we went to Chicago to play on New Year's Eve with the Gin Blossoms, and I just felt miserable. I was shaking and having these panic attacks, I felt dizzy, and I hadn't slept in a few days." He saw a doctor who prescribed sleeping pills. "Nothing seemed to work, and that's when I really started doing the heroin. It was like there was a switch in my mind, and I said, 'I'm just going to start doing this whenever I can, and when I can't get it, I'll just deal with it.'"

Steven's bandmates knew about his drug use, but he managed to mask the extent of his problem for several years to come. "The way that Steven does drugs, he could be doing booze, he could be doing heroin; it's just entertainment for him," Wayne told me in 1994. "Steven knows what he's doing; he doesn't have a drug problem." A decade later, Wayne admitted he'd been in denial. "We all were, but Steven was very, very good at never letting any of that shit interfere with work, in the studio or on tour, so it was hard for us to really know how bad things had gotten."

Wayne always had fostered an atmosphere in the band that tolerated everyone's habits, good or bad, as long as they got the job done, but Ronald frowned on Steven's excessive partying, and he especially disapproved of the heroin use. Tensions between the two youngest members of the band grew while recording *Clouds Taste Metallic,* and drugs were only part of the problem. "Steven would play things that sounded more classic rock, and Ronald wanted to be more tripped-out, New Wave," Wayne said. "We were secretly veering more toward Steven's way of doing it, and there was some true psychic stress there. It was like, 'How are we going to tell Ronald that this part he just spent four days working on isn't going to be used?' All bands must struggle with that, but with someone like Ronald, who couldn't communicate, it was always worse. Any time someone gains confidence, the whole dynamic of a group shifts." Steven was starting to move from being "merely" a great drummer to serving as the driving force of the band in crafting melodies. "He was starting to think more about writing songs."

"If there was an idea of mine that was used, there was a little bitterness there, and if there was an idea of Ronald's that was used, I would be like, 'Well, damn,'" Steven said. "And he was just getting crazier and crazier the older he got." Added Wayne, "We felt like we knew him to a certain extent, but as the years went on, whatever the thing is that he's got—I call it a mild form of schizophrenia, though there's no proof of that—it seemed like it came in cycles, and it did get worse."

The Flaming Lips first saw a change in Ronald during the sessions for *Transmissions from the Satellite Heart,* when the singer from his old band, Snail, died in a car wreck. "That was the first big chink in the armor," Steven said. "I could tell it was really fucking with him." Distraught, Ronald showed up at Booker's apartment. "I opened the door, and he immediately started crying, just sobbing and literally sitting in my lap," Booker said. "I just held him, and he cried for like thirty minutes."

Ronald had never liked traveling, and his bandmates said he grew increasingly paranoid during the extensive touring of 1994 and 1995. He sometimes thought the police were following the van, or that the group would be jailed at an international checkpoint. "Obviously, it's a valid reason to worry about crossing borders when someone in the party is carrying drugs," Steven said. "I understand that, but he also started becoming paranoid about weird shit that we just couldn't understand. He really thought people were out to get him. We'd go into a restaurant and the waitress would ask for his order last, so it was, 'There's a conspiracy because I'm black.' Maybe some of that was real—it sure as hell is possible—but he became more and more on the edge, more uncomfortable dealing with things. And on some real basic level, Ronald started to hate Wayne."

In his typically confronsational style, Wayne probed Ronald about his burgeoning spirituality. "I think Ronald felt Wayne specifically picked on him and was beating up on him or being confrontational with him, as opposed to 'Why don't you confront Steven about the shit he does?'" Steven said. "Wayne needled everybody, but Ronald just took it a lot more personally and started to internalize this paranoia and hatred."

One night on tour, Wayne was bunking with the guitarist when Ronald bolted upright in bed, convinced that someone had entered their hotel room. "I was like, 'Dude, that's not real; you have to believe me,' but I couldn't convince him otherwise," Wayne said. "I remember flicking on the lights and saying, 'Ronald, how could someone come in here?' but he was like, 'I don't know how they got in here, but they were here.' That sort of thing got worse and worse until he was building his own reality and you couldn't combat it."

Ronald adored the work of Australian musician Richard Davies, the former leader of a psychedelic revival band called the Moles, and the Flaming Lips often covered the Moles' "What's the New Mary Jane?" onstage. In 1994, Davies made a self-titled album called *Cardinal* with classically trained trumpeter Eric Matthews, inspiring a surge of interest in the indie-rock world for orchestral pop. The next year Davies launched a solo career, and Ronald encouraged the Flaming Lips to undertake a club tour serving as the singer-songwriter's backing band, as well as playing a set of their own material. "I remember the Lips calling me from the studio when they were doing the *Clouds Taste Metallic* album and saying, 'Ya got any ideas?'" Davies said, laughing. "They said, 'We've run out of ideas, and we've got all this time and money in the studio; what do we do?' I said, 'I haven't a clue!' But that's how that relationship started."

The shows the band performed with Davies in the spring of 1996 were inspired. "To me, it was just like being in the Moles," Davies said. "Wayne was very visual in his way of thinking about music, and I could relate to that." From Wayne's perspective, the partnership wasn't quite as rewarding. "While we had loved his earlier stuff, I didn't necessarily like the music that he was doing at that time, and I didn't like Davies after that tour. He's an egotistical putz, the sort of guy who thinks that he's not a normal person, and one of those rock-star idiots."

The Flaming Lips planned to take the summer off after the tour, with three high-profile exceptions: gigs at the Roskilde Festival in Denmark, the Phoenix Festival in Ireland, and the Reading Festival in England. The English press had shown some enthusiasm for *Clouds Taste Metallic,* and Booker hoped to build the band's following in Europe. But a week before rehearsals for Roskilde, Ronald visited Steven's apartment. "He didn't call before, which I thought was kind of weird, because Ronald wasn't the kind of guy to just show up. He had this little plastic bag, and in the bag was everything I'd ever given him, from a piece of paper with a little drawing on it making fun of something, to a cassette of the *Tormato* album by Yes, down to a little necklace."

Ronald repeated this ritual with everyone in the band, returning anything they'd ever given him, but he broke the big news to Steven first. "He told me he didn't want to see me anymore, and if I didn't leave the band, he was leaving the band," Steven said.

For the second time in their history, the Flaming Lips called a formal band meeting—"The first time was about getting Keith Cleversley out of the organization," Steven said—and Ronald repeated his ultimatum. "I told the guys, 'I'll quit if it'll make Ronald stay; I'll get off drugs,'" Steven said. "I don't think I was being sincere, because I was enjoying the band too much, but that's what I said. But Ronald decided, 'I'll do these last three festival shows, and that's going to be it.'"

Ronald's playing seemed especially fiery after he announced his decision. The Roskilde show ranked with the band's best, featuring a fierce cover of "Baba O'Riley" by the Who and a Kraftwerk-style jam during "Take Me ta Mars" that found Ronald mimicking the Germans' synthesizers with his guitar. In contrast, the Reading show, before fifty thousand people, was a disaster. "There was something so depressing about it, and Michael was just playing like shit," Steven said. "Wayne was looking at me and Ronald with this look of contempt, and it was kind of a soul-destroying experience. And that was it—bam!—the last show with fucking Ronald Jones."

Ronald went on to play guitar on *Telegraph,* Richard Davies's 1998 solo album, but the guitarist didn't tour with Davies to support it, and the two fell out of touch a short time later. "We were very good friends, but by the end of the *Telegraph* album, I think I was starting to get on his nerves as well," Davies said. "Ronald is a very sensitive soul, and his ability to create things goes completely with the fact that he's a sensitive person. I think that the only way for him to get over living, breathing, and thinking about music pretty intensely for three or four years was to hit the stop button completely and turn off the stresses of dealing with the entertainment industry. That was part of his personality and his artistic sensibility, and because of that, he really only had a certain shelf life in the music world."

Ronald hasn't spoken to anyone directly connected to the Flaming Lips since he left the band. He has never commented publicly about the group since he quit, and with a few rare exceptions such as running sound or contributing a guitar overdub to local Oklahoma City bands, he has kept his distance from the music business. He refused to be interviewed for this book.

During the previous twelve years at Wayne's side, Michael had suffered only one crisis that prompted him to consider quitting the Flaming Lips—six years earlier, after *In a Priest Driven Ambulance,* when he fell in love for the first time. "Here was an actual relationship that I was in, and there was sex involved with it, too—a double bonus!—and, my God, I was twenty-seven by the time that happened. For being a guy who you'd think had all the cards lined up right—'He's in a band, he puts records out, he tours all around the place, and he's a nice guy'—I never got it together to have the sex part in rock 'n' roll happen until I was actually pretty old. I was the geeky guy, Anthony Michael Hall in *The Breakfast Club,* except I was actually in the band." Money had been tight at the time, the band didn't seem to be going anywhere, and Michael's new girlfriend wanted him to return to college and pursue the sort of career his parents always expected he'd have. The quiet bassist agonized over the notion of quitting for several months, a period that Wayne and Booker call "Michael's lost weekend."

"Basically, I reached a crisis point where I was trying to decide, 'Hey, what are you going to do with your life?' and it was all wrapped up in this relationship," Michael said. "That falling-in-love thing—whatever that drug is, they need to bottle it. It's as bad as heroin or speed or any of that, because that shit will fuck you up. That song 'When a Man Loves a Woman'—people play that at their weddings, but they obviously don't listen to the lyrics, because that's what love is: You will fuck your friends over, you'll fuck your family over, you will change the way you live. That's what that song is saying, and that song is true."

Michael claimed he never actually left the Flaming Lips—that Frid-

"WHEN I SAW HER, I THOUGHT SHE WAS THE MOST BEAUTIFUL WOMAN IN THE WORLD." MICHAEL AND CATHERINE DOBIESZ, 1994.

mann and Booker prevailed upon him to stick it out a little while longer—though Wayne said his original partner did indeed quit, albeit briefly. "It wasn't because we didn't like each other; it just reached a point where he sort of wanted to have a life and a job without living with the band," Wayne told me in 1995. "One day, I just went to where he was working and talked to him for a while, and Michael finally said, 'I know, it's just bullshit; I'm not leaving.' We had known each other for so long that we didn't really even think about it as being in a band together. It was just how we always did stuff."

By the time the group started work on *Hit to Death in the Future Head*, Michael had recommitted as steadfastly as ever, and his first romance ended shortly thereafter. A few years later, while performing in Chicago in 1993, he met Catherine DoBiesz, who had grown up in Detroit and road-tripped to a show at Metro with her friend Heidi Olmack, a writer for *Cake* fanzine. The usually introverted bassist mustered the courage to start a conversation— "Without being too cheesy, when I saw her, I thought she was the most beautiful woman in the world"—and the two began a long-distance relationship. In the summer of 1994, Catherine moved to Oklahoma City, though Michael traveled constantly with the band, and he disliked leaving her behind. Catherine didn't know anyone in Oklahoma, and aware of the way that Michael's earlier relationship had put a wedge between him and the group, the band's extended family warmed to her slowly.

Now, in the uncertain days after Ronald's departure in the summer of 1996, Michael once again wrestled with questions about whether the band had a future, and if he still had a role in it at age thirty-three. "I know that as far as Wayne is concerned, he's never doubted what he's doing. There were a couple of times when the band should have broken up, and it just didn't happen, but for me, I actually consciously had to make choices and not just go along for the ride because, 'Well, it seems like I've got nothing better going on,' or 'Boy, if I don't do this, I've got nothing.'"

As the two quietest members of the band, Michael and Ronald had often roomed together on tour, and Michael confessed to being drunk and ruining the group's last show with Ronald at Reading. "There's just no excuse, but I guess his leaving really did affect me. I guess because I talked to Ronald a lot or roomed with him, people thought we were in cahoots somehow: That he was going to quit the band and I was going to quit as well. I remember being as depressed as I can get."

Wayne always had valued loyalty above everything other than hard work; according to Nathan Roberts, the band's leader had questioned his commitment just because he lived in his own apartment two doors away from the duplex the rest of the group had shared. As the Flaming Lips grappled with the void left by Ronald, Wayne came to believe that Michael considered edging him and Steven out of the band and continuing in some new configuration with Ronald. Everyone close to the group found it hard to believe that Wayne could suspect Michael of being capable of such a plot, or that Michael would even consider it, much less pull it off. Wayne admitted he never confronted Michael about his suspicions, but added, "He knows I know."

"That just never was in my mind, and I certainly don't think it was in Ronald's mind," Michael insisted. "It's pretty obvious that if you don't have Wayne in the Flaming Lips, it's not going to be the Flaming Lips." Michael maintained that Wayne misread his desire to branch out into recording and producing other bands, which came as an extension of his love for all things technological and his concern about his role on the band's recordings, since Steven had begun to play most of the bass parts in the studio.

The fact that Wayne could harbor such a suspicion about the band's other founding member and one of his oldest friends is indicative of the precarious state the Flaming Lips were in after Ronald's resignation and the failure of their seventh album. "In general there was a crisis in the whole band of 'Jesus, what are we going to do now?'" Michael said. "It didn't seem quite as easy to just find another guitarist. Bands were getting dropped left and right at this point, and the alternative thing was totally dying. That movie *Spinal Tap* is supposed to be a 'mockumentary,' but to me it's not funny; it's reality. We worried that we'd end up being some forty-five-year-olds banging out some heavy-metal bullshit at the state fair, and we didn't want to do that."

These fears loomed large for Michael, Steven, and Booker as the band left England after performing at the Reading Festival. But before they'd even landed in Oklahoma City, Wayne had started talking about a new and very unusual plan.

CHAPTER 8

THE CAPTAIN'S BEING BOLD ABOUT IT

ZAIREEKA (1997)

NEWLY shorn of his trademark mop of ratty brown hair and wearing a bright yellow raincoat on a sweaty afternoon in March 1997, Wayne Coyne stood on a milk crate in the center of the second floor of a covered parking garage at Seventh and Brazos streets in Austin, shouting directions through a bullhorn.

The eleventh South by Southwest Music and Media Conference had drawn more than nine thousand journalists and music-business insiders to the Texas capital for the industry's largest annual gathering, with three days of panel discussions at the Austin Convention Center and four nights of showcase performances by five hundred bands at three dozen clubs across the city. Word spread that the Flaming Lips would be putting on a different kind of gig, and fifteen hundred curious spectators turned up for what Wayne called Parking Lot Experiment No. 4.

Flaming Lips manager Scott Booker had recruited thirty volunteers in thirty cars equipped with thirty tape decks for the first "road test" of an automotive symphony that the group had already attempted three times since the fall of 1996 in the covered parking garage of an office building near Oklahoma City's Penn Square Mall. Following Wayne's directions, I pulled my white Chevette into a space in the corner of the Austin garage. Sizing up the Avis vehicle and noting that the rental car's sound system was nothing special, he assigned me the relatively unimportant part of Car No. 22. My contribution to the two songs comprising the concert/performance-art piece would consist of what sounded like an elephant snoring, ping-ponging between the left and right speakers, occasionally coming together in glorious stereo.

Steven Drozd handed each of the thirty drivers a different cassette with a different prerecorded part, and Wayne explained that we should all roll down our windows, turn the volume up to its maximum level, and simultaneously hit play on his command. It took an hour to arrange the cars in a giant circle—drivers had to carefully navigate through the growing crowd of fans—and another thirty minutes to test the setup with two trial runs that found each auto announcing its number, more or less in order ("This is Car No. 1," "This is Car No. 2," and so on).

Several times, Wayne had to remind the drivers to keep their electrical system turned on but their ignition turned off so that listeners wouldn't be asphyxiated by exhaust fumes. "On top of worrying about the music going well," Wayne said, "I was really concerned about somebody dying or getting run over." The fans didn't seem to mind waiting during the elaborate preparations. Leaning against the hood of my car, an aging Austin hippie said the scene reminded him of a vintage sixties happening, "and back then, the anticipation and the hint of danger were always part of the fun."

"ON TOP OF WORRYING ABOUT THE MUSIC GOING WELL,
I WAS REALLY CONCERNED ABOUT SOMEBODY DYING OR GETTING
RUN OVER." WAYNE AT THE CENTER OF PARKING LOT
EXPERIMENT NO. 4, AUSTIN, TEXAS, 1997.

Finally the moment came when Wayne screamed, "One, two, three—play!" The weird symphony came together in a swirling, circular fashion that filled the ramp with otherworldly sounds. The first piece, "Altruism, or That's the Crotch Calling the Devil Black," consisted of an ambient swoosh that brought to mind the Orb meets My Bloody Valentine, or Aphex Twin jamming with Public Enemy's Bomb Squad. This combined with the ecstatic sounds of a female orgasm, which built to an eardrum-rattling crescendo as it echoed off the steeple of the Episcopal church across the street. Dubbed "The March of the Rotten Vegetables," the second piece featured a catchier instrumental theme, interrupted by a recording of Steven playing a garage-shaking drum solo in the style of Pink Floyd's "A Saucerful of Secrets."

Like many of the Flaming Lips' wildest ideas, this one had started simply enough: In 1978, a seventeen-year-old Wayne had walked through the parking lot of the Lloyd Noble Center in Norman before a concert by KISS and Uriah Heep and noticed the strange effect of different cars blasting the same tune on different eight-track players at the same time. "This led to the idea that we could have all these separate entities playing this big piece of music," he said. If things went well in Austin, he hoped to take the experiment on the road to college towns, and he said it had suggested the direction for the band's next album: a multidisc set designed so that fans could play all of the CDs at once.

"I'm doing a weird step that's outside of what we normally know as listening. You can have this enormous sound of a live orchestra, but eventually everything gets reduced to coming out of the left and right speakers. There are other ways to hear things, and that's what I'm playing with. I don't know if I can make it happen, or even if it will be worth listening to if it does happen, but I'm gonna try it."

In the Austin garage, Car No. 16, a van with the most high-powered stereo system present, blew a fuse and ruined the finale, leaving the frustrated composer standing on the milk crate, trying to explain through his bullhorn what listeners *should* have heard. Wayne was the only musician at South by Southwest to complain that too many people came to his gig: The garage had been so crowded that spectators couldn't walk around in between the cars, which he said enhanced the surround-sound experience.

The Flaming Lips' leader was also the only person in the garage dissatisfied with the experiment, and listeners gave the band a wildly enthusiastic five-minute ovation. The group had pulled off a show unlike any of the other four hundred ninety-nine during the music conference, claiming a place in the pantheon of avant-garde sonic pioneers somewhere between Karlheinz Stockhausen, who wrote a string quartet to be played from four helicopters; John Cage, of the famously doctored pianos; and Carl Stalling, who arranged and conducted the music for Warner Bros.' "Looney Tunes" cartoons.

One day in 1931 a British electrical engineer named Alan Blumlein attended the cinema with his fiancée and asked if she noticed how the actors moved about on-screen while their voices remained stationary. "Well, I have a way of making the voice follow the person." His famous patent called it "Binaural Sound," since humans have two ears. Under the more popular name of stereo, it would become the predominant way we listen to recorded music, though it was never the only or necessarily the best method.

As Blumlein developed his new system, engineers at Bell Laboratories across the Atlantic tested ways to capture more of the lush sounds of Leopold Stokowski's Philadelphia Orchestra. They used three channels on 78 rpm wax disc recordings to simulate the concert experience, with the sound coming from left, right, and center. By the early fifties, movie theaters utilized a variety of systems stemming from their discoveries, most with four but some with as many as seven channels. But when "high fidelity" audio equipment arrived in homes a few years later, it employed only two channels, because phonograph records at the time simply couldn't accommodate more sonic information.

In the early seventies, improvements in the manufacturing of vinyl LPs led to the birth of quadraphonic sound. When the Flaming Lips' heroes Pink Floyd recorded their phenomenally successful 1973 album *The Dark Side of the Moon*, they mixed it for four speakers. The band had been playing with the idea in concert for years, since its live-sound engineers developed the fancifully named Azimuth Coordinator, a joystick device that they manipulated to move the music coming from the stage between speakers surrounding listeners in each corner of the hall. Unfortunately, competitive audio manufacturers could never agree on a standard format for quadraphonic sound, which confused and frustrated consumers, who failed to embrace it. But the four-channel concept returned in the early eighties with the advent of home theater equipment and a new system called surround sound.

The Flaming Lips always had strived to present as much sound as possible on their recordings, ranging from the brilliant combination of symphonic music and ambient effects on songs such as "The Abandoned Hospital Ship" to ambitious but unsuccessful sound collages such as "Hell's Angels Cracker

Factory." In the fall of 1996, the band knew that relatively few of its fans owned high-end audiophile gear, but everyone seemed to have more than one CD player: the conventional stereo-system component, augmented by a computer player and perhaps a boom box or two. Wayne began talking with Dave Fridmann about how listeners might duplicate the multisource sonic swirl of the Parking Lot Experiments at home in a simple and low-tech way.

The Flaming Lips' leader initially hoped to release ten CDs designed to be played simultaneously, but Booker, who faced the challenge of packaging the music so that Warner Bros. could sell it, and Fridmann, who had to record the daunting multidisc epic, prevailed upon him to settle for the more realistic number of four.

The artists weren't the first to play with this idea. Conrad Schnitzler, "the mad genius from Berlin," had helped to spur the Krautrock movement of the early seventies, working with the German bands Tangerine Dream and Cluster. In concert as a pioneering electronic solo artist, he augmented his synthesizer with the *Kassettenorgel* (cassette organ), six tape decks mounted in two cabinets wired to a stereo output. When technology allowed him to record compact discs, he replaced the tapes with CDs.

A fount of knowledge about esoteric sounds and artistic subcultures, Jon Mooneyham had schooled his friends the Flaming Lips about avant-garde composers such as Stockhausen, Cage, and Brian Eno, though he never introduced them to Schnitzler. "If you're honest about it, some of that stuff is really unlistenable," Michael Ivins said. "But the liner notes are spectacular: They really make it seem like something is going on here and that something important is happening, and I think Wayne really took that to heart with *Zaireeka*."

In his own liner notes, which are as entertaining as the music, Wayne explains that the title of the band's eighth album combines the words "Zaire" and "eureka." He intended the exclamation to convey the sense of discovery in hearing music in a different way, while he chose the name of the war-torn African nation Zaire because he considered it synonymous with "trouble," "confusion," and "paralyzing chaos"—words that also described the state of the band after the departure of Ronald Jones.

For the first time in thirteen years, the supremely confident bandleader wrestled with self-doubt. "Instead of knowing more, I feel like the more work I do, the less I know," Wayne wrote in a long letter he sent me in December 1996. "Instead of finding limitations or answers, I seem to have found endless possibilities and more questions. With a lot of music we've done in the past, we've had points of reference either intentional or accidental: It is a guide, a way to do things. With this there is no guide. With this I truly do not know what I'm doing. I don't know how it can succeed. I don't know how I would know if it has already failed."

With the melodramatic flair of a man playing a mad genius, Wayne complimented my mental health while questioning his own: "You are a nice guy who writes about a lot of 'insane' people who most definitely for the moment is 'sane.' This is good for you, 'cause what I'm doing seems to be goin' just the opposite." But as strange a project as *Zaireeka* appeared to be, it also represented a shrewd strategy.

The Flaming Lips had decided it would be impossible to replace Ronald, and that they wouldn't even try. Working with former Chainsaw Kittens guitarist Trent Bell at his studio, Bell Labs, in Norman, Steven had recorded a song called "Headphones Theme from Seemingly Infinity" for the 1997 album *Flyin' Traps*, a compilation featuring instrumental compositions by alternative-rock drummers. In addition to playing drums, Steven used guitar, piano, and Mellotron to create a one-man symphony as impressive as any Ronald had built. Together with the many contributions he made to *Transmissions from the Satellite Heart* and *Clouds Taste Metallic*, this track convinced Wayne and Michael that Steven could play any instrument the Flaming Lips would need in the studio. But they still had to solve the problem of how to perform onstage.

"When Wayne had the idea for the parking-lot shit, he was like, 'Let's start making this weird music and see if we can get some cars together and make this some sort of viable act, something to keep us busy for the next six months,'" Steven said. "It just seemed like a really good way for us to bide some time."

Warner Bros. continued to be wracked by corporate upheaval. Booker knew that with their marginal sales, the Flaming Lips couldn't count on the label to provide full-scale promotion for a new release, and they wouldn't survive another flop like *Clouds Taste Metallic* with their contract intact. They had nothing to lose by going underground, and Wayne compared the band to a bug that scurries for cover when the lights come on. "You know that T-shirt, 'Jesus Is Coming'? We hear that," he told *Raygun* magazine in July 1999. "We hear the ax coming down and we know we're underneath it and we just start moving around so when the ax falls, we're not where we used to be."

The group started recording in April 1997 at Tarbox Road Studios, which Dave Fridmann had just opened in Cassadaga, New York, not far from the old student facility in Fredonia where he'd helped the Flaming Lips make some of their best music. Now, Michael joined him in tearing out, rewiring, and reconfiguring much of the equipment he'd just installed, jury-rigging a system to record and mix four separate stereo masters at once. The group recorded on two eight-track ADAT (Alesis Digital Audio Tape) machines running in conjunction with the twenty-four-track analog tape machine, then mixed to four stereo DAT machines wired to eight speakers.

"All of that stuff at any given time was never more than forty tracks [of music]," Fridmann said. "We would just choose which ones to turn on for which CD." The producer has since heard of fans mixing the four CDs to one stereo disc, "but they're missing the point. When we would turn on all the tracks, it would sound like crap. They were purposefully meant to be an experiment, like, 'Here are two different things in two different keys. If you put them together, they don't work, but if you put them in two different sets of speakers, they have a weird relationship that actually does sound good.'"

Solving the technological problems proved to be easier than creating music that justified all of this trouble. After three months at Tarbox Road, the band had spent half of the budget Warner Bros. had allotted for the group's next "real" album without completing a single song for its arty side project. One afternoon, following his tenth cup of coffee that day, Wayne exploded. "Look, we don't have to be friends, we don't have to like each other, we don't have to be in each other's lives on that level anymore, but we *have* to make this record!," he barked. "Somebody has to come up with an idea now!"

"It was the most frustrated I've seen him, before or since," Fridmann said. "At that point, everybody was sort of beating around the bush, like, 'I don't want to say anything, but this idea is going nowhere.' He just cut through it: 'No, fuck that! We have to do something. Somebody get out there and fail, but *do* something!' It was a great, liberating thing for all of us, because we were like, 'Oh, we don't have to be friendly? We can just cut to the chase and quit pussyfooting around and actually say what we think? Cool. Let's do it!' And we got to the bottom of it."

The band discovered that instead of imposing the four-CD format on its usual songwriting, it had to write specifically for the new medium. This realization freed everyone up, and the songs began to flow. Not all of them fit the unique sonic requirements of *Zaireeka*, but those that took shape as more traditional pop songs were earmarked for the next conventional album, and shifting between the pop songs and the experimental tracks relieved the tension. By August, the group had completed eight tracks for *Zaireeka*, as well as several lushly orchestrated pop songs that would stand as some of the most beautiful they'd recorded, including "Race for the Prize" and an epic tune called "The Captain Is a Cold-Hearted & Egotistical Fool."

Wayne had written "The Captain," as it was alternately known, on his own at the Compound, though he maintained that "it was really Steven who brought it to life." The song starts with a portentous trumpet, sawing strings, and crescendos of orchestral percussion—all played by Steven with samples triggered from a MIDI keyboard—before the dramatic fanfare gives way to acoustic guitar, vocals, and grand piano during the minimal verses. Like the title track of Brian Eno's *Here Come the Warm Jets,* the song builds slowly, lulling the listener with its hypnotic melody. An insistent bass drum and violent cymbal crashes add to the growing urgency as Wayne repeats the single line in the chorus: "Instead of being bold about it / The captain's being cold."

"I had this idea that this captain guy wasn't listening to the ship's doctor, who was saying, 'I know we've got this journey, but this devoted crewman is too ill, and we need to stop,'" Wayne said. "The crew members have all given their lives to this captain, because they trust him, but when he doesn't stop for this other guy, their attitude changes. I think somewhere in there was this inner story of whatever it was that I was doing at the time, and me worrying about whether I was worthy of these people's devotion, or if it would turn into some kind of *Apocalypse Now* scenario where I would wind up getting my throat cut."

In addition to offering another way of hearing music, Wayne had two goals for *Zaireeka.* One was to create a group listening experience at a time when the musical community represented by Lollapalooza at its peak had dissipated and fans were becoming increasingly segregated and isolated. "It's probably easier for people to get four CD players together at one time than to get four friends, but if you try the two together, I think it's intriguing," Wayne said. "I want people to perceive this as something they have to participate in: that it's different and unique and it does take a bit of a hassle. I'm looking for this to be a little bit of an event."

The other goal was to illustrate the unexpected pleasures of what Eno called "happy accidents." Contrary to manufacturers' hype, all CD players do not run at the same speed, and the subtle differences in synchronization guaranteed that every *Zaireeka* listening party would be a different experience. "We've tried it with a lot of different CD players around here just to see what the variables would be," Wayne said. "We've had them virtually tight in sync for three or four songs in a row, then they start to develop a mind of their own, and part of that is built into the music, so the rhythms and things, what appears to be wrong, could be just different. With anything like this, I think the audience has to take a little bit of a leap with the artist."

Fans weren't the only ones required to make a leap of faith. The general manager at Warner Bros., Jeff Gold, hated the idea of the four-CD set and wanted to drop the band from the label, according to its A&R rep, David Katznelson. Booker knew he'd need every bit of his Will Rogers charm and no-nonsense business acumen to sell the notion to Steven Baker, who had become president of the label at a time when fearful executives summarily rejected any offbeat and potentially unprofitable idea. The fact that Katznelson was a friend of Baker's family helped, as did Baker's respect for the group's work ethic and resourcefulness. "I was dealing with bands coming to me and saying, 'We need a backdrop that costs ten thousand dollars' or 'We need these lights that cost twenty grand,'" Baker said. "I'd be thinking, 'You assholes, look at the Flaming Lips: They have a better light show, and it came from Ace Hardware! Don't you get it? This is your career, and you have to do it yourself.'"

A masterful salesman since his days managing Rainbow Records, Booker crafted his pitch: For an advance of two hundred thousand dollars, the band would deliver two albums, the experimental *Zaireeka,* which it wouldn't count as one of the seven albums required by its contract, and the next pop disc. "I told Steven Baker and David Katznelson that I felt the Lips were making a really great record, and that this could be the one," Booker said. He played them "Race for the Prize" and "The Captain" and had a ready answer when the executives asked why the pop disc shouldn't be released first. "Up to this point, all their reviews have been like this: 'Gosh, these guys are weird! What a bunch of psychedelic weirdos! They've got some good songs, but man, oh man, are they weird!' If we put *Zaireeka* out, everyone is going to get tired of saying we're weird. They'll all get it out of their systems with this record, and then they can talk about what a beautiful album the next one is."

A week before meeting with the president, Booker worked his way through every department at the label, collecting the numbers to bolster his case. "I did my homework: I asked, 'What are our packaging options? What are the costs? How can the label make money?' I figured out a way to do it so that if we sold twelve thousand copies, Warners would break even, and they'd start earning money after that. They thought they'd be lucky to sell that many, but then advance orders came in for fourteen thousand. I went through every single aspect of this before I took it to Baker, and the last thing I said to him when I walked out the door was, 'Just think, you'll go down in history as the first person who released four CDs that had to be played at once.' And he just laughed and said, 'Okay.'"

"I didn't okay it with some ulterior motive, like 'I'm going to show the world how amazing and how creative the Flaming Lips are,'" Baker said. "It's a good indication of the way Scott works that he sold it in a way that made sense, and I just thought, 'I can do this. I'm not having any fun here, and this is something that will be fun and will make this label look cool again.'"

Warner Bros. released *Zaireeka* as a specially priced boxed set in October 1997. A short time later, the label's revolving door spun again, and Baker left to become president of DreamWorks Records, but his faith in the Flaming Lips hadn't been misplaced. The album didn't win the band any new fans, garner any radio play, or broach the *Billboard* charts, but supporters held listening parties at rock clubs and record stores across the country, generating a tremendous amount of "Aren't they weird?" press coverage, just as Booker had predicted. To date, the album has sold twenty-eight thousand copies, more than double the number the record company needed to turn a profit.

In the tradition of *4'33"* by John Cage, which employed four minutes and thirty-three seconds of silence to shift listeners' attention from the stage and prompt them to hear the ambient sounds around them, and *Metal Machine Music,* the 1975 album by Lou Reed that featured four vinyl LP sides of nothing but grating feedback, *Zaireeka* is partly an inspired audio experiment, and partly pure P. T. Barnum hucksterism.

Hints of the gorgeous sounds that would flower on the band's next album can be heard on four of the eight songs, and despite Fridmann's claims to the contrary, these do work as conventional stereo mixes, though there are certainly added dimensions in the eight-speaker format. "Riding to Work in the Year 2025 (Your Invisible Now)" is a hook-laden, multipart orchestral suite with lyrics that tell another of Wayne's science-fiction tales: A secret agent tries to stop a plot to end the world but ends up "reporting back to nothing" when his headquarters is destroyed.

A similarly dire story unfolds in "Thirty-five Thousand Feet of Despair," a spare and creepy tune with symphonic flourishes. It opens with one of Wayne's most memorable images—"Another moth disintegrates/Hovering in the bead of a searchlight"—then goes on to paint an unsettling portrait of a pilot who loses his mind and hangs himself in midflight. Like "The Captain," the tale mirrors Wayne's own predicament at the time, especially if you accept the reading of "Moth in the Incubator" from *Transmissions from the Satellite Heart* as an allegory about the band.

The group revisits familiar terrain with the other two "conventional" tracks, "A Machine in India" and "The Big Ol' Bug Is the New Baby Now."

Based on an acoustic guitar decorated by Steven's synthesized flute, the melody of the former owes a substantial debt to "The India Song" by the power-pop band Big Star. "I'm goin' to India over and over again/I'm standin' in a cylinder/Seein' all the bleedin' vaginas," Wayne sings. In the liner notes, he explains that the lyrics stemmed from a conversation with his significant other, Michelle Martin, "about the 'other world' she is in during her menstrual period and the kind of dull and depressing mild insanity that seems to possess her."

Following the model of "U.F.O. Story," the story-song "The Big Ol' Bug Is the New Baby Now" pairs a musical coda with Wayne's spoken-word account of how the couple's three rambunctious dogs "adopted" a plastic grasshopper that they treated as if it were their offspring, sparing it the fate of being chewed to death. The track ends with an audio assault of barking dogs, which Steven recorded while riding his bicycle as a pack of canines nipped at his heels.

The remaining four tracks exist to showcase the eight-speaker format, and they really can't be appreciated unless you take the trouble of arranging four CD players. If you do, sounds zip around the room, weird noises erupt from unexpected places, and unlikely melodies come together and mutate in bizarre ways. "Okay I'll Admit That I Really Don't Understand" is a one-chord drone that finds Wayne repeating the title mantra-like; "The Train Runs Over the Camel but Is Derailed by the Gnat" combines three unrelated melodies and a swirl of ambient noise; "March of the Rotten Vegetables" is the electronically doctored drum solo from the Parking Lot Experiments; and "How Will We Know? (Futuristic Crashendos)" is distinguished by irritating high- and low-frequency drones. "Can cause a person to become disoriented, confused, or nauseated," Wayne cautions in the liner notes. "Make sure infants are out of listening range."

⸱

The Flaming Lips had emerged from their most difficult recording sessions since *Telepathic Surgery* with a disc that, if not a complete artistic success, certainly contains moments of greatness, and which has to be admired for its sheer ambition. Of course, *Zaireeka* did nothing for their finances. Touring always had been the group's only reliable source of income, and in early 1998 Wayne figured out a way to perform in support of its oddest album.

Starting in February 1998 and continuing through the fall, the band brought the Boom Box Experiments to midsized rock clubs across the United States and Europe, traveling with forty portable cassette players and forty tapes for each song on the set list. The musicians corralled friends and fans in each city to sit onstage in two groups with the boom boxes in their laps. Wayne "conducted" the twenty operators on the right, instructing them to raise or lower the volume at different points in each tune. Steven directed the twenty on the left, and Michael stood in the center, manipulating a mixer that fed lines from all of the boom boxes into the house PA.

In the wake of his second brief crisis of confidence, Michael had skipped the Parking Lot Experiment at South by Southwest. "I'm going to admit now that I was just plain wrong, but back then I really didn't think there was anything to it and it didn't make any sense for me to go down to Texas. Looking back, I should have been there—I'm usually all over weird art stuff like that. Here's the thing: I like fiddling with stuff, and I just didn't think there was anything for me to do in the parking lots."

"WHAT THE HELL WAS WAYNE THINKING WHEN HE CAME UP WITH THIS BOOM BOX THING?" WAYNE AND STEVEN "CONDUCTING" THE BOOM BOX EXPERIMENTS, 1998.

The Boom Box tour was the Flaming Lips' lowest-budget excursion in years: The three musicians traveled in one van with one roadie, Michelle Martin's girlfriend Jennifer Flygare, who loaded, unloaded, and maintained the forty tape players, bestowing a nickname on each of them. Money woes kept everyone on edge. "Scott was just all freaked out the whole time," Flygare recalled. "He was like, 'What the hell was Wayne thinking when he came up with this boom-box thing?'"

After two tests of the system, each concert featured six mostly instrumental tracks. Every concertgoer received a program with notes written by Wayne explaining the inspiration behind and the order of the night's selections, which included "The Big Ol' Bug Is the New Baby Now"; "Altruism, or That's the Crotch Calling the Devil Black"; "A Winter's Day Car Accident Melody," a haunting dirge augmented by the sounds of eighty wailing sirens and eighty car crashes; "Heralding in a Better Ego," which built from two or three trumpets to more than forty; "Realizing the Speed of Life," another sad and tuneless drone; and "Schizophrenic Sunrise, or The Loudest Blade of Grass." Wayne described the genesis of the last of these pieces in his program notes:

> Ronald Jones, our former guitar player . . . always had an over-sensitive awareness of sounds. Once while driving through some busy city traffic, he was listening to the different car horns all beeping and determining their pitch. Another time we were recording a song and he seemed bent on having a sound he was calling "mosquito wings" accompany the rhythm track. To me it was and still is inaudible in the song, but I think he could hear it clearly. "Schizophrenic Sunrise, or The Loudest Blade of Grass," while not directly about Ronald, is about a man with a similar talent or affliction, depending on how you look at it, who, over the period of one summer, goes from being normal to being schizophrenic. As he sits at his bedroom window watching the sunrise he hears every bird chirping, every insect buzzing. As the summer rolls on his sensitivity is exaggerated. He hears flowers growing, and even the sun itself rising. By late August he is, like Ronald with the car horns, trying to determine which blade of grass is the loudest.

Unfortunately, Wayne's notes were more interesting than the music, which consisted of about six minutes of choir members drawing breaths at different times as twenty harp players plucked different notes, followed by the invasion of an army of whirring lawn mowers.

The volunteer orchestras were often sprinkled with indie-rock celebrities—Kevin Shields of My Bloody Valentine, Pete Kember (aka Sonic Boom of Spacemen 3), and Miki Berenyi of Lush all participated in London—and the Boom Box Experiments generated rave reviews congratulating the band for its ambitions; especially lavish praise greeted a performance at the College Music Journal Music Marathon in New York, for which the Lips brought their boom boxes to Lincoln Center. But the show I witnessed in Chicago at Metro, an eleven-hundred-capacity club that sold out at ten dollars a ticket, was a huge letdown after Parking Lot Experiment No. 4. The sound was hardly as overwhelming as the band intended: The boom boxes themselves weren't very loud, and most of the volume came from the PA, which had the same stereo configuration as at every other concert. It may have been an interesting experience for the volunteers onstage, but the other thousand concertgoers had nothing to watch. As he had during the shows as a duo after Richard English quit, Wayne relied on his charisma to carry the day, but it wasn't quite enough.

At the height of the band's success with *Transmissions from the Satellite Heart,* Wayne had espoused an anti-elitist philosophy that contrasted with the self-important pretensions of many indie art rockers. "If someone walking on the street likes Lynyrd Skynyrd, Led Zeppelin, and Stone Temple Pilots, I want them to be able to hear Flaming Lips music and not think that it's subversive or weird, but just think that it's rock 'n' roll," he told me in 1994. During the Boom Box Experiments, the Flaming Lips seemed to be falling prey to the snobbish, art-for-art's-sake attitude that they had once condemned. "Wayne Coyne has always said he wants his music to be challenging but still accessible to the average rock fan, unlike the avant-garde experiments of a Sonic Youth, but the six pieces the band played at Metro were tuneless, pretentious, pointless, and boring," I wrote in the *Chicago Sun-Times.*

My review encouraged fans to skip this tour, and that struck a nerve with Wayne, prompting a confronsational debate about the relationship between criticism and art. "I was never trying to trick people, Jim," Wayne told me the next time we met. "You have an image of me that I could make Goo Goo Dolls records and be as successful as they are, but that's a magical accident that they're having success, the same way it would be for me. I make the music I make, and I know there's consequences and there's opportunities that aren't open to me because of that, but in the end, I take the risks, whether it's with the boom boxes or the parking lot thing. Don't beat me up for taking this type of risk; the day I come to you and make a Goo Goo Dolls record, *then* you can beat me up."

Years later, Wayne admitted that the situation had been fairly desperate: The Flaming Lips still faced the prospect of being dropped by their label before they could release the pop album intended to follow *Zaireeka,* and their financial straits were as dire as the days before Warner Bros., when they sold blood in order to pay the rent. "If we're not diligent about making money, we won't make any, and you have to make money to pay the people who've put their faith in you and buy the things you need to buy to accomplish what you want to do," Wayne said. "We have to be lusting after as much money as we can get, or we're never gonna make any, and I felt like your review was taking money out of our pockets."

Of course, the critic's responsibility is to worry about the fan's wallet, not the artist's, and he or she has a pact with readers who trust that they're getting an honest opinion. As a critic and a fan, I believed the Flaming Lips were capable of better music—more melodic, more emotional, and more inventive—than what they delivered during the Boom Box Experiments. "Listen up, Wayne: It's time to take whatever you've learned with these experiments and apply it to music that moves us," I had written in my *Sun-Times* review. The band was about to do exactly that, and to an extent that fans had never heard before.

CHAPTER 9

WAITIN' FOR A SUPERMAN

THE SOFT BULLETIN 1999

TOM COYNE'S health had been failing for some time when the doctors finally diagnosed his cancer in October 1996. It started in his pancreas and spread through his body over the next three months, although he refused to stay in the hospital until the very end. "He just didn't believe in it," his son Wayne said. Tom's illness devastated everyone in the family, but Wayne seemed especially distressed that a disease could render such a strong, vibrant, and hardworking man so fragile and in such pain.

As their father lay dying, Wayne joined his older brother Kenny to run around Lake Overholser, about fifteen miles from the Compound in northwestern Oklahoma City. With winter coming on, an eerie silence clung to the otherwise deserted jogging path. "It's getting pretty heavy with Dad, isn't it?" Wayne asked as the two brothers ran late one fall afternoon. "What do you mean, 'It's getting heavy'?" Kenny said. "We're in it: This is as heavy as it gets."

"Something about those experiences just shakes you down to your core," Wayne said. "We never got to the point where we were looking at each other with a certainty of him dying. We sort of arrived at it slowly—walking toward the grave, in a way—but when that person is in front of you, to imagine them dead while they're still alive, you just have some sort of a block."

During the long period when the Flaming Lips simultaneously crafted the four CDs for *Zaireeka* and started the new set of pop songs for their next album, Wayne clipped a photo of Pink Floyd founder and notorious acid casualty Syd Barrett from *Mojo* magazine and taped it over producer Dave Fridmann's mixing console, where it hung as a talisman throughout the sessions. The caption: "It's heavy in here, innit?"

Early on, Steven Drozd had come up with a melody on acoustic guitar that he thought sounded like prolific indie-rock heroes Guided by Voices. He tried it on piano, transposing it from the key of A to B-flat. "I would play it at the studio all the time, until Wayne finally asked what it was," Steven said. "I'd do that a lot if I had a tune that I was especially proud of, just keep playing it until he finally noticed and decided to put some words to it." After his father died on January 4, 1997, Wayne wrote an inspired set of lyrics, which started by re-creating his conversation with Kenny at the lake.

As the title implies, "Waitin' for a Superman" includes an element of the playful fantasy world that had always been present in Wayne's lyrics, but it's coupled with the knowledge that sometimes even a superhero can't save the day, and people have to look for superhuman strength within themselves. "Tell everybody waitin' for Superman that they should try to hold on the best they can," Wayne sings in one of his most emotional vocals. "He hasn't dropped them, forgot them, or anything / It's just too heavy for Superman to lift."

"I remember thinking, 'I hope that Wayne comes up with something really cool to sing with this,'" Steven said. "I had no idea that what he'd come up with would drive the song so much more and take it to a place that I would never dream of."

By February 1999, after nearly two years of intermittent recording sessions, the Flaming Lips finally had finished their first pop effort since *Clouds Taste Metallic* in 1995. Always eager to expand the colors on their sonic palette, the musicians consistently had embraced new technology. They had used digital recorders as far back as *In a Priest Driven Ambulance,* and ADAT machines had been essential during the complicated process of recording *Zaireeka,* but with *The Soft Bulletin,* they jumped into the digital domain head-first. Before, they essentially had been limited to twenty-four tracks; now, they had hundreds. "It finally occurred to us that we are not performers, we are recording artists," Wayne wrote in an essay sent to reviewers with advance copies of the group's ninth album. "I don't mean this in a pompous way. What I mean is, if someone was to ask me what instrument do I play, I would say, 'The recording studio.'"

With Steven creating lush layers of sound comprising dozens of synthesized orchestral instruments, "The Captain Is a Cold-Hearted & Egotistical Fool" showed the band another new way of working—one that, ironically, they thought Ronald would have loved. "A lot of times before, you would lay down ten tracks on a song, and it would be pretty good, but you'd lay down five more, and it would ruin the whole thing," Wayne said. "But when we did

'The Captain,' even if we did a hundred tracks, it just got bigger and bigger and better and better, and as it piled up, it became this monstrous pyramid with laser beams shooting out at the top. We'd bring people in and say, 'Can you believe this? We just did it with keyboards!' Even six months earlier, we couldn't have done a song like that, but after we had done 'The Captain,' we were off on our own trip."

While "The Captain" provided the musical template for *The Soft Bulletin*, the group ultimately left it off the album. "It just didn't seem to fit," Wayne said. (The group later floated it on the Internet as a free download, and it finally officially became available in 2005 on the 5.1 surround sound edition of the album.) After the lighthearted whimsy of much of *Clouds Taste Metallic*, Wayne had vowed to dig deeper in his lyrics—"to communicate 'real' expressions, not just references, about the nature of existence, outer space, love, death, reality, melancholy, madness, self-doubt, the victory of optimism, the wonder of things," as he wrote in the press release—and the band scrutinized the words on its new effort as rigorously as the music, demanding a level of emotional honesty and a thematic unity.

"By the time we hit *The Soft Bulletin*, there was an actual concerted effort for all of it—music, song structure, and lyrics—to be more cohesive," Michael Ivins said. "If we had a song that was supposed to be sad, we were basically going to let you know all the way through it. There was no irony, no 'We're being a little coy here.' It was, 'This is a sad song, and we're going to do it with the chords, we're going to do it with the melody, and we're going to do it with the words.'"

Along with "Waitin' for a Superman," "Race for the Prize" is the other key track epitomizing the disc's melancholy yet hopeful mood. Steven had developed the melody six years earlier during the sessions for *Transmissions from the Satellite Heart*, and the band had gotten as far as recording a version with the guitar-bass-and-drums lineup of the time, but the song never gelled. "It sounded like a car commercial, or the sort of thing that you'd hear at the beginning of a football game," Wayne said. Steven resurrected the tune circa the first Parking Lot Experiment, playing it on a keyboard with a patch duplicating the homely string sounds from an early-seventies Mellotron. "Now it was a whole other story," Wayne said. "Suddenly it seemed like it could be Frank Sinatra on one side and Led Zeppelin on the other." The first version the group recorded at Fridmann's Tarbox Road Studios utilized Steven's typically massive John Bonham drum sound throughout, but the approach robbed the song of subtlety. Then the group hit upon the idea that it could record different drum kits for different parts of the tune, with a small jazz set or a tight

R&B sound augmenting the bombastic rock drums. From that point on, some songs would utilize four or more different drum sets.

The lyrics of "Race for the Prize" chronicle the efforts of two determined scientists "locked in heated battle for the cure that is the prize"—a vaccine to prevent AIDS, a solution to the ozone problem, or perhaps a cure for cancer. "During that time I started to feel that we take a lot from the world, but we haven't really stepped up to the plate and said, 'Here's what we have to offer,'" Wayne said. "We act like this music is the biggest deal ever, but it's all self-serving: None of it helps the world. Our generation never cared about these things; it was always about us. Like with cancer, we think, 'Someone is going to find a cure.' Not us, but someone, and in fact, it's never going to get done if we don't do it."

As the Flaming Lips' new pop songs came together, their manager, Scott Booker, periodically sent them to Warner Bros. By late 1998, the company had a version of the completed album. "The label reacted to the record the same way it had reacted to *Clouds Taste Metallic*," the group's A&R rep, David Katznelson, said. "I was really worried. After *Clouds*, you had people who wanted them dropped, and right at that time you had that horrifying story in *Rolling Stone* including them on the list of 'the top five one-hit wonders of the last ten years.' Some people at the label were saying, 'Why bother with these guys? The only hit they ever had was a fluke.'" Katznelson heard potential singles in "Race for the Prize" and "Waitin' for a Superman," but he thought the tracks needed tweaking to assure their potential, as well as to placate the band's detractors at the label. He gave the group a list of producers who could remix the songs to be more radio-friendly, and Wayne balked.

"There were moments on *The Soft Bulletin* when we weren't really talking," Katznelson said. "There was a four-month gap between when the remix was brought up and when it happened. Wayne made a very valid point when he was angry with me: 'What do you know? You signed the Boredoms!' We all know the Boredoms had no potential of ever having a hit, and here I was saying to him, 'This is how you have a hit.' But finally Wayne came into my office, sat down, and said, 'I hear that people think we're arguing, but it's great that we can talk and express ideas.' In the end, there was no deviation from the plan."

"They gave us a list of these producers, and almost all of them were people who worked with alternative rock bands," Booker said. Once the Flaming Lips had reconciled with the idea of remixing some of the tracks they'd completed with Fridmann, they chose the most unlikely name on the list: Peter Mokran, a computer programmer and remixer best known for working with

R&B artists such as Prince, Michael Jackson, Lisa Stansfield, and R. Kelly. "We literally picked the name that had the biggest hits next to it," Booker said. "We figured it would be an experiment. Also, it was like a placebo: You give them the sugar pill and they say, 'Gosh, my headache went away.' If that's what it took, twenty grand to have this guy do not much to our songs but to make the label feel like they're hits, then let him."

When Mokran started work with the band at the Chicago Recording Company, he was astounded by the number of tracks the musicians had used to build each tune. "Unlike when artists usually come to me looking for me to come up with all the ideas, this was the opposite," he told rollingstone.com. "They had so many ideas that I had to rein them in, and I was more of a re-ducer than producer." For the band, the most interesting aspect of working with Mokran was hearing his stories about the bizarre behavior R. Kelly and Michael Jackson displayed in the studio.

Ultimately, the differences between Mokran's mixes of "Race for the Prize" and "Waitin' for a Superman" and the ones the group did with Frid-mann were extremely subtle and hardly noticeable to casual listeners, though the group and Fridmann swear that their versions are superior. The finished album includes both mixes of "Race for the Prize" and "Waitin' for a Super-man," as well as Mokran's mix of another tune, "Buggin'," which appears only once on the album. "Wayne didn't even want to include it, but I guess Warner Bros. thought that was a hit, too," Booker said.

A bouncy pop throwaway and the only song that doesn't fit the concept of *The Soft Bulletin*, "Buggin'" finds Wayne bemoaning the scourge of every picnic and backyard barbecue. "All those bugs buzzin' round your head/Well, they fly in the air as you comb your hair/And the summertime will make you itch the mosquito bites," he sings. "That song could have been on *Clouds Taste Metallic*," Steven said, "but since we recorded it in the middle of the *Soft Bul-letin* sessions, it didn't hurt as bad to sing another song about bugs or ants."

After "Waitin' for a Superman" and "Race for the Prize," the album's most striking track is "The Spiderbite Song." It came together early in the ses-sions, during the summer of 1997, but toward the end of the process, the band did a different mix, making it less of a sixties-influenced, baroque pop number and more of a strange, ambient electronic tune. In the first two verses, Wayne recounts two harrowing incidents that threatened the lives of his bandmates. One day in 1996, in the midst of compiling the tapes for the third Parking Lot Experiment, Steven arrived at Stately Wayne Manor with an ugly, festering wound on his left hand. He told his bandmates that while rum-maging around in a storage shed, he'd been bitten by a brown recluse spider.

Known as "fiddlebacks" in the Southwest because of the violin-like marking on their backs, the spiders are rare, tiny (less than an inch long), and extremely poisonous: Their venom can cause an ulcer that eats through soft tissue and leads to gangrene. Steven wound up in the hospital for five days, and at one point doctors considered amputating his hand.

Around the same time, Michael had come to a stop at an intersection while driving in Oklahoma City when a stray tire came rolling toward his windshield at forty miles per hour. "It hit the corner of the car on the hood and went bouncing down the street, but if I had been pulled up another foot, it would have come right through the windshield," he said. "It hit hard enough on the driver's side of the car that it actually locked me in, and I was sitting there going, 'What the fuck just happened?' I never even saw the other car!" Wayne exaggerated an already frightening tale in his lyrics.

The third and final verse of "The Spiderbite Song" offers a more general comment on the devotion of an unnamed lover, possibly Wayne's significant other, Michelle Martin, though it also could refer to his bandmates or family members. All three verses are punctuated by the heartfelt emotion of the choruses, which find the singer expressing his own needs more frankly than he ever had before: "I was glad that it didn't destroy you, how sad that would be/'Cause if it destroyed you/It would destroy me."

"We're not touchy-feely people, me and Wayne," Michael said, "but I was touched, and I still am to this day very touched, by that song. I know a lot of times we really don't express to each other how much we really care about each other. I think we've decided that it's implicit in our actions, but it's very obvious what Wayne is saying in that song, and it's all reciprocated, of course. We can't have lived this life and not have a deeper feeling that goes beyond friendship, beyond family, in a way that we're just linked so deeply."

The Flaming Lips included two instrumentals on the album, a practice that would pay off in an unexpected way on their next disc. "The Observer" is a fragile and wonderfully moody song driven by what sounds like a beating heart, a concept Pink Floyd used on *The Dark Side of the Moon*. Originally part of a longer instrumental for the Parking Lot Experiments, "Sleeping on the Roof" is a somber meditation with a backing track of chirping crickets echoing Brian Eno's *Another Green World*, as well as "There You Are" from *In a Priest Driven Ambulance*. It would have ended the album if the disc hadn't included the alternate mixes of "Race for the Prize" and "Waitin' for a Superman."

In "The Gash," Wayne's lyrics pay homage to the last volunteer who battles on in the face of a dramatic but undefined struggle. Musically, the tune is most notable for the dramatic crashes on a giant gong—an instrument that became an effective prop in the new stage show—and Steven's complex orchestrations of a melody that evokes a Russian military march. A similar Eastern European–sounding riff drives "The Spark That Bled," a possible reminder of Steven's roots in Houston's community of Czech immigrants. The latter song begins with Wayne recounting a simple but mysterious incident—"I accidentally touched my head/And noticed that it had been bleeding"—and offering a surreal and ominous explanation: "What kind of weapons have they got? The softest bullet ever shot." The song dramatically shifts into another march before finally erupting in an unexpected moment of triumph as Wayne declares that he stood up and shouted "Yeah!"

"'The Spark' is like three or four different songs jammed together, and you get these great sweeps of mood where one part shifts into the other," Wayne said. "Little by little, we started thinking, 'We can do that, and instead of it being awkward or noisy or patched together with feedback, whatever solutions we used before, we can rely on the emotions we're putting across in the music and the singing.'"

For every album, Wayne had chosen one song to inspire the cover art; this time it was "The Spark That Bled." The band's friend George Salisbury had become a graphics artist and computer wizard, and he manipulated an already atmospheric photo that Wayne found in an old Time-Life book about psychedelic drugs. The digitally altered shot resembles Wayne in the yellow raincoat he wore during the Parking Lot Experiments, as well as evoking the image of a beleaguered soldier, rescue worker, or astronaut contemplating the dark shadow he casts on the ground.

"I imagined that you could look at that and listen to 'The Spark That Bled' and it would really enhance the experience," Wayne said. As the Flaming Lips developed an ever-more-elaborate show to support *The Soft Bulletin*, "The Spark That Bled" became a particularly theatrical moment, with Wayne concealing a small bottle of stage blood in his hand, pouring it on his forehead, and letting it run down over his face—a striking tableau that he said was inspired by another black-and-white photo, a famous shot of Miles Davis dripping blood on his elegant white suit after an altercation with police outside a jazz club in the fifties.

The risks that Wayne took with his vocals on "The Spark That Bled" encouraged him to be even more daring on some of the other songs. "We really did treat 'The Spark' like a Frank Sinatra song, trying things with the vocals that we would have never done before, and the same with 'Feeling Yourself Disintegrate,'" he said. The rhythm of the latter is established by Steven vocalizing a snare-drum march; the real drums don't come to the forefront until the song expands into a beautiful chorus that finds Wayne crooning the title phrase. Similarly, "What Is the Light?" builds from the barren soundscape of Wayne's voice and some ringing bass notes on the piano into a regal chorus that underscores the album's most direct and optimistic lyric: "Looking into space, it surrounds you / Love is the place that you're drawn to."

Floating along on Steven's synthesized strings and flutes, "A Spoonful Weighs a Ton" and "Suddenly Everything Has Changed" are both sad tunes that bring to mind the aftermath of the Oklahoma City bombing. "And though they were sad they rescued everyone / They lifted up the sun," Wayne sings in the former, while the latter considers how the universe can change completely during an otherwise mundane moment, when you're unloading the groceries or folding your laundry. "'Spoonful' has to be, not the day of the funeral, but the day my dad died, when all these people got together to bring us food and stuff. It is such a little thing to do, but the meaning is huge. People are just saying, 'We are here and we are in this thing together.' That's what the spoonful is. 'Suddenly Everything Has Changed' is the same thing, where after my father died, I felt like my whole world was different. It's in those times when there isn't another drama going on—moments of boredom, where your mind isn't filled up by thinking about a million things, you're just putting the groceries away—that these devastating changes really hit you and you realize, 'I really am different now.'"

When it was released in June 1999, I heard *The Soft Bulletin* as a concept album about millennial tension: As the turn of the century approached, alarmist fears about "Y2Kaos," dire warnings of terrorist attacks, and talk of the coming "end-times" among some evangelical Christians and other fringe groups dominated the media, providing fodder for a diverse list of artists ranging from pop gods the Backstreet Boys to R&B giant Prince, from trip-hopper Tricky to rappers the Goodie Mob, and from arena rockers U2 to avant-garde chanteuse Björk. "There's an element of that for sure," Wayne said, but the more direct inspiration came from the flood of emotions unleashed by his father's death, a subject that he only began talking about as time went on and he started hearing from fans who told him the album had helped them through their own emotional trials.

"People at funerals, people going through childbirth, people who are depressed, they seem to gravitate towards *The Soft Bulletin* and find their own meaning in it. There are a lot of records like that—even a Britney Spears album can do that—and maybe it's just that Flaming Lips fans are more expressive or have a bigger stake in their internal life, where they feel like they have to share that with me. It was just a matter of timing and all those things coming together—a lot of people's dads die, and they don't make good records—but some sort of existential optimism does seem to come through."

For many of the Flaming Lips' fans, cynical Gen-Xers as well as newly won members of Generation Y, *The Soft Bulletin* is an intensely personal and emotional album that offers hope and solace during trying times. In the mid-sixties, the Beach Boys' soulful orchestral masterpiece *Pet Sounds* had done something similar for their Baby Boomer fans, and in late 1999 the HBO TV series *Reverb* recruited Wayne to interview Brian Wilson. The Beach Boys' musical genius had returned to touring as a solo artist, performing many of the songs from *Pet Sounds* after years of inactivity stemming from his notorious emotional breakdown. As in many of his interviews, Wilson seemed uneasy, anxious, and uncommunicative, despite Wayne's friendly

approach, and the chat never aired, though it did contain one revealing exchange.

"Do you ever get tired of being known as this 'crazy guy' who wrote these 'crazy songs'?" Wayne asked.

"Yeah, I do," Wilson said, and Wayne nodded knowingly.

In March 1999, two years after the biggest and most celebrated of the Parking Lot Experiments in Austin and three months before the release of *The Soft Bulletin,* the Flaming Lips returned to the South by Southwest Music and Media Conference and performed once again as a conventional rock band, though the multimedia extravaganza they presented was anything but ordinary.

"*The Soft Bulletin* IS WHERE THE SHOW PART OF IT REALLY KICKED IN." THE FLAMING LIPS PERFORM AT TREES IN DALLAS, MARCH 1999.

The high-profile showcase paired the group with Sparklehorse and Grandaddy, two indie rock bands strongly influenced by the Flaming Lips, and Mercury Rev, the new group led by Wayne and Michael's former bandmate Jonathan Donahue. David Baker had quit Mercury Rev in 1993 after the release of its dark second album, *Boces*, leaving Jonathan as the group's primary singer, songwriter, and driving force. In the fall of 1998, the band—including Fridmann, who produced the group and played on its recordings but no longer performed live—released the most successful album of its career, *Deserter's Songs*, a set of lushly orchestrated psychedelic folk rock. (*Deserter's Songs* arrived in stores several months before *The Soft Bulletin*, though Mercury Rev began recording well after the Flaming Lips started crafting their ninth album; while the two discs share many similarities, Fridmann maintains that Mercury Rev never heard the Flaming Lips' work-in-progress.)

At South by Southwest, a capacity crowd including much of the national music media filled the cavernous, hangarlike space of La Zona Rosa to hear how Mercury Rev would render the complicated arrangements of *Deserter's Songs* onstage, and to discover how the Flaming Lips had reinvented themselves after more than two years of experimenting with car stereos and boom boxes. Mercury Rev played a solid set as a standard guitar-bass-and-drums lineup augmented by keyboards and theremin, but the Flaming Lips emerged as something else entirely. Steven and Michael added backing vocals and alternated between live guitar, bass, pedal steel, and keyboards, playing in sync with tapes that included Steven's drum parts and the layers of synthesized orchestral instruments that he'd crafted in the studio. Meanwhile, Wayne eschewed the guitar he'd hammered for the last fifteen years to focus on his singing, rendering the songs in a more dramatic style than he'd ever attempted in concert before, and serving as the flamboyant master of ceremonies.

Wayne had always been a cheerleader, comedian, and entertaining storyteller, steadily growing into his role as front man since his brother Mark left the band in 1985. Now, with the new confidence in his showmanship gained during the Parking Lot and Boom Box Experiments, he morphed into a combination of a giddy psychedelic guru—Timothy Leary at his most playful, or Ken Kesey leading the Acid Tests of the sixties—and a postmodern composite of the Rat Pack's Frank Sinatra, Dean Martin, and Sammy Davis Jr., the ideal ringmaster for a gonzo multimedia circus. "*The Soft Bulletin* is where the show part of it really kicked in," Wayne said. "I've always said I'm not that great of a singer. Most of the singers I really, truly love, like a Gladys Knight or a Sade or people like that, they just kill ya. It's only by appearance and default that

I'm a singer, so part of it is the three-legged-dog aspect: People appreciate what I'm doing just because I get up there and do it, even though I'm not very good at it. The other part of it is, 'Well, since I can't really sing, I'll try to entertain ya,' like Louis Armstrong or whatever."

Of course, Satchmo never pounded a massive gong, threw mountains of confetti into the crowd, generated dense, billowing clouds of fog with a smoke machine, mimicked his vocals with a hand puppet, or benefited from a giant video screen. The Flaming Lips opened their succinct but mesmerizing set in Austin with "Race for the Prize," its musical statement made even more powerful by a barrage of videos compiled by Wayne and George Salisbury and controlled onstage, along with the backing tapes, by Steven. Footage of the nuclear tests of the fifties was interspersed with a frenetic Leonard Bernstein, who seemed to be conducting both the band and the horrifying symphony of mushroom clouds.

The show included the two most musical songs from *Zaireeka,* "Riding to Work in the Year 2025 (Your Invisible Now)," accompanied by science-fiction footage of a futuristic, Orwellian society, and "Thirty-five Thousand Feet of Despair," which cut between clips of open-heart surgery and test film of a 747 that had intentionally been crashed so engineers could study the impact. The set also featured reworked versions of two of the most reliable tunes from *Transmissions from the Satellite Heart,* "She Don't Use Jelly"—the crowd cheered the inclusion of the band's only hit and the video of Michelle rolling around in the psychedelic bathtub—and "Slow Nerve Action," which featured a clip of Steven playing drums in the living room at Stately Wayne Manor.

Two more songs from *The Soft Bulletin* completed the performance, and though few concertgoers had heard the new album yet, these made the biggest impact musically and visually. "Feeling Yourself Disintegrate" became even more creepy and enigmatic as the group performed in front of images of sperm struggling to inseminate an egg, while Wayne crooned "Waitin' for a Superman" to a hand puppet of a nun as the video screen flashed footage from a whimsical but melancholy children's film.

In a link to the Boom Box Experiments, the Flaming Lips had loaned sixty portable stereo sets to the sixty fans who lined up first, and these listeners tuned in to a short-range FM radio broadcast of the live sound mix. Wayne claimed that this added frequencies that enhanced the music, while the headphones yielded greater stereo separation and a feeling of being "inside" the mix, but I didn't hear anything special, and I passed my headset to another listener midway through the show.

The group had performed in its new incarnation only once before, in Dallas two nights earlier. That gig had been awkward and nerve-wracking—the VHS projector and the digital tape decks that played the musical backing tracks offered numerous possibilities for things to go wrong—but everything worked perfectly at La Zona Rosa. The crowd greeted the show with ecstatic cheers, indicating that they'd been ready for the next step in the band's evolution, and that the group had once again outdone itself.

"Once we got through the first couple of songs, it was like, 'It looks like this is gonna work,'" Wayne recalled. "After doing something like the Parking Lot Experiments, where there was no ceiling or floor and nothing to compare it with, we were just like, 'What the fuck.' By the time we were doing the *Soft Bulletin* shows, we knew we had some cool visual stuff going on—I was throwing confetti, I had the puppets, we had the videos—and at the time, after all those years of these grunge bands just getting up there and playing, we felt like somebody should be doing something different. By the time we got done, we got this standing ovation, and people acted like, 'God, we've never seen anything like this before.' It isn't that hard to do something people haven't seen before; I don't know why sometimes we're the only ones doing it."

As impressed as everyone else, Jonathan reconnected with Wayne backstage after the gig. They had crossed paths several times since Jonathan quit the Flaming Lips in 1992, and any ill feelings had long since dissipated. The two bandleaders now shared a friendly but unspoken rivalry, and they quickly fell into their old repartee as Dingus and Louis. "We don't hang around that much, but whenever me and Jonathan are around each other, in two seconds we're right back where we were," Wayne said. Jonathan agreed. "People were saying that South by Southwest show was a reunion of sorts between old, estranged friends. It didn't really strike me that way; I'd just take the 'e' off of 'estranged' and leave it at 'strange.' If you heard us talk on a phone conversation tomorrow, you wouldn't be able to tell if it was 1987 or 2005."

The Flaming Lips had been building their following in the United Kingdom since the late eighties, but in 1999, Mercury Rev was much more popular there. *Deserter's Songs* had spurred a surge of interest in orchestral pop and indie rock from America, and in some cases, ill-informed English reviewers even claimed that the enigmatic New Yorkers had inspired the Flaming Lips, instead of the other way around. "We purposely released *The Soft Bulletin* in the U.K. first," Booker said. "*Deserter's Songs* had been such a big deal over there, my idea was, 'Maybe we can ride on those coattails a little bit.'"

Taking a cue from Mercury Rev, Booker hired Nigel Harding, an independent radio promoter at Alan James Public Relations. The company had represented many of the biggest Britpop bands, and it had helped make *Deserter's Songs* a hit. "The *Deserter's Songs* album really changed the musical climate in the U.K.," Harding said, "but in 1998 the Flaming Lips were just a footnote. Then Scott FedExed *The Soft Bulletin,* and it just blew our minds. They had the remixes that Peter Mokran did that were readymade for radio, and we knew we could work with it." Warner Bros. had an in-house staff to promote its releases in the United Kingdom, and it was reluctant to cede the band. "So Scott got some guy on his last day at Warners in America to sign off, and in fact we ended up invoicing the American label," Harding said. "Scott's very clever."

The Flaming Lips launched the album with a tour opening for Mercury Rev throughout the United Kingdom in April 1999. "We kind of felt like Jonathan knew he was doing us a favor," Booker said. "It's not like he paid us a lot of money or anything, but it helped us." The openers regularly upstaged the headliners, and they won rave reviews, including a piece in the usually cynical *New Musical Express.* "Despite fashioning incredible pop symphonies since 1985, the Flaming Lips have been consistently overlooked, at least commercially, until now," *NME* wrote. "As an example of the sheer depth of possibilities that music can offer, they're currently unbeatable."

"We owe a lot to Jonathan for that," Wayne said. "I never felt like he owed us anything—if anything, I owed him—but he brought us on tour and he let us do whatever we wanted, and playing to their crowd, a lot of nights I felt, 'Damn, I wouldn't have wanted to play after us!'"

By the end of 1999, *NME* had named *The Soft Bulletin* the album of the year, the Flaming Lips had scored chart hits with the Mokran mixes of "Waitin' for a Superman" and "Race for the Prize," and the album had gone gold with British sales of a hundred thousand (the United States defines gold sales as five hundred thousand). "Jonathan Donahue, for all his mystique, could come across as quite cold," Harding said. "Not that many people liked him that much, whereas everyone who met Wayne completely fell in love with him. People had a warm, friendly feeling toward the Flaming Lips, and they wanted them to succeed."

The buzz in England crossed the Atlantic, building excitement for the domestic release of *The Soft Bulletin* in June 1999. The group's new publicist at Warner Bros., longtime fan Rick Gershon, tirelessly promoted the disc, and contrary to the music-industry truism that press doesn't sell records, he believed the efforts paid off. "Press is something you can't put a price tag on," Gershon said. "The Flaming Lips have had hit singles in virtually every part of the world except America, so I do think that press has been an important part of the awareness here, purely for the fact of how outspoken Wayne is, and how interesting and colorful. There is nobody else like them."

As Booker had predicted, reviewers finally dropped the "Flaming Lips are weird" angle. *Spin* rated *The Soft Bulletin* a nine out of ten, *Entertainment Weekly* gave it an "A," and *Rolling Stone* deemed it one of the best recordings of 1999. The majority of critics agreed. When the *Village Voice* published its annual "Pazz and Jop Poll" of a thousand music journalists, the disc ranked as the fourth-best album of the year, behind Moby's *Play*, the Magnetic Fields' *69 Love Songs*, and Beck's *Midnite Vultures*, though Robert Christgau, who oversaw the poll as the self-proclaimed "Dean of American Rock Critics," remained a rare naysayer. "People love [*The Soft Bulletin*] because it's neopsychedelic in such an American, wide-open-spacey way—generous by nature, jerry-built on principle, and hopeful beyond all reason," Christgau wrote. "What puts me off is that Wayne Coyne evinces so much more sweetness than brain."

T he pop-music landscape had changed considerably between the time when "She Don't Use Jelly" finally became a hit in late 1994 and the release of *The Soft Bulletin* in mid-1999. In many markets, modern-rock radio stations either had slipped in the ratings or disappeared from the dial entirely, and lowest-common-denominator gangsta rap and teen pop from the likes of the Backstreet Boys, *NSync, Britney Spears, and Eminem dominated the pop charts and what little time MTV devoted to airing music videos in between reality programming and teen soap operas.

The Flaming Lips made two inspired videos with director Bradley Beesley to support the album. The clip for "Race for the Prize" features two of Wayne's brothers—Marty on his motorcycle and Kenny running with assorted medical monitors taped to his chest—as the three band members front a mini-orchestra entirely comprised of tuba players in yellow raincoats. The video for "Waitin' for a Superman" is even more striking, telling an allegorical tale of a young boy (Marty's six-year-old son, Rayce) who finds a superhero's cape on the playground, uses his newfound powers to heal the bloody head wound of a man who walks into a street lamp (his uncle Wayne), then gives the magical garment to another man sitting distraught on a park bench (a haggard-looking Steven).

Neither video garnered significant airplay, nor did the singles score a hit on American radio, but even without those traditional engines, album sales climbed steadily. *The Soft Bulletin* eventually sold two hundred twenty-seven thousand copies—fifty thousand fewer than *Transmissions from the Satellite Heart*, but enough to please Warner Bros. and to mark the Flaming Lips as one of the few groups to survive the end of the alternative era with an audience that was growing instead of shrinking.

"Sonic Youth, the Beastie Boys—there are a few bands that have been around as long as we have that keep thinking about what they do and how they can present it to the world," Wayne said. "I think we're lucky. In more ways than one, the Priest Driven Ambulance has always arrived at exactly the right time: with the *Priest* album, with 'She Don't Use Jelly,' with *The Soft Bulletin*. As much as people seemed to like *The Soft Bulletin*, it wasn't selling in America at first, but little by little, we kept touring and it started to click. It was a combination of luck and hard work."

As in the past, the band toured relentlessly, from mid-1999 through the end of 2000, including several trips to Europe and a tour of Japan; in the United States, the group filled several supporting slots and headlined its own Music Against Brain Degeneration Revue. This four-band package tour found the Flaming Lips loaning six hundred personal stereo sets to fans each night—these would be the last shows to feature this added audio bonus—and headlining thousand-seat venues in a sort of scaled-down, indoor version of Lollapalooza, which had come to an end in 1997. "The idea was to duplicate those old Motown shows, or the kind of concerts they put on at the Fillmore in the sixties," Booker said. "I felt that it was important for us to help some bands that we liked, but at the same time it elevated us even higher than a lot of people on the scene at the time. I feel like a jaded rock manager saying we were just so much better than anyone else out there, and I don't know if Wayne felt like that, but I certainly did when I was putting the bill together. Part of me felt, 'I want to show what we are, compared to everyone else.' I thought we could take on any band in the world."

When the revue came to Chicago in July 1999 for the first of two sold-out shows at Metro, Wayne introduced each band and gave an inspired speech at the start of the night, encouraging listeners to go home afterward and try to resolve a dilemma that had previously eluded them. "It is a scientifically proven fact that listening to complex music can strengthen the ability to think abstractly and solve complicated problems," he said. The show kicked off with Sonic Boom, a veteran of psychedelic rockers Spacemen 3, who played an odd set of electronic music on a Speak & Spell, a children's computer toy. Venerated cult hero Robyn Hitchcock, who led the first psychedelic revival in the eighties with the Soft Boys but now performed as a solo troubadour, followed, then sensitive indie rockers Sebadoh. Finally, the Flaming Lips delivered their overwhelming multimedia assault, which ended with the three musicians walking offstage as the Scarecrow from *The Wizard of Oz* sang "If I Only Had a Brain."

As two of the smartest and most eloquent musicians the underground rock scene ever produced, and as songwriters who both favored whimsical or dadaist lyrics at times, Wayne and Hitchcock seemed to have the most in common. But as Richard Davies had learned, Wayne didn't necessarily like to share the spotlight, and as anyone who'd served in the band's road crew knew, the Flaming Lips' leader expected everyone who toured with him to work as hard as he did. This caused some friction with Hitchcock, who at forty-six was eight years older than Wayne, and accustomed to less of a do-it-yourself ethic. "He's a baby, a whiner," Wayne said of Hitchcock. "I would have to go and say, 'Get your ass out there; let's go, man!' He would say, 'Oh, I'm so hot, I'm so tired. Can't you put me on later?' And I was like, 'No! What do you think this is?'"

Hitchcock laughed when he heard Wayne's version of events. "You could incur the wrath of Wayne, and I wouldn't want to be caught napping with him. He cracks the whip, but he is also very helpful . . . He has an ego, but he hasn't got that sort of aura that successful rock musicians develop. He is still very much himself, and I do admire him for that." Nevertheless, Hitchcock dreaded landing in the hot seat next to the Buzzard on the tour bus. "There was a point when Wayne decided I was a nut he wanted to crack. He probably did break a few pieces of shell off, then, like a crab trying to break something off underwater, he wandered off again. There was no point in him reducing me to a completely pulverized state. I enjoyed the whole social whirl of that tour, and I'd be up for doing it with him again . . . but the whole atmosphere with the Flaming Lips was not really what I first glimpsed it to be, and Steven was in a very strange state."

Although Hitchcock was too discreet to spell it out, Steven's heroin addiction had become an increasingly serious problem. During the Music Against Brain Degeneration Revue, Steven had been scheduled to back Wayne and Hitchcock in performing several songs on *Sound Opinions,* my radio show with Greg Kot, but no one could find him for the Sunday-afternoon taping because he had wandered off to score, leaving Wayne embarrassed and angry. Four years into his habit, Steven's addiction was beginning to interfere with his obligations to the band.

From their first EP through *Zaireeka,* the Flaming Lips equally shared songwriting credit and the ensuing publishing income. Recognizing the new way songs came together, Wayne instituted a different formula starting with *The Soft Bulletin.* The two largest cuts were divided equally between him for writing the lyrics and Steven for writing the music, while smaller stakes went to Michael and producer Dave Fridmann, with the exact percentages shifting depending on their contributions. The new split acknowledged Steven's crucial role in the way the band now worked, though he hadn't pushed for the change, and was too oblivious at the time to grasp the show of confidence on Wayne's part.

"To Wayne's credit, I was at my worst, and he could have said, 'Well, fuck Drozd,'" Steven said. "Not that I didn't help with the songwriting, but he could have said, 'I'm going to take 75 percent and just give him 25 percent,' and he never did that." In fact, with Steven spending virtually everything he earned on heroin, some of those closest to him believed the band should have cut him off.

Raised in Tulsa, Becky Stokesberry had begun dating Steven in 1991, when she was twenty-one and he was twenty-two. They moved in together shortly after he joined the Flaming Lips, but the constant touring put a strain on their relationship, and his drug use made things worse. "I think it first hit me, how serious it was, at Christmas, 1994," Becky said. "Before that, I was pretty stupid: I just didn't want to see it, but nobody did. It started out for him as something fun—he thought it was cool and glamorous—but he was self-medicating. Depression runs in his family, and I think that had a lot to do with it. It was a way to divorce from things he didn't want to remember."

After two years of living together, Steven broke up with Becky in July 1995. "He wasn't ready to have a family or get married, and I was," she said. "He wanted to do drugs and not hear somebody bitching at him all the time." She moved to Saint Louis and taught elementary school, then relocated to Los Angeles, though she and Steven remained close and spoke often. "I remember one Christmas telling him that if he were to get off drugs, I'd seriously consider a relationship with him again, but he was still using at that point, so it was impossible for us to make any serious plans. I was mad at Steven, and I wanted to blame it on someone, so I blamed Wayne."

When Becky saw the group in Los Angeles in 1996, she confronted Wayne about enabling Steven. "Wayne just gave me the argument, 'He's a big boy, he'll do what he wants,' and he was right. Wayne understands addiction, because it's happened in his family, too. I didn't have anything like that in my family, so I didn't fully understand his thought process. My thinking was,

'They treat Steven like a machine: Put in a quarter and he'll pop out a tune.' But it wasn't like that. I want to get it straight that I was wrong, and I just needed somebody to be angry at."

"With Steven on the dope, I think a lot of people were really mad at us because we kept giving him money," Booker said. "Wayne and I would talk about it a lot, but we felt in a way that if we fired him, it would only make things worse. He probably would have died. At least when there was enough money around to buy drugs, there was still money for him to eat and to pay rent, so there was some semblance of a regular life. And the bottom line to us was very cut and dried: It was his money. It wasn't our money that we decided to give him, it was money that he had earned. You can't say, 'I'm not giving you your money,' even though you may not like what he's going to do with it."

During the sessions for *The Soft Bulletin*, Steven lived with Wayne and Michelle at the Compound. "It was hard for me, because I was friends with Becky," Michelle said. "Steven essentially chose the dope, and it was devastating for her. I'm getting choked up just talking about it, but you ask everyone you know, 'What do you do?,' and they all tell you that you can't do anything. You can't take someone to a rehab; they have to do that on their own. I just felt more comfortable knowing he was here in the house. Maybe he was upstairs blacked out on dope, but he wasn't lying in a ditch, getting robbed or raped, getting sick or sharing needles or whatever. I know a lot of people thought it was selfish, but it was selfish for emotional reasons. Wayne will never say that he cared about Steven doing the drugs, but this is something where what you see is not what is really there. Wayne was really scared for him."

Nevertheless, in mid-1998, not long after Steven returned from a fruitless month spent in New York working on an aborted solo album by former Pixies bassist and Breeders bandleader Kim Deal, Michelle discovered Steven's works—his spoon and syringes as well as his stash of heroin—sitting out in the open in the upstairs bathroom, and she and Wayne asked him to leave. "I just couldn't have that here," Michelle said. "My sister would visit, and she was only nine years old." Steven was nonplussed. "They both told me, 'We don't care how high you are in the house, but you can't bring that shit in here.' I couldn't blame them for asking me to leave."

After three years of denying the extent of his problem, Steven's bandmates concluded that he had to bottom out, confront his addiction, or die, a realization that Becky had reached some time earlier. "The spider bite was the thing that sent me into a tailspin," she said. During the remix sessions with Mokran, Wayne probed Steven about the mysterious incident that nearly cost him his hand, and Steven confessed that he hadn't been bitten by a fiddle-back, he'd suffered a staph infection caused by shooting up with a dirty needle. The concern for his partner that Wayne expressed in his lyrics was real, but the incident at the heart of "The Spiderbite Song" was a lie.

CHAPTER 10

I THOUGHT THAT TIME WOULD PROVE YOU WRONG

<u>YOSHIMI BATTLES THE PINK ROBOTS</u> (2002)

AS IF the home Wayne Coyne shared with Michelle Martin hadn't already stood out in Oklahoma City's Classen-Ten-Penn neighborhood, in the spring of 2002, the Flaming Lips' bandleader purchased a ten-thousand-gallon white fiberglass tank from a local junk-yard—salvaged from beneath the pumps at an old gas station, the oblong cylinder measured twenty feet long and eight feet in diameter—and hauled it on a flatbed truck to the backyard of the Compound.

Combining the obsessive devotion of Dustin Hoffman's *Rain Man* and the artistic vision of sculptor Simon Rodia, who built "Nuestro Pueblo," better known as the Watts Towers, out of garbage found on the streets of Los Angeles, Wayne proceeded to saw several holes in the gigantic gas tank; rig it with yards of tubing and wiring, old computer parts, and blinking lights; and attach it to some upended acrylic hot tubs and the revolving door from a photographer's darkroom. Now, a dozen friends and aspiring filmmakers from Oklahoma University scurried about, climbing ladders or crawling on the ground in an effort to position the battery of lights to make it look less like a mountain of scrap and more like a space station on Mars.

The auteur in the paint-splattered orange jumpsuit wasn't satisfied. "I've gotta find that damn light," Wayne said as he ran into the house, frantically searching for a particular fluorescent lamp. He rushed past the kitchen, where Michelle, ever the unflappable den mother and gracious hostess, prepared a giant salad and two dozen turkey burgers for the cast and crew, and through the living room, where a bemused Steve Burns struggled into a homemade spacesuit.

Best known as the wide-eyed guy in the striped polo shirt who hosted *Blue's Clues*, the Nickelodeon children's show that found him helping a big, blue cartoon canine solve puzzles and riddles, Burns recently had quit to pursue more adult dramatic roles. He had first heard the Flaming Lips a few months earlier, when someone played *The Soft Bulletin* at a party in Manhattan, and he'd immediately left to buy the CD. A few days later, he had called Wayne and struck up a friendship, and the actor didn't hesitate for a moment when Wayne asked him to drive from New York to Oklahoma City. "I would have driven all the way to California to be in this film," Burns said. (Later, Steven Drozd returned the favor by helping Burns craft a solo album, *Music for Dust Mites*.)

"We're thinking about doing a movie—not just a movie soundtrack, but actually making a movie ourselves," Wayne first told me in early 2000, six months after the release of *The Soft Bulletin*. Two years later, he already had spent close to thirty-five thousand dollars and shot more than thirteen thousand feet of sixteen-millimeter film. "I figure we're about a third of the way finished," said his collaborator, Bradley Beesley, who couldn't be sure, because neither he nor any of the actors had ever seen a script. "Wayne gives me codirector credit on the movie, although it's certainly his baby."

Raised in Moore, Oklahoma, Beesley studied art at Oklahoma University a few years behind Michelle. "She was way too fucking cool for me, and I was frightened to talk to her or Wayne," he said, though in the small and incestuous world of artistically inclined Oklahomans, the Flaming Lips inevitably tapped him to help with their homemade music videos. "I was the kid in art school who laid down a thousand bucks to own his own film camera. Our relationship was spawned out of that and geographical convenience."

Except on the rare occasions when Warner Bros. persuaded the band to work with a "name" director, as with Michael Lavine on "Turn It On," or when the group turned to a celebrated pal such as Sofia Coppola, who shot "This Here Giraffe," Beesley and Wayne co-directed all of the band's videos, including the memorable clips for "She Don't Use Jelly," "Race for the Prize," and "Waitin' for a Superman." After making his first documentary in 1999, *Hill Stomp Hollar*, a portrait of bluesman R. L. Burnside, Beesley filmed *Okie Noodling*, a critically acclaimed look at fishermen in rural Oklahoma who dive to the bottom of muddy rivers and catch giant catfish with their hands. The Flaming Lips recorded the soundtrack, which Wayne described as "epic country and western," an unlikely merger of Glen Campbell and Pink Floyd.

When Wayne first approached Beesley in 2001 with the idea of making a feature-length movie, the filmmaker balked. "I told him on the first shoot that I would give it a try, but I didn't feel confident doing feature work. When we shot the first time and watched the footage back, I said, 'See how fucking shitty this looks? Everything about it is bad!'" Wayne disagreed. He loved the

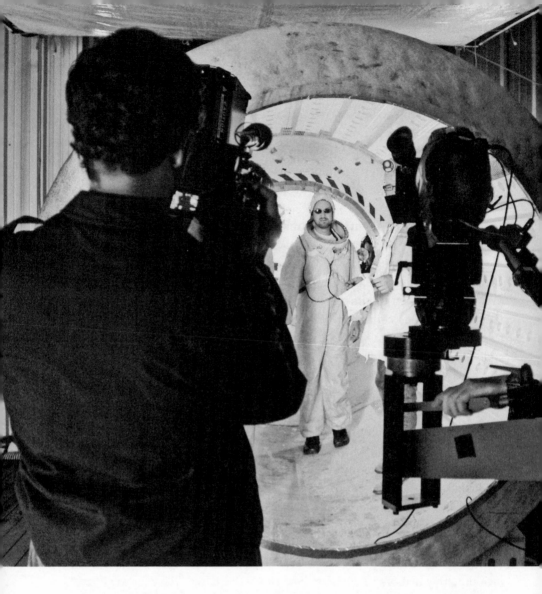

results, which evoked *Eraserhead*-era David Lynch shooting *2001: A Space Odyssey* without a budget, and he convinced Beesley to persevere, working for several days at a time every few months, moving the set from its first locale, in an old cement factory, to the backyard of Stately Wayne Manor, and utilizing a crew of volunteers and a cast of friends and family members.

Wayne wrote the dialogue for each scene by hand and gave it to the actors the morning of the shoot. "I think he's treating the movie the same way he approaches doing a painting or an album: 'We'll find out where we're going when we get there,'" Michelle said. When pressed, Wayne sketched the barest outline of a plot: A depressed space colonist (Steven Drozd) wonders whether he is losing his mind when he encounters an alien (Wayne in green-

face and antennae) who is helping celebrate Christmas and the birth of the first infant on Mars after another astronaut (Michael Ivins) commits suicide. "I do know where it ends," Beesley said. "Michael accidentally blows himself up and explodes everywhere, and then Wayne, the all-knowing, magical, alien Santa Claus, puts him back together, and it turns out it was all a dream"—no surprise, given Wayne's enduring belief in the magic of Christmas and his fondness for *The Wizard of Oz.*

"If I'm good, people will walk away thinking they saw a movie about an optimistic guy who decides to celebrate Christmas even though the space station is careering toward certain doom, but that's not really what it's about," Wayne said. "To me, there's some abstract quality that you can get in moviemaking where the image and the sound and the music all combine to elevate a moment into something super-emotional. Even when you watch a bad movie, like *My Dog Skip,* you still wind up crying, because it's that powerful. *Christmas on Mars* is really about the idea of belief: that if people around you believe in you, it influences what you can do."

A half hour after starting his search, Wayne finally found the elusive light, Burns climbed into the gas tank, and the crew filmed several takes of the actor expressing dismay at some cosmic dilemma, improvising his lines after some minimal direction from Wayne. "Mostly I said things like 'What did you do? Do you know what this means? We're fucked!'" Burns recalled. "There was also a lot of technobabble, such as 'Delta nozzle four . . . Delta nozzle four . . . check.'"

Another twelve-hour day ended with *Christmas on Mars* a few minutes closer to completion, though despite the postcards the band sent promising "a psychological fantasy adventure featuring the Flaming Lips, available Christmas 2002," the film wouldn't arrive that year. In fact, the next three holiday seasons would pass without its release, prompting Wayne to joke that he might wind up doubling the three-year ordeal Francis Ford Coppola underwent while making *Apocalypse Now.*

Work dragged on partly because the filmmakers gained more experience with every shoot, inspiring them to revise scenes they'd shot earlier, or to attempt even more ambitious visions when work reconvened. Wayne also found it hard to resist when Hollywood talents tracked him down as Burns had done and volunteered their services. In order to shoot a scene with Adam Goldberg, a Flaming Lips fan and an actor whose credits included *Dazed and Confused* and *Saving Private Ryan,* Wayne rented the flatbed again and hauled the gas tank four hundred miles to Austin, Texas, when Goldberg attended the South by Southwest Film Festival in March 2004. Scott Booker spent the rest of that year trying to coordinate schedules to accommodate roles for Goldberg's girlfriend, actress Christina Ricci, and former hobbit Elijah Wood, who fell in love with the band while making *The Lord of the Rings.* But the biggest reason Wayne couldn't finish his strange home movie came when the group released its tenth album, launching the busiest and most successful period of its career.

Just as the recording sessions for *Zaireeka* had taken the pressure off the Flaming Lips as they simultaneously started *The Soft Bulletin,* filming *Christmas on Mars* and recording the soundtracks for their own movie and *Okie Noodling* overlapped with work on their next album through 2001 and 2002, to the extent that even producer Dave Fridmann couldn't recall when recording actually began on *Yoshimi Battles the Pink Robots.*

"The movie wasn't such a big priority—it still isn't—but I really don't even know how *Yoshimi* started," Fridmann said two years after the disc's release. "It wasn't really focused: Wayne just brought in the latest stack of CDs he'd been listening to and said, 'Okay, I like Björk, I like Madonna, I like all these different elements of these different things,' and I had been of a similar mind that if we were going to start something, this seemed like as good a way as any other to try something new."

Wayne, Michael, and Steven always had listened to music from a wide range of genres—from mainstream pop to the most obscure underground recordings—and studied the way the records were made; they can wax rhapsodic about the snare-drum sound on a Britney Spears album without unduly worrying about the abysmal schlock that surrounds it. Madonna's 2000 album, *Music,* and Björk's 2001 effort, *Vespertine,* both had drawn inspiration from the electronic dance underground to craft conventional pop music from unconventional sounds. Together with more abrasive electronic artists such as Aphex Twin and popular techno DJs such as the Chemical Brothers—with whom the Flaming Lips would collaborate on the 2003 single "The Golden Path"—these discs inspired yet another new way of recording, with the band primarily relying on computers.

"Wayne would give me the shell of a song or his four-track recording and we would basically spend as long as it took to come up with a sound that was like, 'Okay, *that* is what the song is,'" Fridmann said. "There were a couple of times where I would spend days in the control room programming until I would stumble upon something, and once that was done, everyone would file back in and we'd beat the heck out of that and play real things on top of it. We'd record twenty-four tracks, keep the best three, and start all over again. That became easier to do with the technology that had become available, so that whenever we thought, 'I'm not sure about that,' it would be, 'That's fine—just throw it into the computer and save it; we can always come back to it.'"

Michael always had taken an intense interest in the recording process, and he had been sliding into the position of assistant engineer since *Clouds Taste Metallic* in 1994. Five years later, whenever the band took a break from touring, he worked as an apprentice at Tarbox Road Studios, helping Fridmann record other groups, many of whom were surprised to find the Flaming Lips veteran running cords and checking microphone placement. At the beginning of work on *Yoshimi Battles the Pink Robots,* Michael and Catherine moved to Fredonia—the couple had married in September 1998, at a ceremony where Booker served as the best man—and Michael blossomed in his new role behind the controls, helping Fridmann with programming and perfecting the sounds, recording his bandmates, and archiving the growing mass of musical data, a shift he put in terms of his beloved *Star Trek:* If he had once been Spock, the reserved sidekick to Wayne's Captain Kirk, he was now Lieutenant Commander Geordi La Forge, the brilliant chief engineer of the USS *Enterprise*-D.

"By then I had come to grips with, 'If I'm not going to be the guy who gets looked at whenever it's time to put a bass part down, what am I going to do?' The answer was, 'I'm going to really throw myself into this end of things,' especially because it had always been fun to be in the studio, and I had always been fascinated with the mechanics of it. There was more work than ever to be done on that end, and that could be my contribution, beyond being in the band, playing live, helping tour-manage, roadie, and drive, and being the general cheerleader, tap-of-approval, throwing-ideas-out-there kind of person."

Even for many in the band's camp, the partnership between Wayne and Michael and the specifics of what Michael adds to the group can be hard to define, but the best insights came from their producer and from Wayne's significant other. "When you are continuously, purposefully confronting the unknown psychic ball of energy as Wayne does, you need somewhere to go with that, someone who will have the perspective of the last twenty years to play off of," Fridmann said. Added Michelle, "If we bought a bicycle, the first thing Michael would do is open up the instructions, read them, see how it should be put together, get all his tools, line them up very neatly, then methodically begin with step one. Wayne would take the front wheel out to the yard and start rolling it down the street. That is why they work so well together."

Through many of the sessions for the new album, Steven continued to wrestle with his heroin addiction. Though he rose to the occasion whenever his bandmates needed him to contribute keyboards, guitar, bass, drums, or backing vocals, he felt he let them down. "I know I played most of the instruments and wrote a lot of chords and melodies and stuff, but I really don't feel like my heart was into it with *Yoshimi*. I don't feel like I was a driving force like I was during *The Soft Bulletin*." Countered Michael, "If that is Steven letting me down, give me more of that."

Indeed, if *Yoshimi Battles the Pink Robots* lacks the overall emotional impact of its predecessor, there are moments that better *The Soft Bulletin*, and the combination of that album's orchestral arrangements with the more electronic sounds and rhythms—many of them played by Steven on acoustic drums, then sampled, looped, or remade via computers—seems like a decisive step forward, rather than the consolidation of ideas that *Clouds Taste Metallic* represented after *Transmissions from the Satellite Heart*.

The band's tenth album opens with the portentous announcement "The test begins *now*," borrowed from the tapes for the Boom Box Experiments, before launching into the fat synthesizer bass, typically propulsive drum part, and reliable acoustic guitar of "Fight Test," a Wayne tune that captures the adolescent uncertainty of whether it's better to run or to stand and fight, even if you know you're going to lose. The protagonist doesn't battle to win the object of his affections—"So it came time to fight/I thought, I'll just step aside/And that time would prove you wrong," Wayne sings—and the result is illustrated in the video, a rare example of literal storytelling. Wayne's nephew Dennis not only loses his girlfriend, he's pushed facedown into a pile of horse manure. Wayne maintained that the horse shit was real—the video was filmed in a barn in Paul's Valley outside Oklahoma City—though Beesley insisted that chocolate mini-donuts had provided a sanitary substitute.

Steven conceived the next song as a piano ballad in the mode of Lionel Richie's "Hello." He played it for Wayne over the phone from New York, and by the time Wayne arrived at the studio from Oklahoma City, he'd written the lyrics, which link up with several other tunes to comprise the story invoked by the album's title and the painting Wayne did for the cover. "One More Robot—Sympathy 3000-21" portrays a robot that "learns to be something more than a machine . . . feeling a synthetic kind of love." I initially heard the disc as a concept album about preserving humanity against encroaching technology, but Wayne—who doesn't own a computer and never has used e-mail—said he intended the exact opposite, championing machines that are more "human" than people. The idea sprang from a TV documentary he had watched about robotic dogs providing solace for aged shut-ins, as well as from the unquestioning devotion of the trio of flesh-and-blood canines at Stately Wayne Manor.

"We have one dog that doesn't come in the house, and we came home around midnight on Christmas and the other two dogs had beaten that dog up. We took him to the vet and he almost died, and these things just crush you. Me and Michelle have always had this sort of philosophical argument about these animals and whether they love us, and I was the realistic guy: 'It's not love, we're just the people who feed them.' But when that happened, it occurred to me: 'What is love?' If you perceive that you're loved, you probably are. If you think your animals or a robot or God or whatever loves you, you're probably happier than people who don't have any love."

The album's title character, Yoshimi, admires the loving Unit 3000-21, but she fights the robot nonetheless: She's a super-heroine, that's her job. While it's not obvious in the lyrics, as Wayne envisions the story, Yoshimi doesn't defeat the robot; it allows her to win, committing suicide because it has fallen in love. "We had this weird instrumental that didn't have a name, but we had invited Yoshimi [Yokota] from the Boredoms to scream on it, and since it sounded like a fight was going on, I thought that was a great title: 'Yoshimi Battles the Pink Robots.' It's psychedelic, and that suited me fine. At the same time, Steven had this nice melody, just this unrelated thing that we

"I NEVER FELT LIKE ANYONE WOULD THINK OF IT AS
YOSHIMI FROM THE BOREDOMS." STEVEN AND YOSHIMI
YOKOTA IN THE STUDIO IN AUSTIN, 2001.

were working on, and I started singing this ridiculous story: 'Oh, Yoshimi,
they don't believe me/But you won't let those robots defeat me.' Without
giving it much thought, it became this neat little pop song."

The Flaming Lips first met the Japanese art-rock/noise-punk band the
Boredoms in 1994, when the two groups toured together as part of Lollapalooza. "Our backstage areas were very close," Boredoms drummer, trumpeter, and vocalist Yoshimi wrote me in an e-mail interview conducted
through a translator. "All the Flaming Lips were very nice to our broken English. Also the Lips had a guitar player Ron whose mother is Filipino. Something about him and Boredoms is very similar. His guitar play was so fun to
watch. And he had so many polka-dot T-shirts! He gave one to our guitar
player Yamamoto [Seiichi]. It did not look good on him, but Yamamoto liked
the shirt and was wearing it for a long time."

Yoshimi had joined the Flaming Lips onstage several times during Lollapalooza, blasting discordantly on her trumpet, and she'd been happy to record
some trumpet and vocals when Wayne booked time at a studio in Austin

after she traveled there to play with her side band, OOIOO, at South by Southwest in 2001. But she never expected to see her name appear in the album title. "What happened to the Lips? I still do not know the reason. It was surprise to me, too!" Yoshimi wrote.

"I don't think she likes it," Wayne said, "but I never felt like anyone would think of it as Yoshimi from the Boredoms. I just wanted to create a different identity, a character who wasn't me, where you'd get the feeling that she has some sort of mystical, kung-fu quality, but you wouldn't know exactly what her super power is."

The instrumental half of the epic story-song packs an impressive rhythmic wallop—"I told Steven, 'Think of yourself as Stevie Wonder and John Bonham is playing with you,'" Wayne said—but Steven disliked the second part of the Yoshimi epic. "I think it sounds like a cheap attempt to sound really electronic and techno. I wish 'Funeral in My Head' was on the record instead, but Fridmann agreed with Wayne that if that had been subbed for 'Yoshimi Battles the Pink Robots Pt. 2,' the album would have been too much of a downer."

A sad but beautiful song rife with crashing gongs, orchestral flourishes, the sound of a thunderstorm, and dramatic vocals—"But if I go mad/No one will know it," Wayne sings—"Funeral in My Head" joined "Jets" and "The Captain Is a Cold-Hearted & Egotistical Fool" among the best Flaming Lips tracks never released on album.

Underscoring Steven's feeling that he played less of a role in the songwriting, the next four tunes all originated with Wayne, though Steven made significant contributions. For the first time, Wayne abandoned his trusty acoustic guitar and toyed with developing melodies on an imitation Moog synthesizer. "With 'Ego Tripping at the Gates of Hell'—and that is such an awesome title for such a silly nothing of a song—my nephew Dennis borrowed the synthesizer and came up with that bubbling sound. I put it into my digital recorder, played one chord and an element of that bass line, and when Steven came by, I said, 'See if you can make this something we could sing over.' I went out for a bike ride, came back, and he had something perfect, a synthesizer/Motown crossover, and I just came up with some lyrics about longing and not seizing the moment."

"Are You a Hypnotist?" sounded like a country ballad when Wayne demoed it, but the song evolved into a much stranger tune as Steven and Fridmann tried a half-dozen approaches to the rhythm, arriving at a pastiche of several different acoustic drum kits and electronics. Musically, "In the Morning of the Magicians" sprang from another keyboard melody that Wayne discovered and a bridge that he thought sounded like Bob Seger's "Night Moves." It drew its lyrical inspiration from *The Morning of the Magicians,* a proto–New Age tome published by French columnist Louis Pauwels and physicist Jacques Bergier in 1960 espousing a philosophy they called "Fantastic Realism." Wayne never read the book, just a lengthy review—which is typical of his reading habits and the way he has always soaked up information and shaped his own philosophy.

"I don't really read novels or philosophy," Wayne said. "I just grab books or articles with things that pertain to me. I'll carry around the same book for ten years and just read the same things over and over, like listening to a record. The way I read is really just grabbing or bits and pieces of other people's opinions of the world."

The musicians started recording "In the Morning of the Magicians" with their old friend Trent Bell at his studio in Norman before moving on to Tarbox Road. "It's Summertime" also originated at Bell Labs. During the Japanese tour in support of *The Soft Bulletin,* the Flaming Lips connected with two devoted fans, Mutsuko Nagai and her sister, who followed them from show to show and touched everyone with their devotion. "Then, almost as soon as we got home, we got an e-mail from one of these women, and her English was almost indecipherable, but she said, 'Mutsuko is dying,'" Wayne recalled. "We were like, 'We just saw her; what happened?' After three or four days of e-mailing, she said, 'My sister is dead,' and we never really knew exactly what happened." (Mutsuko died as the result of a chronic heart condition.)

"It's Summertime" contrasts the beauty of the season with the realization that death can strike at any time, like a tornado in the Oklahoma summer, and it serves as an introduction to the next two tunes, both sublime pop songs as well as examples of the odd mix of romanticism and existentialism inherent in Wayne's worldview.

In "Do You Realize??," Wayne asks a disturbing question at odds with a beautiful melody that evokes the John Lennon of *Mind Games*—"Do you realize that everyone you know someday will die?"—but he provides an uplifting answer that underscores his belief that we are all responsible for creating our own happiness: "Let them know you realize that life goes fast / It's hard to make the good things last."

"I didn't know it was going to be a smash, but I instantly knew I loved it," Steven said of the first time he heard the song on Wayne's demo. "There are times you know Wayne has a real winner, and you just try not to fuck it up. He had this one intact, and I just helped give him a little twist in the chords at the end of every stanza." Wayne scoffed at Steven's modesty. "It was really more of a back-and-forth," he said. "Take away Steven, and I am just a guy playing chords. All of these songs require Dave Fridmann and Steven to give us everything they've got to make them work."

The next tune began as one of Steven's melodies, with Wayne adding lyrics that follow the model of "Do You Realize??" in using cosmic musings to make a point about life on earth. Over a minimal backing of piano and ambient noises, Wayne sings about a time traveler who arrives from the future to announce that "All We Have Is Now," amplifying another of his favorite themes: The challenge in life is to make the most of every moment, because you never know if it will be your last.

After delivering three heavy philosophical statements in a row, the album ends with a more lighthearted tune whose title returns to the fantastical realm of the Yoshimi song cycle. "Approaching Pavonis Mons by Balloon (Utopia Planitia)" is a lush instrumental with a wordless vocal recorded by Yoshimi buried deep in the mix, à la Clare Torry's orgasmic crooning on Pink Floyd's "The Great Gig in the Sky." Pavonis Mons is a volcano on Mars, while Utopia Planitia is the location where NASA's Viking 2 probe landed and first explored the red planet in September 1976. The song had been recorded for the soundtrack of *Christmas on Mars,* but Wayne cut the scene from the movie and decided to include the tune on the album, "just to provide a different atmosphere, and to give listeners a break from my dumb voice." It would prove to be a fortuitous decision.

During the first week of release in July 2002, *Yoshimi Battles the Pink Robots* sold twenty-six thousand copies, more than a quarter of the hundred thousand copies *The Soft Bulletin* had sold to that point, indicating that the Flaming Lips had built a strong new following more loyal than the one created by "She Don't Use Jelly." By the end of 2005, album sales approached half a million, the band's first domestic gold record, but that number would be the result of two and a half more years of touring instead of a hit single.

"Fight Test," the first single chosen by Warner Bros., once again made little impact on modern-rock radio; the second single didn't do much better, despite an elaborate video by Mark Pellington, who had directed *The Mothman Prophecies.* "'Do You Realize??' got radio play, just not as much as Korn or Limp Bizkit," Booker said. Some Warners staffers speculated that the pop audience may not have been ready for a song that asked them to consider the meaning of life and the fact that they'll all die, but the band has since heard stories of "Do You Realize??" being played at funerals and wakes, where it has provided comfort and injected a note of optimism. Grover Biery, who had risen to the post of senior vice-president of promotions, maintained that "it should have been a big, huge, fat, fuckin' hit. I bet you someone will cover it one day and it will be; it's just one of those songs."

Warner Bros. continued to suffer corporate turnover at the time, and the Flaming Lips lost one of their most reliable allies, A&R rep David Katznelson. Another ally, Russ Thyret, was edged out as chairman and CEO, and the label was waiting for his replacement, the supposedly artist-friendly Tom Whalley, to extricate himself from a contract with Interscope. Meanwhile, David Kahne was running the show as the head of A&R, and he would be vilified during the period for his role in driving Wilco from the label. The Flaming Lips got lost in the shuffle as this executive drama played out. "We were all frustrated that we couldn't get 'Do You Realize??' played, and it might have been different if Tom [Whalley] had already arrived, but for Scott, the manager that so believes in this band, it was especially frustrating," Grover said. "The Lips were always respectful, because they knew that we were doing all we could, but at the same time it was hard for them to deal with it or to accept that we were doing all we could, particularly because *Yoshimi* was doing so great otherwise."

By the fall of 2001, midway through recording *Yoshimi Battles the Pink Robots* and six years into his heroin addiction, Steven had hit bottom. He lived alone in an apartment in Norman with no electricity or running water, sleeping on a mattress on the floor amid the usual junkie's squalor of discarded fast-food wrappers, empty beer cans, used syringes, and burned spoons. He had sold his car, his stereo, his keyboards, and all of his guitars, including the prized Fender Jazzmaster he'd used on *The Soft Bulletin*. He regretted ruining his relationship with Becky Stokesberry, and as he neared age thirty-two, he realized he'd end up dead or in jail if he didn't kick his habit soon.

Interviewed for the documentary *The Fearless Freaks*, Steven asked director Bradley Beesley to borrow fifty dollars in return for agreeing to be filmed while shooting up.

A few days later, on October 6, Wayne expected Steven to arrive at the Compound at seven a.m. to leave for the eighteen-hour drive to Cassadaga, New York, where they'd resume working with Dave Fridmann on the new album. Hours passed as Steven scoured Oklahoma City looking for a connection. When he couldn't score, he cooked the heroin he had left on hand and vowed that it would be his last shot, though he had said that many times before and had never quit for more than two weeks. Wayne considered leaving without Steven—"If he had left, I really don't know what would have happened," Michelle said, fearing that it could have meant the end of Steven in the band—but the Flaming Lips' leader stood waiting on the porch with his arms crossed, silently fuming when his bandmate finally showed up five hours late. "He looked so fucking pissed off, and I'd never seen him look like that before," Steven said.

Michelle had celebrated her thirty-third birthday the night before, and Steven handed her a card he'd made on a piece of notebook paper. "Steven's saving grace is that he can be doing something right in front of you that makes you hate him, but he has this charm that makes it hard to be mad at him," Michelle said. "That day, it wasn't hard to be mad at him." The van pulled off with Wayne behind the wheel and Steven in the hot seat. They had only gone a few blocks when Steven tried to shrug off the delay, pulling out the road atlas and making a show of tracing the route, even though they had made the trip many times before. "Okay, so we're a couple of hours late," he said. "But we're leaving now, so we should make it there by—"

Wayne grabbed a bottle of water out of Steven's hand, threw it in his face, and unleashed a flurry of punches to his bandmate's head before pulling to the curb. "Everything we've worked for is going to fall apart, and I'm going to have to make a choice before too long," Wayne barked. "If these guys say, 'We can't in good conscience work with Steven anymore,' I'm not going to side with you over Scott Booker or Dave Fridmann. You've got to get your shit together!" That night, Wayne called Michelle and told her what had happened. "He said, 'I regret it,' but I told him, 'You weren't just hitting him for you; you were hitting him for a lot of people.'"

"That was the turning point," Steven said. "I had no more options except to quit doing drugs. When Wayne punched me in the head, that solidified my thinking." Wayne downplayed his role. "I don't believe me hitting him did anything; he had already started to convince himself. If he was nine-tenths of the way to quitting already, maybe hitting him just pushed him the last little bit. I was the one in the wrong—I hit him, he didn't come at me—but there are people who are so civilized that they aren't friends because they won't punch each other, and then there are fuckin' hillbillies who'll be friends when they are a hundred years old, and they're fighting every other weekend."

After the band finished the latest sessions at Tarbox Road, Steven stayed in Fredonia; he knew he would be less likely to score heroin in rural western New York than in Oklahoma City. He didn't attend a twelve-step program, and he didn't quit drinking—"For the first month and a half, I basically stayed on Michael and Catherine's couch and drank all their booze," he said—and he later became a fixture at B.J.'s Bar in Fredonia. Otherwise, he withdrew cold turkey.

"Have you ever seen *The Man with the Golden Arm*?" Steven asked. "Kim Novak locks Frank Sinatra in the closet, and he says, 'No matter what I do, don't let me out.' It's so hokey and melodramatic, but it's based on some truth. I honestly wouldn't recommend doing it that way to anybody, especially if you don't have the kind of friends I do. I didn't have any money, I was helpless, I was having these freakouts, I was uncontrollably crying all the time—I was like a baby. If it wasn't for Michael and Catherine and Dave and Mary Fridmann, I don't know if I would've gotten out as easily as I did."

Michael and Catherine hadn't hesitated when Steven asked if he could stay with them. "We said, 'Please, stay on our couch, stay in our home, we will help you,'" Michael said. "For two weeks when there was nothing going on in the studio, I woke up every morning with Steven, and Catherine and I both sort of tag-teamed with him. Then I had to go to work, and I'd be gone for twelve hours a day, and it was really Catherine who basically baby-sat him for about four months and helped him, because he just had to work through so much stuff. For someone like me that actually finds talking about things

"THERE WERE TIMES WHEN HE COULDN'T EVEN SPEAK ON THE PHONE, HE WAS SO EMOTIONAL." STEVEN AND BECKY STOKESBERRY ON THEIR WEDDING DAY, 2003.

fairly difficult . . . He had a lot of stuff that he needed to work through without the buffer of a drug that makes you feel good, and I don't know if I could have done that. But Catherine did." Added Catherine, "It just had to be done. Steven needed help; he was a friend; we could do it, and we were happy to."

In late January 2002, Steven visited his sister in Houston, then flew to Oklahoma to shoot some scenes for *Christmas on Mars*. He gathered the few possessions he'd left in Norman and drove back to Fredonia, where he found an apartment and continued the struggle to keep clean while facing some deep-seated issues he'd never addressed, including the deaths of his mother, who had succumbed to a drug overdose in late 1986, and his brother Bubba, who had committed suicide in 1989. "There were times when he couldn't even speak on the phone, he was so emotional," Becky Stokesberry said. "When you are sedated for that long, every emotion that you erased over the past few years comes up to the surface. His family history is something he hadn't dealt with, and it was really hard."

In February, Becky visited Steven in New York, and the couple began to

"FLAMING LIPS . . . YOU'RE UP."
MICHAEL AND CATHERINE ON
THEIR WEDDING DAY IN 1998
(LEFT), AND WAYNE AND
MICHELLE IN JUNE 2005 (BELOW).

rebuild their relationship, but she had gotten an offer to spend a year teaching in Japan, and she accepted. When Steven's sister, who also struggled with addiction, stole a shotgun and took her own life in the fall of 2002, Becky returned to be at his side, and he visited her in Japan at Christmas. After her year overseas, she moved in with Steven in Fredonia, and in the fall of 2003, the Flaming Lips' last bachelor wed. (Wayne and Michelle had long considered their partnership a common-law marriage, and she now uses the name J. Michelle Martin-Coyne.) Michael served as the groomsman, and Wayne acted as the best man. In 2005, Steven and Becky moved back to Oklahoma City, bought a house a few miles from Stately Wayne Manor, and celebrated the birth of their son, Daniel. Steven had been free from heroin for four years, and he had never relapsed.

The backstage area at the Flaming Lips' shows always had been chaotic, with the musicians joining the roadies to untangle yards of Christmas lights, rig the film projectors, prepare bucketfuls of confetti, and inflate dozens of big balloons, but from early 2001 on, things got even stranger. Every night, Cory Franklin, a veteran roadie since 1993, donned a Santa Claus outfit and threw himself into his new role as "animal wrangler," recruiting fans at each concert to dress in a colorful array of thirty furry costumes, as well as ten special inflatable outfits, including a giant smiling sun.

Steven and Michael also wore costumes, though they avoided the animal headpieces because they had to sing, while Wayne took to dressing in light-colored suits that he besmirched at each show with a torrent of fake blood. At first, he shopped at thrift stores, but when he discovered that the blood washed out more easily from more expensive clothing, he turned to Armani and Dolce & Gabbana. He washed his designer suits each night in cold water in the hotel bathtub and dried them with a hair dryer.

The furry menagerie grew from a gig at Oklahoma City's Will Rogers Theater in February 2000, when the band's friend George Salisbury persuaded one of his pals to dress as a pink bunny rabbit. People assumed the costumed character walking through the crowd was part of the show, so Wayne embraced the idea, buying a frog costume and a "dog/bear thing" for fans to wear onstage. By the time the group started touring behind *Yoshimi Battles the Pink Robots* in 2002, it owned two road cases crammed with enough outfits to dress an army of living cartoon characters rivaling any theme park.

While this spectacle added a sense of childlike wonder, the concerts still boasted unsettling images of nuclear mushroom clouds and dissected eye-balls, as well as non–politically correct touches such as strippers. "Anybody that doesn't see that naked women are a great, beautiful wonder of the world, I just don't get that," Wayne said in response to the musicians' occasional feminist critics, including some of their spouses. "It's just breasts, people! It's fun! Free yourself up!"

The costumed animals also had a sexual connotation as the subject of one of the more distinctive fetishes that thrive courtesy of Internet interest groups. The subculture describes itself in a lexicon defined on several Web sites: "Plushophiles" enjoy being intimate with stuffed animals or "plushies"; "zootaphiles" are excited by people wearing animal costumes, aka "fursuits" or "furries"; "toonophiles" get their kicks from cartoon characters; and "furverts" enjoy all of the above. "While outsiders find the combination of cute childhood imagery and sexuality to be disturbing, furverts have no inter-est in sex with children," wrote sexologist Katharine Gates, the author of *Deviant Desires: Incredibly Strange Sex*. "This is about 'growing up' childhood dreams and fantasies."

Consistently curious about the oddities of human behavior, Wayne hadn't let this phenomenon escape his attention. "Yeah, sure, I know about that," he said with a grin, "but I didn't think anyone would read all that much into the costumes. I just think it adds to the show in general, because if you're not used to it, it's the greatest thing ever to be up there with your favorite band and feel all that love. And it's contagious: You see someone going crazy, and it allows you to go a little bit crazy, and it all just builds."

With rare exceptions—the more reserved Scandinavian countries could be problematic, Franklin said—the outgoing animal wrangler usually found more furry volunteers than he needed, including such well-known names as actress Juliette Lewis, who danced onstage in costume with her sister, and singer Justin Timberlake, who dressed as a dolphin to join the Flaming Lips for a taping of the BBC's *Top of the Pops*. "I won't lie: I've gotten a few dates out of this job, but I try to keep things on a professional level," Franklin said. "The big challenge is to keep them from hitting or knocking over Steven's keyboard, which has happened too many times to count."

The Flaming Lips hit the road shortly after the release of *Yoshimi Battles the Pink Robots*, promoting the album as relentlessly as they had supported *Transmissions from the Satellite Heart*. With relatively short breaks in between, they embarked on the Unlimited Sunshine Tour with Cake, Modest Mouse, and Kinky; a tour opening for and supporting alternative-rock hero Beck; a string of gigs headlining twenty-five-hundred-seat theaters; a West Coast tour opening for the Red Hot Chili Peppers; a headlining tour in England and Europe; and tours of Australia and Japan. The band also did a series of shows with the String Cheese Incident, and it began to build a following by playing festivals catering to the "jam band" or "baby Dead" hippie rock crowd. But the Beck dates garnered the most attention by far.

In September 2002, Beck Hansen released his fifth and most mature album, *Sea Change*, inspired by the end of a longtime romance. The notion of the Flaming Lips backing Beck had been the idea of Beck and his management, putting an indie-rock twist on Bob Dylan's tours with the Band, and garnering some buzz at a time when Beck bordered on becoming old news. Beck claimed to be a Lips fan. "There's an emotional quality to their music," he told the *San Diego Union-Tribune*. "Wayne has always had an amazing ability to communicate with an amazing lack of pretension. He's one of those people who can just say whatever's on his mind, and they don't come off cliché. And they have a sense of humor about what they do." But that attitude was more difficult to deal with than Beck had anticipated, and the tour didn't quite work out for him as he'd planned, which he could have predicted if he'd investigated the only other tour the Flaming Lips did backing another artist, Richard Davies, or the difficulties with Robyn Hitchcock on the Music Against Brain Degeneration Revue.

The Oklahomans expected Beck to work as hard as they did, with the same self-effacing humor and down-to-earth attitude, but despite the image he fostered as a fun-loving underground eccentric, the Los Angeles native and practicing Scientologist operated more like a self-indulgent seventies superstar than an eighties indie-rock road warrior. "The fact that the Flaming Lips even finished that tour is a testament to Wayne's patience," Michelle said, "because nobody gets away with that crap."

Maintaining their usual pace, the Flaming Lips filmed three videos the weekend before arriving in Burbank, California, in early October 2002 for two weeks of rehearsals with Beck. Steven flew directly from his sister's funeral in Houston, but the star proved to be an elusive presence. "Beck just operates on his own rules," Wayne said. "We were supposed to show up for rehearsals at noon, but he wouldn't show up until five. After the third time, we said, 'Look, if you are not going to be here, just tell us,' but he wouldn't." When Beck did arrive, he'd spend two hours eating dinner, sending his food back to the kitchen when it didn't meet his standards. "All the guys I talked to who've worked with him said he's always been a prima donna and high maintenance."

At first, Beck's manager didn't want his client's new backing band to per-

"THE FACT THAT THE FLAMING LIPS EVEN FINISHED THAT TOUR IS A TESTAMENT TO WAYNE'S PATIENCE." WAYNE AND BECK PREPARE TO PERFORM ON *Late Night with Conan O'Brien*, HALLOWEEN, 2002. WAYNE HAD ASKED THE MAKEUP ARTIST TO GIVE HIM A BLACK EYE, BUT HE TOLD PEOPLE THAT BECK HAD HIT HIM.

form its own material, just help Beck deliver his, but Booker argued that the fans would expect the Flaming Lips to play some of their songs, and with tickets costing sixty dollars, they deserved it. The group envisioned a seamless performance, with its set preceding and flowing into Beck's, but Beck demanded a break in between, which sometimes stretched to forty-five minutes. His crew had promised to haul the Flaming Lips' equipment, but they reneged after the first gig in Minneapolis, and Booker had to scramble to rent a truck. At the same time, Beck's manager complained that it looked unprofessional when Steven chewed gum onstage. "He's chewing gum so he doesn't

"I AIN'T SEEN NOTHIN' LIKE THIS." WAYNE IN THE "SPACE BUBBLE" AT COACHELLA, 2004.

shoot heroin!" Booker said. "Is this some weird Scientology rule we didn't know about?"

Despite the tension backstage, the shows were revelatory, and the Flaming Lips brought an exciting garage-rock edge to Beck's music. Although the group hadn't performed as a conventional rock band for six years, Steven deftly handled guitar and many of the keyboard parts, along with second keyboardist Greg Kurstin, who'd been hired by Beck. Wayne added guitar noise, burbling electronics, backing vocals, and cheerleading; Michael anchored the flowing grooves on bass; and Kliph Scurlock, the latest addition to the Flam-

ing Lips' entourage, replaced Beck's former drummer, Joey Waronker, an acclaimed session player and the son of former Warner Bros. exec Lenny Waronker.

Throughout the tours supporting *The Soft Bulletin*, Wayne adamantly denied that the group had lost something by no longer having live drums in concert, despite jibes to the contrary from Fridmann. In the spring of 2002, Wayne and I had an hour-long debate about the visceral power of acoustic drums in an era when electronics seemingly made them unnecessary. He vowed that the Flaming Lips would never use "real" drums again, but a few months later, Steven began to make cameo appearances behind the kit at every show, drumming on "Race for the Prize" and "A Spoonful Weighs a Ton."

Twenty-nine years old, a native of Topeka, Kansas, a talented drummer, and a Flaming Lips superfan, Kliph had won a job on the road crew after volunteering to hand out headphones during the *Soft Bulletin* show at South by Southwest in 1999. When Beck needed a drummer, the Flaming Lips suggested their roadie. The star resisted and held auditions, though he didn't bother to turn up for them; meanwhile, Kliph drummed during rehearsals. Beck never got around to hiring anyone else, so Kliph landed the gig. Twenty minutes before the first show of the tour, Wayne told him he should play drums during the Flaming Lips' set, too, augmenting Steven's taped rhythm tracks.

"From my perspective, I didn't even really care that much that I was playing with Beck," Kliph said. "It was more like, 'Fuck! I'm actually playing drums with the Lips!'" He would continue playing drums onstage along with Steven's taped rhythm tracks from that point on, though Steven still played all of the drums in the recording studio.

The tour with Beck won the band a new level of mainstream attention, including a controversial profile by Tom Junod in the March 2003 *Esquire* that featured Wayne ranting about the headliner's rock-star behavior, offending Beck and angering his management. (The title of the piece stated, among other things, that "Beck is a dick.") Beck responded to the magazine a year later in a letter written with a self-deprecating sense of humor that contrasted with the attitude the Lips had derided. "Your insights really brought to light the depths of my character and showed all the world who I truly am," Beck wrote. "As I do blow off a copy of your magazine backstage and burn through the $200+ million I made off my last record of folk ballads, I have been given cause to reflect on what may be important in my life and what may be irrelevant."

When Wayne ran into Beck backstage at the Coachella Fest in Indio, California, in May 2004, shortly after his delayed response to *Esquire*, the Flaming Lips' leader tried to bury the hatchet, and he led the crowd in singing "Happy Birthday" to the child Beck was expecting with his new wife, actress Marissa Ribisi. Beck didn't seem placated. (He has generally refused to discuss the Flaming Lips in interviews since the tour, and through his publicist, he declined to be interviewed for this book.) Despite problems with the monitor crew that limited their set to four songs, the Flaming Lips grabbed most of the headlines from Coachella when Wayne climbed into a giant clear plastic "space bubble" and rolled over the heads of sixty thousand fans.

Realizing that the band had little hope of denting radio or MTV, Booker had begun to look for other ways to reach a broader audience. The dogmatic anticorporate mindset that prevailed during the indie-rock eighties had begun to erode during the alternative era, though cynical Gen-Xers continued to sneer at the concept of "selling out." In the new millennium, that notion hardly registered anymore for older Baby Boomers, many of whom didn't even scoff when Bob Dylan appeared in a 2004 ad for Victoria's Secret, or for many younger members of Generation Y, who were as likely to discover new music in television commercials as they were via radio or the rock press. In the most famous example of this new paradigm, techno-pop artist Moby had sold each of the eighteen tracks on his 1999 album *Play* to one or more TV commercials or film soundtracks, and he'd been rewarded with a hit that sold ten million copies worldwide.

Of course, there are ways to use advertising and Hollywood that are creative as well as remunerative, and ways that are much less successful, and the Flaming Lips experienced both.

When Booker forged a pact with Hewlett-Packard, the computer company featured the white-suited Wayne in the center of its print ads, while a TV spot called "The Green Room" found actor Abe Vigoda of TV's *Barney Miller*, model Rachel Hunter, the magical-comedy duo Penn and Teller, an actor portraying Abe Lincoln, and New York Yankees pitcher Randy Johnson awaiting a mysterious summons to stardom. When the door opened, the producer called, "Flaming Lips . . . you're up," and a beaming Wayne answered the call, followed by two costumed rabbits, to the strains of "Do You Realize??" The campaign might not have been successful for HP—some viewers couldn't tell what it was selling—but it served as a million-dollar promotion for the band.

In contrast, the Mitsubishi Galant ad featuring "Do You Realize??" was just another boring TV car commercial; instead of creating a left-field hit, as Volkswagen did with Nick Drake's "Pink Moon," it only cheapened the band's existential pop song. Similarly, the band's guest appearance in a 2002 episode of *Charmed,* the occult melodrama starring Alyssa Milano, Holly Marie Combs, and Rose McGowan, had none of the camp appeal of its cameo on *Beverly Hills, 90210* years earlier. Much cooler was the song the Flaming Lips recorded for *The SpongeBob SquarePants Movie,* "SpongeBob & Patrick Confront the Psychic Wall of Energy." The accompanying video featured the musicians dressed as pirates and cavorting in a giant foam-rubber mouth dripping with fake saliva in a clip every bit as surreal as the wickedly subversive cartoon.

In early 2005, Nickelodeon paid the group $100,000 to perform two songs at an invitation-only corporate party; the band had barely earned that much during its first ten years of touring, and the money funded projects such as *Christmas on Mars.* On the other hand, when the Flaming Lips accepted $120,000 to perform a show for Mazda, the gig turned out horribly. Originally it was to be a private affair, but the promoters decided to admit the public. A heavy-handed bouncer berated the fans who showed up, admitting only those who met some nebulous dress code, and even hassling the musicians themselves.

In each of these cases, the Flaming Lips had been approached by longtime fans who'd achieved a measure of success in the corporate world or in Hollywood—Milano herself had called Wayne about *Charmed*—and the musicians trusted their admirers to portray them in the right way. This didn't always happen, and the band members justified their more questionable decisions in several ways. "We can talk about *Pet Sounds* and the Beatles as art, but it's all pop music, because it ends up being entertainment," Michael said. "We fell victim to that integrity question for a long time, the whole thing about selling out: We would have liked to sell out, but no one had been buying. Britney Spears isn't worrying at night about what people think about her. People like her, and she likes the music she's making, and that's the end of the story."

"I feel like I am being subversive when I get a Lips song on a Mitsubishi commercial," Booker said. "It is slightly self-serving to say that, but I want people to know about the Flaming Lips, by any means necessary, and gosh, to get paid for it, too—how much better can life get?" But there are lines the band wouldn't cross. "Would we want [George W.] Bush to use one of our songs? No, and we wouldn't let him."

"I just go from my own experience," Wayne said. "We can all go back to when [the Beatles'] 'Revolution' was used in a shoe commercial, but I still think that's a kick-ass song, and that didn't change the meaning of the song for me at all." He is also reluctant to turn down any opportunity because of preconceived biases. "I'm hoping that we do things that are interesting, and obviously, we want to make money. Who wouldn't?"

By early 2005, as a successful mid-tier major-label rock band, the Flaming Lips were themselves a corporation generating millions of dollars a year—"though we've never had a million dollars in the bank at one time," Booker noted—and they had reached a new level of fame. Wayne and Michelle invested in several other properties in their neighborhood, extending the borders of the Compound, and Wayne had met rock-star heroes such as Paul McCartney, Robert Plant, and David Gilmour of Pink Floyd, who treated him as a peer and professed to be fans of his music.

Booker, his second wife, Jennifer, and their two-year-old son, Harrison, moved to a new home in suburban Edmond, and the band's manager converted a former 7-Eleven nearby into the impressive new offices of Hellfire Management and Marketing. Scott and Jennifer joined Michael in achieving Trekkie nirvana when Flaming Lips fan Connor Trinneer of *Star Trek: Enterprise* arranged for them to appear on the show as extras, portraying oppressed miners in an episode directed by LeVar Burton, Lieutenant Commander Geordi La Forge himself.

In August 2003, Michael and Catherine bought a house near her sister's in Kentucky, just across the Ohio River from Cincinnati, and devoted themselves to helping raise their niece, Mary Elizabeth, or M.E., who was born in January. Around the same time, Steven paid a debt to his first musical inspiration, inviting his father to play sax during the Flaming Lips' appearance on *Austin City Limits*. "It was the greatest gig of my life," Vernon Drozd said. Steven found himself lauded by his own fan club, the Steven Drozd Appreciation Society; recruited by Adam Goldberg to co-score his film *I Love Your Work;* and feted by Goldberg, Giovanni Ribisi, and Christina Ricci on Jon Favreau's talk show, *Dinner for Five.*

Approached by some fans from the theater world who envisioned a musical based on *Yoshimi Battles the Pink Robots*—a cross between the Blue Man Group, *Rent,* and the Monty Python–inspired *Spamalot*—Booker entered talks with Des McAnuff, who had directed *The Who's Tommy.* "The Flaming Lips on Broadway: Is that weird or what?" Booker asked. Even stranger, in February 2003, the band claimed a Grammy for Best Rock Instrumental Performance, besting jam-band favorites Gov't Mule, progressive rocker Tony Levin, virtuosic guitarist Joe Satriani, and Guns N' Roses veteran Slash to win for "Approaching Pavonis Mons by Balloon (Utopia Planitia)," the song they'd included on the album as an afterthought.

Well aware that conservative Grammy voters often overlook groundbreaking musical accomplishments while honoring commercial achievements, the Flaming Lips had no illusions that the award recognized their artistry; it simply acknowledged that they finally had landed in the mainstream. "There's a lot of stuff about winning a Grammy that's really kind of silly," said Wayne, who appeared at the ceremony sporting a Band-Aid on his cheek. ("Wayne just loves to wear Band-Aids," Michelle said.) Booker displayed Wayne's golden gramophone at the Hellfire office, Steven gave his to his father, and Michael placed his in his home office. But the group would find that its increased profile had its downside.

The musicians often had appropriated riffs, melodies, chord patterns, and sometimes even snatches of recordings from a wide range of artists they loved, twisting the end results so the origins could hardly be recognized. Rock 'n' roll had cannibalized itself from its inception—critic Lester Bangs famously pointed out that the three chords of "La Bamba" by Ritchie Valens were recycled for "Louie Louie" by the Kingsmen, "You Really Got Me" by the Kinks, "No Fun" by the Stooges, "Blitzkrieg Bop" by the Ramones, and, we could now add, "Smells Like Teen Spirit" by Nirvana—but Wayne differed from many artists in that he owned up to it, and his frankness got him in trouble.

Although the finished version of "Fight Test" sounded almost nothing like "Father and Son," the 1970 tune by singer-songwriter Cat Stevens, Wayne had pointed out the similarities in several interviews—"There's definitely a reference to the cadence, the melody," he told *Rolling Stone*—and a BBC DJ began playing the songs back to back. Adopting the name Yusuf Islam, Stevens had famously turned his back on many aspects of Western society, though not its fondness for litigation. When he read Wayne's comments, he sued.

"It was a pain in the ass," said the Flaming Lips' longtime attorney, Bill Berrol. "It was completely innocent of them, but nonetheless, you learn your lesson: You listen to your sister's records twenty years ago and become influenced by them and incorporate those influences into a song where somebody is an Islamic activist and, in my mind, an artistic firebrand, and you are buying into a little bit of trouble there."

Eventually, the two sides reached a settlement to permanently divide royalties from the song 75 percent in favor of Stevens/Islam, ensuring a link in perpetuity between the man who wrote "Morning Has Broken" and "Peace Train" and the band behind "Jesus Shootin' Heroin" and "Oh My Pregnant Head (Labia in the Sunlight)."

CHAPTER 11

WE'VE GOT THE POWER NOW, MOTHERFUCKERS

AT WAR WITH THE MYSTICS (2006)

LOOKING TO ESTABLISH their own planet, or at least claim a small corner of this one, members of the Spiritualist church in Laona, New York, purchased eighteen acres of farmland in the southwestern corner of the state not far from Lake Erie in 1879 and founded what they called the Cassadaga Lakes Free Association, a religious assembly of psychics, mediums, and faith healers. In 1906, they changed the name of the settlement to the Lily Dale Assembly, and a century later, Lily Dale still thrives as a private, gated town of charming Victorian gingerbread mansions, including its own post office, volunteer fire department, hotel, library, and museum. The sign at the entrance proudly heralds "the World's Largest Community for the Religion of Spiritualism," and several dozen residents stand ready to help paying customers divine their future or communicate with loved ones who've left this world and allegedly gone to a better one.

Three miles away, in the town of Cassadaga just outside Fredonia, where the Flaming Lips first recorded with their longtime producer Dave Fridmann at the SUNY Fredonia School of Music's Sound Recording Technology studio in 1989, the band was working on their eagerly anticipated eleventh album in early August 2005 when Wayne Coyne took a break one sunny afternoon for a drive in a rented white minivan. "It's nothing but fortunetellers and healers and stuff—a New Age community," he said as we toured Lily Dale. If the irony of his band recording an album called *At War with the Mystics* five minutes away at Tarbox Road Studios struck him, he didn't mention it. "I just like it 'cause it's an old community. This is the way people used to live."

Wayne had first scribbled the title for the new album two years earlier as an interesting phrase for a lyric he never finished. "There's something about a man struggling with the things that are mysterious to him, where once you defeat the mysteries, you've defeated something wonderful," he said. "We're not at war with the people who think they're mystics, but with our own mystical perceptions. It's just the idea of trying to get to the truth of what's real and what isn't."

This already had been the theme of two of the Flaming Lips' best albums, *In a Priest Driven Ambulance* and *The Soft Bulletin,* as well as many of the strongest songs throughout the rest of their now considerable catalog. During more than twenty years of writing about popular music, I've never encountered a group that is less nostalgic or more determined to continually break new ground. Nevertheless, the musicians had spent the last year taking stock of where they'd been, through Bradley Beesley's documentary *The Fearless Freaks*; Jay Blakesberg and J. Michelle Martin-Coyne's photographic history, *Waking Up with a Placebo Headwound*; *VOID (Video Overview in Deceleration)*, a DVD compilation of the Flaming Lips' music videos that also serves as a

"THERE'S SOMETHING ABOUT A MAN STRUGGLING WITH THE THINGS THAT ARE MYSTERIOUS TO HIM." STEVEN AND WAYNE WORK ON A GUITAR PART AT TARBOX ROAD STUDIOS, AUGUST 2005.

greatest-hits collection (though most of the songs never actually charted); and a new edition of *The Soft Bulletin*, remixed like the *VOID* songs, for the latest high-end audiophile format, 5.1 surround sound.

In prerelease interviews, Wayne's consistent buzzwords for the new album were "more organic." His bandmates, Michael Ivins and Steven Drozd, stated the goal more directly: The Flaming Lips wanted to rock again, though they insisted this desire had nothing to do with returning to the past. "There would be times when I'd be transferring something [for the 5.1 surround sound remixes], and Wayne would go, 'What's that?,' and I'd be like, 'It's us,'" Michael said. "But I don't like to think we're coming full circle or digging from the past or anything. Usually, the formula for a band is 'If it ain't broke and it works, just keep doing it,' but we always just start getting bored. We could've continued on with *Clouds Taste Metallic* forever, but even without Ronald [Jones] leaving, it was like, 'This is the same trick; we've done this already.' The same thing with the Björk or Aphex Twin electronic stuff."

"To me, the obvious electronica stuff sounds cheap now," Steven added. "It doesn't sound cheap when you put something fresh with it, but I just didn't want to do *Yoshimi* again. We wanted to have those electronic elements, but with more guitars and drums that were actually played [live]. I'm breathing a sigh of relief, because at least half of this shit sounds like new music to me—here is what is happening now, instead of taking the elements of *The Soft Bulletin*, shuffling them up, and turning that into ten 'new' songs."

Continually forging ahead with new sounds doesn't come quickly or easily, however. From 1993's *Transmissions from the Satellite Heart* on, the time between the band's albums had grown increasingly longer, partly because of unexpected setbacks such as Ronald's departure and side projects such as *Christmas on Mars*, but primarily due to the group's efforts to broaden its audience through extensive touring. The band tried to balance this goal with the impatience of hardcore fans who might see it perform essentially the same set half a dozen times, but with *At War with the Mystics* projected for release in March or April 2006, the wait for a new album stretched to more than three and a half years since the release of *Yoshimi Battles the Pink Robots* in July 2002.

Eric Fritschi, who has been the band's product manager and primary liaison at Warner Bros. since *The Soft Bulletin*, tried to bide time and keep fans satisfied with a flurry of EPs and CD or DVD singles full of remixes, live tracks, and rarities. (The *Fight Test* EP, released in the spring of 2003, received a Grammy nomination for best alternative-music album of 2004, despite the fact that it wasn't an album. It didn't win.) Among the many tide-over treats: "Funeral in My Head," "Assassination of the Sun," "I'm a Fly in a Sunbeam (Following the Funeral Procession of a Stranger)," and "Sunship Balloons," all outtakes from *Yoshimi Battles the Pink Robots*; "Syrtis Major" and "Galactic Melancholy," from the soundtrack of *Christmas on Mars*; "At the Fish Fry & the Biggot's Drunk" from the soundtrack of *Okie Noodling*; the wonderfully goofy new track "Thank You Jack White (for the Fiber-Optic Jesus that You Gave Me)," and covers of "The Golden Age" by Beck, "Knives Out" by Radiohead, and "I Can't Get You Out of My Head," which dance diva Kylie Minogue had borrowed from seventies glam rockers Mud. But by the summer of 2005, Fritschi and many others at Warner Bros. were eager for a new album.

"The Lips now are like a cultural phenomenon, and everybody at the company is in love with them," Fritschi said. "We may have been hoodwinked by some of their crazy ideas, but one night when I'd had a few cocktails, I told Scott Booker that in a way, the band has helped to shape what Warner Bros. is today. They keep bringing these absolutely insane ideas to us—the kind where anyone who takes the phone call will start out with a big sigh—and then you hear Scott explaining to you how it is going to work, and every time we've gone with their muse, it has worked out, and we've won. That's been their secret, or at least the secret of our success with them."

In the sixteen years since he'd first recorded the Flaming Lips, and largely because of his work with them, Fridmann had become one of the busiest and most sought-after producers on the underground rock scene, with credits including Modest Mouse, Lake Trout, Mogwai, Beth Orton, the Delgados, Low, Luna, and Sleater-Kinney. He had built his dream studio by converting a comfortable, wood-sided home on a tree-lined country road, setting the main recording space in a large room with a vaulted ceiling two stories tall and a balcony accommodating a set of timpani, tubular bells, three drum sets, and part of his extensive collection of vintage keyboards. The rest of the first floor housed various isolation booths, workshops, storage spaces, a kitchen, and the control room, while the remainder of the second floor served as an apartment for client bands, because the nearest motel was twelve miles away.

Fridmann generally booked Tarbox Road months in advance, though he always tried to clear the calendar for the Flaming Lips. "There are a lot of bands I like to record with, but the Lips are my favorite, bar none," he said. "It's always challenging and rewarding, and they're the only band I've ever worked with where you can come out of a twelve-hour day and say, 'I feel

"THERE ARE A LOT OF BANDS I LIKE TO RECORD WITH, BUT THE LIPS ARE MY
FAVORITE, BAR NONE." DAVE FRIDMANN, CENTER, PREPARES TO RECORD
STEVEN'S GUITAR AS MICHAEL ASSISTS AT TARBOX ROAD, AUGUST 2005.

better now than I did going in.'" Added Wayne, "He's in on this with us:
We've become part of his self-expression. I'm sure I could ask Dave to work
with us for a year for free, and he would."

The band began working on *At War with the Mystics* in the spring of 2004,
and the first sessions produced rough versions of three new songs, though

with its busy drum groove and burbling electronic keyboards, "Zolly Golly" sounds more like an outtake from *Yoshimi Battles the Pink Robots* than a step forward, and it was soon earmarked for a future B-side or bonus track. Consisting of a spacey instrumental that serves as the backing for one of Wayne's science-fiction monologues, the story-song "Time Travel!? . . . YES!" also covers familiar ground. "It's not that different from 'U.F.O. Story,' but we were listening to the OutKast album [2003's *Speakerboxxx/The Love Below*] which has all these little skits on it, and we thought, 'We should do that,'" Wayne said. The band considered having the voiceover recorded by one of its most famous fans, Dave Eggers, author of *A Heartbreaking Work of Staggering Genius* and founder of the literary journal *Timothy McSweeney's Quarterly Concern,* but actor Steve Burns asked to give it a shot, and the group used his take.

More of a departure musically—Wayne described it as "space-age jazz"— "Mr. Ambulance Driver" points to a fresher direction. The spare, atmospheric tune focuses on the low-key, intimate-sounding vocals and Steven's straightforward drum part and tinkling piano, while the lyrics portray a man kneeling beside his dying girlfriend, wishing he could trade places with her. It was inspired by a scene Wayne had witnessed years earlier, when he was riding his bike to work at Long John Silver's one frigid morning and saw an ambulance that had just arrived at a bloody car wreck. The next day, he read that the ambulance had collided with another car en route to the hospital, killing the victim the paramedics thought they'd rescued.

Wayne had drawn inspiration from the incident before, for "A Winter's Day Car Accident Melody" in the Boom Box Experiments, and the ambulance as a metaphor for the fragility of life had been central to *In a Priest Driven Ambulance.* "We revisit these things, and it's like, 'Oh, yeah, the Lips sing about ambulances.' I think we're still going back to that Bloodrock record, 'D.O.A.,' because there's just something about the eeriness of a rock band taking on death. This song was just an excuse to tell this weird story, but my mom also got sick around then, and there were times . . . they were just the grimmest. If you've ever known someone who's been given a death sentence, those are just horrible days."

In July 2004, not long after the sessions that yielded "Mr. Ambulance Driver," Wayne's mother died from ovarian cancer. Dolly's six children gathered for her funeral—the musician son whose tours she'd booked; Linda, now happily remarried and living in Iowa; Kenny and Mark, who'd taken over their father's business; Marty, who still worked as a mechanic in Oklahoma City; and Tommy, who attended the service on a furlough from prison in the midst of his latest term for drug possession—and as they had after their father's death in 1997, they talked about the traits they'd inherited. "My mom was optimistic to a fault, and we knew that; even when she was dying, she bragged about not going to the doctor for forty years," Wayne said. "She was delusionally optimistic, but that's beautiful, and all of us are."

When the band returned to Tarbox Road for two more rounds of sessions in the summer of 2004, it recorded its cartoonish contribution to the soundtrack of *The SpongeBob SquarePants Movie*; a hauntingly pretty cover of "Gates of Steel" for an unreleased Devo tribute album; and "Bohemian Rhapsody" for *Killer Queen: A Tribute to Queen*, released in August 2005. The musicians and Fridmann spent eight days on the Queen cover, and their version of the epic mock opera is alternately more understated and more over the top than the original, with the computer's auto-tune program helping to re-create the many layers of stacked backing vocals down to the last "mama mia."

The group returned to *At War with the Mystics* during its next sessions, in February 2005, starting with a lovely ballad called "Your Face Can Tell the Future," which had been written by Wayne. "I liked it, but it didn't sound like we were going anywhere new," Steven said. Wayne also had recorded a demo for a song called "It Overtakes Me." The keyboard bass line brought to mind vintage Stax/Volt, and as Steven fleshed out the instrumentation to create a sexy and slinky groove, Wayne added some of his strangest vocals ever, with singsong rapping spinning off the title phrase: "It overtakes me . . . It master-slaves me . . . It wakes and bakes me/Oh, yeah."

"I wanted to write a song for Gwen Stefani to sing, and I was thinking of her dreaming of outer space while masturbating, though I couldn't say that, so it became 'master-slaves,'" Wayne said. Added Steven, "He's got a thing about Gwen Stefani."

Finally, toward the end of these sessions, the band made the breakthrough it had been searching for. "The Wand" started out with a simple but catchy five-note guitar riff written by Wayne, and the group initially recorded it as an instrumental. "It had the same sort of really simple but really powerful feel as Black Sabbath's 'War Pigs,'" Wayne said. Insistent electronic percussion joined Steven's propulsive drumming while layers of mysterious digital sounds combined with more traditional rock instrumentation, including a massive fuzz guitar and a trashy garage-rock organ. The tune could have fit on *Oh My Gawd!!! . . . The Flaming Lips*, if the group had rendered its 1987 album with the technology available in 2005, and it seemed both slyly retro and thoroughly futuristic.

When the band returned to Tarbox Road again in the spring of 2005, it built on the sonic breakthrough of "The Wand" and continued honing a simpler, more direct, and more organic sound than those of its last two albums. "My Cosmic Autumn Rebellion" sprang from a grandiose, lushly orchestrated melody that Steven had recorded, and which the band had been using as its concert-intro music under the name "Ta Da." Steven also had written the music for the velvety ballad "Why Does It End?," and now Wayne added lyrics about contemplating the size of the universe: "Stars in the sky shining like they'd always be / Shining down on me . . . When do they end? I don't know." Then the band went back to work on "The Wand."

Hooked by the undeniable melody and the insistent rhythm, Booker, Fridmann, Michael, and Steven had been pressing Wayne to add vocals to the song instead of keeping it as an instrumental. He wrote the words while sitting in the control room, and he surprised his bandmates when he stood before the microphone channeling the profanity-laden revolutionary spirit of the MC5. The lyrics tell the story of an oppressed group that finds a magic wand which enables it to turn the tables on the fanatics who try to rule the world.

"I've got a trick, a magic stick, that will make them all fall," Wayne sings. "We've got the power now, motherfuckers/That's where it belongs."

For the first time in the band's career, Wayne had gotten political, albeit in a fantastic way, and with his usual mix of unblinking realism and wide-eyed optimism. In retrospect, his bandmates realized he'd been moving in this direction for some time, since the group began covering "Seven Nation Army" by the White Stripes in concert after the beginning of the war in Iraq and "War Pigs" by Black Sabbath in the wake of the 2004 presidential election. Wayne already had chosen the art for the new album cover, a digitally doctored picture of an upside-down battleship, "and suddenly, it all clicked in my head: We've got 'The Wand,' we've got this album title, and we've got this image," Steven said. "It wasn't like, 'Fuck, what are we doing?' anymore. We knew where we were going."

"At some point when you're playing all these shows, people always ask you, 'What do you think about this?'" Wayne said. "I don't think 'The Wand' is politics so much as it's just fun to stand up and say some radical shit and get everybody screaming. But I do like the idea of being able to remind people, '*You* have the power. If you don't like the government, *you* can change it. Do something about it instead of just complaining.'"

Many in the band's extended family thought that in "The Wand," the Flaming Lips had crafted a new classic with the instant, irresistible appeal of "She Don't Use Jelly," "Waitin' for a Superman," or "Do You Realize??," and when the musicians entered the studio again in August, the new material continued to flow. "Plinkee" was another instrumental that Steven had recorded for the band to use as an intro in concert; now it became an epic track that begins with a deliberate, plodding opening, shifts into a more expansive midsection, and then ends with the vocal unfolding over a spare acoustic guitar. Retitled "The Gold Mountain of Our Madness"—"It's very H. P. Lovecraft," Wayne said, though he admitted he never really read the horror writer—the lyrics follow the journey of some explorers whose "spirit and strength never run out" as they search for a treasure that doesn't exist. "By the time they got to the peak, they were old and they were weak," Wayne sings, but the song ends by noting that the heroes "decide to treasure what they find and make it golden in their minds."

Another beautiful, spacey meditation on the vastness of the universe, "The Stars Are So Bright" could have fit on *The Soft Bulletin* or *Yoshimi Battles the Pink Robots,* while "The Wizard Turns On" is an unsettling psychedelic instrumental with a fresher sound. "It's kind of like Miles Davis from one of the albums after *Bitches Brew* meets 'Shine on You Crazy Diamond' by Pink Floyd meets Chrome. Maybe we'll win another Grammy," Steven said, laughing.

Echoes of Pink Floyd can also be heard in "Pompeii am Götterdämmerung," thanks to an insistent drumbeat, melancholy organ, and rumbling bass line evoking "One of These Days" from 1971's *Meddle.* "Scott pointed out that part of 'Pompeii' also resembles the German national anthem ['Das Lied der Deutschen'], and I think that's what makes it so powerful," Wayne said. "When we were coming up with the imagery, that opening line—'Running to the station holding hands'—was just so perfect, and I started to get the idea of this distraught nineteen-year-old couple who can't find any satisfaction or peace in this world. Then the volcano erupts, and they like this idea of a great release and a dramatic suicide. It just plays into this whole Wagnerian drama."

The August sessions also yielded two more pop gems, "The Sound of Failure" and "Yeah Yeah Yeah Song," which Warners execs pegged as possible singles. The latter is one of the Flaming Lips' most effervescent tracks ever, and it stemmed from one of Steven's demos; he described it as "Ballroom Blitz" by glam rockers Sweet combined with "Hey Ya!" by the gonzo hip-hop duo OutKast. Wayne added lyrics that followed "The Wand" in examining politics through the realm of fantasy, asking a series of questions—"If you could rule the world with the flick of a switch, would you do it? . . . If you knew all the answers, would you give them to the masses?"—that elicit a giddy choral response of "Yeah, yeah, yeah" or "No, no, no."

"I think that one is obviously, not a novelty song, but a lot different than what we had been doing," Michael said. "There was something about it from the first time it came together, and it has these silly lines in it, but to think that it's a hit—whether it's 'She Don't Use Jelly' or [Britney Spears's] 'Oops! . . . I Did It Again,' who knows? That sort of thing takes a team to make it happen, and we're just worrying about, 'Let's do the best work we can to make it the song it can be.'"

Even with this rush of new material, and fourteen songs now contending for a slot on At War with the Mystics, the band had decided that it needed one more round of sessions, and it returned to Cassadaga in November, after the birth of Steven's son, to polish some of the mixes and attempt several other tunes based on demos that had been recorded by Wayne. (A final, inspired burst of creativity produced the tracks "Free Radicals," "We're Going On," "I Haven't Got a Clue," "You Gotta Hold On," and "Vein of Stars," which Steven described as "a late-sixties, baroque-pop, Bee Gees kind of thing.")

In the age of the listener-controlled iPod playlist, and at a time when a growing number of artists are exploring new ways to release their music via the Internet, the Flaming Lips still hold the album as their ideal canvas, in the sense of presenting a certain set of songs in a particular order taking listeners on a guided tour of a number of different soundscapes. They maintain that this is less out of loyalty to the way they grew up listening to rock 'n' roll than to the album's usefulness as a creative challenge. "What's good about the stuff that happens at the end of a record is that you already know what you've got, and you can just piece [things] together—'Wouldn't this be nice between this song and this song?'" Wayne said.

The end wasn't quite yet in sight when I arrived at Tarbox Road for the first three days of the sessions in August 2005. Michael had driven to Cassadaga from his home in Kentucky in his Mini Cooper the night before, while Wayne and Steven carpooled from Oklahoma City in the rented minivan. The last time they'd made the eighteen-hour drive, Steven's iPod had died. "We talked for like five hours, and then we had nothing left to talk about," Steven said, so he played acoustic guitar while Wayne drove and sang, and they wrote the basis of what would become "The Sound of Failure." The group had spent five days during the spring sessions working on the song, recording a Curtis Mayfield–style guitar solo and a bossa-nova drumbeat that Steven augmented with percussive finger snaps and a rhythm that he pounded out on the couch in the control room. A few weeks later, Wayne thought the song needed something else, and figuring out what that could be became the first item on the agenda in August.

"This will probably take a couple of hours," Wayne said. Instead, it consumed all of the next three days, and watching the Flaming Lips sculpt "The Sound of Failure" into its final form provided an invaluable look at their creative process.

With Wayne singing in the main recording room or Steven plugging into the mixing desk, the work of adding a vocal or guitar overdub remained essentially the same, but the actual mechanics of recording differed considerably from those at Studio Seven a decade earlier during the making of *Clouds Taste Metallic*. Back then, everyone would glance at the twenty-four-track recorder and trust that the massive reels of two-inch tape were capturing the music we heard in the room. Now, thanks to a giant monitor set to the right of the mixing desk, we could all watch the multicolored wave forms as they were feeding into the computer's hard drive, and we were literally staring at sound.

Over the thousands of hours they had logged in the studio, the four members of the Flaming Lips' creative team had grown in their own jobs and in their ability to efficiently work as one. With a speed and agility justifying his growing reputation, Fridmann spent minutes on complicated edits that would take other engineers working on Pro Tools half an hour, or an entire day, if it could be done at all, via the old method of cutting and splicing the master tape. Steven remained an extraordinary musical resource, able to pick up any of two dozen instruments scattered around the studio and add an exquisite new melody or rhythm in one or two takes. Meanwhile, though he resumed his old role by playing bass on "The Wand" and "Your Face Can Tell the Future," Michael primarily devoted himself to meticulously logging every note the group recorded and every bar it edited—an absolute necessity for musicians who work like painters randomly throwing colors at the canvas—while displaying a near-telepathic ability to anticipate and prepare for whatever the group would do next.

At one point, apropos of nothing I noticed or heard, Michael walked into the recording room, set up a microphone and a cymbal, and laid out two mallets. Ten minutes later, Wayne suggested that perhaps Steven should add a cymbal overdub. "Ivins can be kind of spooky that way," Fridmann said.

As for Wayne, he continued to be the captain who steered the ship with an almost imperceptible hand. Day one of work on "The Sound of Failure" started with him re-recording several lines of his vocal with new lyrics that reflected a suggestion from Fridmann. Wayne had written the first draft based on conversations he and Michelle had with some friends whose stepfather struggled with a fatal illness at the same time Dolly battled cancer. "There'd be times when they'd be driving from the stepdad's house and the radio would be on and they'd be enraged about this jubilance in the music they heard—'We're young and nothing can hurt us!'—and they'd just feel like punching these people. The more they heard people singing about joy, the more it would make them depressed."

In the catchy choruses, Wayne initially had sung, "So go tell Britney and go tell Gwen / I'm not trying to go against all them." Steven thought the lyric bordered on goofy—"Here we go again, back to 'This Here Giraffe'"—and Michael worried that it sounded like grousing from an aging indie rocker. "Then Dave said, 'What if you sing it from the woman's point of view?'" Michael recalled, and the change in pronouns prompted Wayne to dig deeper. In the finished song, a female narrator rejects the artificial optimism of Britney Spears and Gwen Stefani because "she is starting to live her life from the inside out," embracing "the sound of failure" and the inevitability of aging and death so that she can fully appreciate the joys of living in the moment.

The group listened to the song five or six times while recording the new vocals, and in the process, Wayne decided he didn't really like the bossa-nova drum groove. Fridmann steadfastly maintained that it had its charms. "Yeah, but what if, just for argument's sake, we tried something else, Dave?" Wayne asked. Well aware that no one ever wins such an argument with Wayne, Fridmann and Michael set about crafting a new drum part on the computer, using samples of live drums that Steven had recorded during other sessions. Meanwhile, Steven and I accompanied Wayne on a supply run to Tops Supermarket in Fredonia, where the band had recorded "There You Are" in the parking lot in 1989.

Tarbox Road had witnessed its share of rock-star behavior—Fridmann recounted the story of some coddled English musicians who decided, while tripping on Ecstasy and toying with air rifles, to shoot up a rental car belonging to a visiting photographer, racking up thirty-eight thousand dollars in damages—but the Flaming Lips never had indulged in such antics. After stocking up at Tops on two hundred dollars' worth of groceries, coffee, and Red Bull, Wayne cooked a dinner of frozen fish sticks, tater tots, and salad, and then Steven took out the garbage while Michael did the dishes.

If you spend any time with the Flaming Lips, they inevitably put you to work. "Tomorrow night, it's your turn," Wayne said, pointing at my waistline. "You look like you know how to cook." I told him that I did indeed, courtesy of my Italian grandmother, and for the next twenty-four hours, he warned me about how their former A&R rep David Katznelson once boasted that he'd cook a great Italian dinner, but after using every pot and pan in the kitchen, he'd produced an inedible mess. I made lasagna on the second night and fettuccine Alfredo with peas and prosciutto on the third, and Wayne paid me two of the highest compliments he ever gives: He ate heartily, and he quit giving me crap for the rest of my stay.

By the time the band returned to the control room after dinner on day one, "The Sound of Failure" had become an almost completely different song, thanks to the new rhythm. "It's really Gerry Rafferty's 'Baker Street' now," Steven said, referring to the 1978 hit. "I didn't realize how much the rumba thing was beating me down, and how it didn't suit Wayne's singing. Now, the best bits—the chorus and the guitar part—sound even better." The day's work ended with some more tinkering on the cymbal rolls and sampled flute flourishes during a dramatic break in the middle of the song. In the course of this, a track that included a snippet of someone talking in the studio was left unmuted, and a mysterious voice fortuitously appeared at exactly the right moment. After Fridmann tweaked the pitch and added some effects, it sounded just like a girl saying "It's dark," and the band embraced what Brian Eno would call a "happy accident."

"I love that!" Wayne said. "I think we've really nailed this one, boys."

By the morning of day two, the band's leader felt otherwise. "You know, it really seems a little slow to me now, Dave. What if we sped things up a bit?" Fridmann obligingly used the computer to increase the speed of the song from 112 to 116 beats per minute, a subtle increase most listeners would barely notice. Wayne declared it a vast improvement. Many engineers would have just used the newly adjusted version of the song, but Fridmann and Michael insisted that the fidelity would be greater if they went into each individual track—there were more than forty, with all of the rhythm, guitar, keyboard, and vocals parts—and increased its tempo, one at a time. It would require five hours of tedious labor on their part, but they swore the results would be worthwhile.

During the downtime, Steven sat at his laptop shopping on eBay. He looked longingly at double-neck guitars for a while, then spied a talk box, the distinctive guitar effect that characterized "Rocky Mountain Way" by Joe Walsh and "Show Me the Way" by Peter Frampton. When he mentioned the device, which operates by feeding the signal from the amp through a tube placed in the guitarist's mouth, he expressed concern that "it might actually be too cheesy to use." Fridmann responded that the best thing about it is that it "completely rattles your teeth and the inside of your head—a totally amazing feeling." Steven was sold, and once the talk box arrived, he'd use it to good effect on "Yeah Yeah Yeah Song."

While Michael and Fridmann continued working on the tempo shift,

Wayne tried to kill time by flipping through the two pieces of reading matter he'd brought from home—*Wisconsin Death Trip*, historian Michael Lesy's 1973 collection of photos taken in Black River Falls, Wisconsin, in the 1890s ("The subject matter ranges from children in coffins, to farm animals, to family portraits of some of the grimmest-looking people imaginable, [designed] to confirm that the good old days were actually awful," the *Library Journal* notes), and the current issue of *People* magazine ("I've gotta keep up," Wayne said)—but he soon grew restless. "Wayne can never sit still for more than ten minutes at a time," Michelle said. "He's like a ten-year-old."

We took a drive to listen to some of the recent rough mixes in the minivan—"It really does sound better at this tempo," Wayne said of "The Sound of Failure"—and returned to find that Fridmann's two grade-school-age sons had come to visit. Wayne spent the next few hours with them trying to catch frogs in a woody marsh behind the studio. He didn't bother to change out of his Dolce & Gabbana; in fact, he never wore anything but the white suit with pink and green stripes during the three days I was there.

On the second night, with "The Sound of Failure" now slightly quicker, Steven began recording the guitar, keyboards, and synthesized flute solo for an extended coda or brief companion tune that Wayne called "It's Dark." On the morning of day three, Wayne added vocals—"She doesn't know where it will take her/ As she's going into the unknown"—and in the afternoon, Steven did a few more instrumental overdubs. "I do believe we might be done," Wayne said, and following several hours spent mixing the tune after dinner, he was finally satisfied.

With the song completed, Fridmann packed it in and went home around midnight on my last day in the studio, but Wayne had been hankering to play some raucous noise guitar—"You know, it's been so long since people have seen me play guitar onstage, I think they might actually be surprised and get a kick out of me doing it now," he said—and he asked Steven and me to set up the drums in the main recording room. Once we did, Steven sat down at a Fender Rhodes keyboard, Wayne wailed on crushingly loud, fuzz-drenched leads, Michael held down the bottom as solidly as ever, and I did the worst Terry Bozzio imitation imaginable as we jammed for thirty or forty minutes on "Black Napkins," a track from Frank Zappa's 1976 album *Zoot Allures* that Michael and Wayne may well have attempted twenty-three years earlier in the meat locker at Tomco, and an instrumental version of "Take Me ta Mars," the tune they'd based on a riff borrowed from German art rockers Can on *In a Priest Driven Ambulance*.

When we were done, Steven and Michael headed off to B.J.'s Bar in

Fredonia for a drink before last call, but Wayne was still wound up, and he suggested that we take a ride to look at the stars. "It's always amazing out here in the country." We drove to the end of Tarbox Road and stared at the early-morning sky, but the heavy cloud cover didn't cooperate, so there wasn't much to see. The conversation turned to the band and this book, and for the third or fourth time in the two years we'd been talking for this project, the Flaming Lips' leader repeated the only concern he'd ever voiced.

"I don't know if what we're doing with this band is worth a book or not, Jim—or really, if it's worth anything at all. We just do what we do, and hopefully you can make it all sound interesting."

I told him that I really didn't think that would be a problem.

Photo Credits

Acknowledgments

THROUGHOUT this book, unless another source is specifically credited, all quotes are taken from my own interviews, which were either conducted for articles I wrote about the band between 1989 and 2002 or were done specifically for this project: thirty additional hours of tape with Wayne Coyne and twenty-five with Michael Ivins alone.

Obviously, special thanks are due for the dozens of interviews, the unfettered access, and the unremitting fact-checking cheerfully endured by Wayne, Michael, Steven Drozd, Scott Booker, Dave Fridmann, and their significant others, Catherine Ivins, Becky Drozd, Jennifer Booker, Mary Fridmann, and the incredibly talented J. Michelle Martin-Coyne, who also served as my primary photographer and photo editor. The generous way they shared their time and the unconditional faith they placed in me to tell their story is a gift I cherish.

I am also grateful to the many others who granted me interviews, some of whom spoke about their experiences with the band for the first time, including Ruben Ayala, Steven Baker, Bradley Beesley, Trent Bell, Deb Bernardini, Bill Berrol, Tom Biery, Steve Burns, Keith Cleversley, Linda Cole (née Coyne), Marty Coyne, Richard Davies, Jonathan Donahue, Ted Drake, Vernon Drozd, Richard English, David Fallis, Jennifer Flygare, Cory Franklin, Eric Fritschi, Rick Gershon, Nigel Harding, Scott Haulter, Gibby Haynes, Bill Hein, Robyn Hitchcock, Gordon Holmes, John Isbell, Linda Ivins, Padraic Ivins, Jo Lenardi, David Katznelson, Jon Mooneyham, Hali Neyland, Chris Nuthall, Roberta Petersen, Nathan Roberts, John Rubeli, Tim Rutili, George Salisbury, Kliph Scurlock, Dick Smart, Thane Tierney, Michele Vlasimsky, and Yoshimi Yokota.

Thanks, too, for the photos and artwork contributed by Jason Campbell, Kenny Coyne, Jennifer Flygare, Katie Fox, Natalie Green, Linda Ivins, Hali Neyland, Marty Perez, and my own lovely and talented photographer-wife, Carmél Carrillo.

In addition to my own reporting, I drew information and insight from the essays and captions in *Waking Up with a Placebo Headwound: Images of the Flaming Lips from the Archives of Jay Blakesberg and J. Michelle Martin-Coyne, 1987–2004* (Warner Bros., 2005) and from dozens of published articles. The following were especially helpful: "Raising Hairballs with the Flaming Lips" by Byron Coley with Mike Monson, *Forced Exposure*, Winter 1986; "Flaming Lips: Hurts So Good" by Fred Mills, *The Bob*, February/March 1988; "Bag Full of Thoughts" by Randy Bookasta and David Howard, *Contrast*, November 1988; "Life as a Lip" by Kory Jay Willis and Steve Kit, *Stage Left*, December 1988; "Life According to the Flaming Lips" by Thomas Anderson, *Oklahoma Gazette*, February 27, 1992; "The Flaming Lips' Van" and "Wayne's World" by Heidi Olmack, *Cake*, January 1995; "Adventures in Hi-Fi" by J. R. Jones, *Chicago Reader*, December 12, 1997; "Candy Store Rock" by Jason Cohen, *Austin Chronicle*, August 6, 1999; "Strange Days" by Jonathan Valania, *Magnet*, June/July 2000; "The Manual Laborer" by George Varga, *San Diego Union-Tribune*, November 28, 2002; "Have You Met the Lips?" by Tom Junod, *Esquire*, March 2003; and Scott Bakal's interview with Nathan Roberts for the Flaming Lips Trading Post Web site.

My colleagues Fred Mills and Jason Cohen also wrote several other extraordinary pieces about the band, and either of them could have written this book, though they not only encouraged me to do it, but shared their notes, interview transcripts, and correspondence. Bradley Beesley also shared much of the footage he didn't use for his powerful documentary, *The Fearless Freaks*. These were selfless gifts indeed.

I also was fortunate to draw on the knowledge of some of the Flaming Lips' most devoted fans. Topping this list is amateur rock critic Tyler Ley, who served as a volunteer editor, tracked down obscure audio and video recordings, shared his extensive collection of ephemera, made connections with other sources, happily engaged in endless brainstorming sessions, and taught me about the culture of life in Oklahoma as well as the difference between concrete and cement (in the years since we first met, he has augmented his standing as Flaming Lips Superfan Number One with a Ph.D. in civil engineering). For some of the same reasons, though we never spoke, I thank Ryan Mulberger, the enthusiast behind the Flaming Lips Trading Post Web site (www.flaminglips.netfirms.com), and Drew Hird, the keeper of the band's official Web site (www.flaminglips.com).

For additional assistance, insight, or support along the way, I also thank Ben Bauer, Brian Beck, Bill Bentley, Jerry Bryant, Andy Cirzan, Ryan Dolan, Bill Gamble, Brett Hickman, Mike Gaertner, Sam Kinken, Marty Lennartz, Damon Locks, Bill Mayer, Sid McCain, Bill Miller, Casey Monahan, Joe Shanahan, David Silva, Anders Smith-Lindall, Cynthia Taylor-Handrup, Jennifer Tillman, James Van Osdol, and Norm Winer; my bandmates, Tony Tavano, Chris Martiniano, and Michael Weinstein; and my friends and colleagues Abdon Pallasch, David Sprague, Jaan Uhelszki, and Robert Wilonsky.

My first radio partner, Bill Wyman, joined me in interviewing the Flaming

Lips during several appearances on WLUP-FM and WKQX-FM in the early nineties. Greg Kot, with whom I am entering my eighth year co-hosting *Sound Opinions,* did the same, as well as inspiring me to make this book as strong as his biography of Wilco, *Learning How to Die.* I also appreciate the support of the rest of the *Sound Opinions* team: Matt Spiegel, Robin Linn, Shawn Campbell, Mike Gaertner, Ray Solley, Dino Armiros, Kate Darling, and especially my Web guru and computer lifeline, Jason Saldanha.

Robin Linn additionally served as my most valuable assistant, chief transcriber, and researcher par excellence, joining my intrepid interns Jenny Grandy and Chris Castaneda in becoming expert on the history of the band as well as esoteric matters such as Oklahoma state statutes, waterspouts, furverts, the *Kassettenorgel,* and brown recluse spider bites. *Staring at Sound* would not have been possible without their help, and they are all such talents that I hope to be lucky enough to one day work for them.

As noted earlier, some of the reporting for this book originally was done for articles that appeared in *Request, Penthouse, Spin, Stop Smiling,* and the *Chicago Sun-Times,* and I am indebted to my editors there, including Keith Moerer, Susan Hamre-Keller, Barbara Rice-Thompson, Sia Michael, J. C. Gabel, and especially my *Sun-Times* colleagues John Barron, Chris Ledbetter, and Thomas Conner, another Oklahoman who enlightened me considerably about the Sooner state.

Following *Let It Blurt,* this book has been the second round for both my editor at Broadway, my hero Gerry Howard, and my literary agent at Sterling Lord Literistic, the inimitable Chris Calhoun, and I cannot thank them enough for their friendship and their faith in me. (Wanna do it again, fellas?) Thanks also to Patrick Dillon, Terry Karydes, Rakesh Satyal, Michael Windsor, Amelia Zalcman, and everyone at Broadway/Random House; Manuel Stoeckl and DongWon Song at Sterling Lord; and Kassie Evashevski at Brillstein/Grey Entertainment.

Very special thanks are due my parents, Helene and Harry Reynolds, for a lifetime of support and encouragement, and Joe and Marcia Carrillo.

Finally, my wife and soul mate, Carmél Carrillo, not only endured my absence during travels to Oklahoma City, Cassadaga, Los Angeles, and Manhattan and the enforced hermitage necessary for writing this book, but as one of the most brilliant journalists and editors I know, she read every draft of every chapter and improved my work immeasurably, as well as listened to the Flaming Lips in near-constant rotation. To her and to our daughter, Melody Rose DeRogatis, I say thank you for loving me.

Index

Page numbers of illustration captions appear in italics.